Effective Employee Assistance Programs

SAGE SOURCEBOOKS FOR THE HUMAN SERVICES SERIES

Series Editors: ARMAND LAUFFER and CHARLES GARVIN

Recent Volumes in This Series

HEALTH PROMOTION AT THE COMMUNITY LEVEL
edited by NEIL BRACHT

**TREATING THE CHEMICALLY DEPENDENT
AND THEIR FAMILIES**
edited by DENNIS C. DALEY & MIRIAM S. RASKIN

HEALTH, ILLNESS, AND DISABILITY IN LATER LIFE:
Practice Issues and Interventions
edited by ROSALIE F. YOUNG & ELIZABETH A. OLSON

ELDER CARE: Family Training and Support
by AMANDA SMITH BARUSCH

SOCIAL WORK PRACTICE WITH ASIAN AMERICANS
edited by SHARLENE MAEDA FURUTO, RENUKA BISWAS,
DOUGLAS K.CHUNG, KENJI MURASE, & FARIYAL ROSS-SHERIFF

FAMILY POLICIES AND FAMILY WELL-BEING:
The Role of Political Culture
by SHIRLEY L. ZIMMERMAN

FAMILY THERAPY WITH THE ELDERLY
by ELIZABETH R. NEIDHARDT & JO ANN ALLEN

EFFECTIVELY MANAGING HUMAN SERVICE ORGANIZATIONS
by RALPH BRODY

SINGLE-PARENT FAMILIES
by KRIS KISSMAN & JO ANN ALLEN

SUBSTANCE ABUSE TREATMENT: A Family Systems Perspective
edited by EDITH M. FREEMAN

SOCIAL COGNITION AND INDIVIDUAL CHANGE: Current Theory and
Counseling Guidelines
by AARON M. BROWER & PAULA S. NURIUS

UNDERSTANDING AND TREATING ADOLESCENT SUBSTANCE ABUSE
by PHILIP P. MUISENER

EFFECTIVE EMPLOYEE ASSISTANCE PROGRAMS: A Guide for EAP
Counselors and Managers
by GLORIA CUNNINGHAM

Effective Employee Assistance Programs

A Guide for EAP Counselors and Managers

Gloria Cunningham

Sage Sourcebooks for
the Human Services Series

28

SAGE Publications
International Educational and Professional Publisher
Thousand Oaks   London   New Delhi

1111821 0

For information address:

SAGE Publications, Inc.
2455 Teller Road
Thousand Oaks, California 91320

SAGE Publications Ltd.
6 Bonhill Street
London EC2A 4PU
United Kingdom

SAGE Publications India Pvt. Ltd.
M-32 Market
Greater Kailash I
New Delhi 110 048 India

Printed in the United States of America

Library of Congress Cataloging-in-Publication Data

Cunningham, Gloria.
    Effective employee assistance programs: a guide for EAP
  counselors and managers / Gloria Cunningham.
        p. cm. — (Sage sourcebooks for the human services; v. 28)
    Includes bibliographical references and index.
    ISBN 0-8039-5205-8. — ISBN 0-8039-5206-6 (pbk.)
    Employee assistance programs—United States. 2. Employees—
  Counseling of—United States. I. Title. II. Series.
HF5549.5.E42C86 1994
658.3'82—dc20   93-41408

94 95 96 97 98 10 9 8 7 6 5 4 3 2 1

Sage Production Editor: Diane S. Foster

Dedicated to the memory of Edward J. Ford
with gratitude for his lessons of love,
support, and personal courage.

CONTENTS

	Acknowledgments	vi
1.	Employee Counseling Services: The Changing Picture	1
2.	The Contexts of Practice	14
3.	A Theory Base for EAP Practice	33
4.	Initiating Services and General Assessment	51
5.	Diagnostic Assessment: Substance Abuse and Chemical Dependence	78
6.	Referral to External Providers	101
7.	Beyond Assessment and Referral	116
8.	Understanding Family Issues	148
9.	Organizational Assistance	169
10.	Personal and Professional Issues	189
	Appendix	203
	References	228
	Index	241
	About the Author	249

ACKNOWLEDGMENTS

It is a firm conviction of mine that two of the most important and frequently overlooked sources of knowledge for counseling and other forms of interpersonal helping are the practitioners themselves and the clients they serve. By virtue of their direct experience of the helping process they provide reality-based insights that often challenge the boundaries of preexisting theory. This book represents an attempt to translate some of these insights into a usable format for other new and seasoned employee assistance counselors.

The practice model described in the chapters that follow owes much of its form and substance to literally hundreds of colleagues, students, alumni, and clients who shared their experiences with me and who must be acknowledged. I am especially grateful to the practitioners and clients who participated in our survey of EAP practice. Special thanks also are due to colleagues from both the EAP field and general clinical social work practice who read and responded to portions of this manuscript: Joan Ferris, Joanne Pilat, Golde Shapiro, Steven Uhrik, and Janice Wiley. Finally, a particular thank you to Joan Allman, who prepared a manuscript of such quality that even the editors at Sage Publications were impressed.

Chapter 1

EMPLOYEE COUNSELING SERVICES
The Changing Picture

A new phenomenon has made its presence felt in the U.S. workplace in recent years: the proliferation of employee counseling services directed toward helping workers and their families deal more effectively with personal, family, and work-related problems. Although the concept itself is not new, the particular form and focus of its most recent stage of development are unique by virtue of its identification with problems of chemical dependency, its association with the employee assistance movement, and its rapid growth and acceptance by all types of organizations and their employees (Blum, Martin, & Roman, 1992). Since 1980 the numbers of U.S. workers having access to employee assistance program (EAP) services has increased from 12% of the U.S. workforce to 36%, and more than three fourths of the Fortune 500 firms have some type of counseling service (Feldman, 1991). Along with this widespread acceptance there has been a diversification in the forms these programs have assumed, the types of problems workers bring to them, the professional backgrounds of the counselors, and the types of clients seeking help. The most common term used to identify these services is employee assistance programs (EAPs), although the term can mean different things to different people.

The emergence and rapid expansion of EAPs generated a number of books, articles, and journals that have been helpful in providing direction and continuing development for EAP practitioners (Akabas & Kurzman, 1982; Masi, 1982; Presnall, 1981). Much of the literature of this period, however, focused on programmatic issues, specifically topics of program design, marketing, and management. Much less information has been available dealing with the core responsibilities of the EAP counselor—the direct counseling of employees and their dependents—except for that aspect of service directed toward the identification and assessment of problems of chemical dependency. Even though other types of problems have surpassed those of alcohol or drug abuse in most EAPs (Leavitt, 1983), an operating assumption for many practitioners seems to have been that they could apply models of substance abuse treatment, more or less unchanged, to any type of problem employees bring to them. This assumption must now be challenged in the light of the increasing diversity of presenting client problems encountered in most EAPs and the growing complexity of the EAP function. Currently EAP counselors are encountering issues and expectations not anticipated by those who entered the field just a decade ago.

This book is designed to address two basic areas of employee assistance: (a) the dramatic changes that have occurred since the mid-1970s and (b) that aspect of service that is the primary focus of most EAP practitioners, which is the counseling of troubled workers who have problems that may include but are not limited to problems of chemical dependency. In addition to changes in clientele and presenting problems, the organizational contexts of EAPs have broadened beyond the traditional in-house management- and union-based programs and now include various models and combinations of models of service delivery. The EAP contractor who provides services to many different types of employers is currently more characteristic of EAPs generally than the in-house management model typical of the earliest programs, but even more complex patterns of service delivery continue to emerge. As program managers and contractors seek to address the common and unique needs of the organizations and employees they serve, they develop modifications and techniques of providing services that move beyond conventional EAP practice.

Another major change occurring has been the increasing dominance of occupational social workers as EAP professionals. Although many other disciplines are represented, the master's-level social worker has emerged as a preferred candidate for EAP positions. Reasons for this include social work's broadly based theoretical and skills training, which encompasses both personal and systems explanations of problems in functioning; the profession's long tradition of offering services at the workplace; and the fact that schools of social work have been the most active of the professions in providing specialized education for employee assistance for more than 15 years. Accordingly, this book is being written from a perspective of occupational social work and the unique knowledge and value elements from the profession of social work that have informed both theory and practice in employee assistance. However, the intent of the book is to provide a realistic orientation to EAP practice usable by anyone currently active in the field or considering it as a career option.

EMERGENCE AND DEVELOPMENT OF EAPs

Historical Perspectives

EAPs developed in this country in the 1940s and were at first concerned exclusively with problems of alcohol abuse. They were staffed primarily by indigenous nonprofessional or recovering counselors (Masi, 1982; Presnall, 1981). Over time, professionally trained alcoholism counselors, often men and women who were recovering from their own alcohol addictions, joined the ranks of EAPs, relying heavily on the "disease concept of alcoholism" and 12-Step self-help programs, such as Alcoholics Anonymous (AA), in their work with employees. These counselors were successful in demonstrating their effectiveness in both human and economic terms, so much so that they promoted the spread of EAP programming throughout U.S. business and helped to generate funding for additional research and demonstration projects.

This process was facilitated by the establishment of federal funding priorities directed at evaluating occupational alcoholism programs (Masi, 1985). In addition, the Hughes Act, which broadened the definition of handicapped employees to include alcoholics, directed attention toward mechanisms that would help identify and assist such victims. On a more subtle level, the early EAP practitioners helped to modify the firmly held belief of many managers that counseling programs of any kind had no place at the worksite. In addition, over time the EAP function has broadened to include help for many other types of employee and organizational concerns.

This change has occurred for a variety of reasons. First, it became clear to managers and line staff that EAP personnel had significant expertise in handling people problems, not just drinking problems, and, with increasing frequency, counselors were asked to deal with a wider scope of concerns. In addition, the success of the EAPs in securing both private and governmental funding attracted professionals from many different helping disciplines—social work, psychology, rehabilitation—who hoped to find new career opportunities at a time when other avenues of client service were drying up. They brought with them different perspectives on the nature of employee problems, which further broadened the scope of EAP services. Their varying theoretical orientations have enriched the EAP field, but they also have contributed to some of the difficulties involved in accurately characterizing the still evolving nature of the work.

Occupational social work's history in the workplace is very different from that of the early EAP movement, and understanding this difference can help to clarify some of the variations in perspectives between social workers and other EAP practitioners. As early as the mid-nineteenth century, companies were hiring social workers or "welfare secretaries" (McGilly, 1985), who received mixed reviews, especially from organized labor (Akabas, 1977). They dealt with problems of illness, economic insufficiency, family breakdown, and the cultural assimilation of new immigrants. Alcoholism was not a major emphasis and it was dealt with in the context of other concerns.

After the 1920s industrial social workers, as they came to be called, no longer constituted a significant proportion of professional social workers in this country. Reasons for this included the cultural laissez-faire attitudes that characterized industrial development in the United States, and the fact that U.S. business was reluctant to cast itself in the role of personal counselor to its workers. Companies were concerned about the ethics of becoming too involved in the private lives of their employees, and the charges of "paternalism" leveled against those few organizations that did establish counseling programs discouraged their continued development (Carter, 1977).

Attitudes and experiences were different in other parts of the world. Since the end of World War II, social workers have become familiar figures in businesses and unions in many European, South American, and Asian countries, where their services are often comparable to those offered by private agencies in the United States (Googins, 1987). In Europe, once peace had been restored, company or union programs provided for their workers many of the standard social services that were no longer available through traditional means. Government and philanthropic agencies were decimated by the war and under pressure to meet the needs of millions of war refugees, so private employers were asked to provide to their workers some of the services formerly available through public or charitable institutions. Today in Europe company-employed social workers often provide a full range of individual, group, and family counseling services in addition to various company-sponsored community organization activities.

Unlike the development of such services in the United States and Canada, however, problems of chemical dependency are not a major focus of their treatment efforts, and professional attitudes toward the assessment and treatment of alcoholism and other drugs are different from those that exist in the United States.

Definition of Terms

As the role of the EAP has expanded over the past 2 decades, the definition of *employee assistance* has lost much of its original precision. At one time the term was virtually synonymous with what is now more commonly designated as an *occupational alcoholism program (OAP)*, a program format designed to deal specifically with the problems of alcoholic employees. Currently, employee assistance is better understood as referring to a program that provides direct service to an organization's workers who are experiencing many different types of problems in their personal or work lives. It is generally understood that these problems often involve substance abuse, and the EAP counselor must demonstrate expertise in the assessment of such problems and in the use of resources intended to address them. Typically EAP services are offered in a work-related context either in on-site management-based services, through unions or membership associations, or through contract arrangements with EAP consultant firms, social service agencies, mental health groups, or private practitioners. Variations of the term employee assistance are used. Unions are more apt to use *members assistance programs* (MAPs) because the phrase employee assistance carries negative connotations as a management device intended to frustrate union organizing activities. For some time the rapid expansion of counseling services for health-care employees spawned the term *hospital assistance program* but increasingly employee assistance program is assuming a generic meaning in the field.

The term *occupational social work* should be understood as describing a broader concept than employee assistance. Not all occupational social workers are employed in EAPs. Unlike employee assistance counselors, occupational social workers may be involved in problems of occupational health and safety, worker compensation issues, corporate philanthropy, child-care contracting, services for the unemployed or underemployed, job training, consumer assistance, retirement programming, or a number of other roles (Fienstein & Brown, 1982; Frank & Streeter, 1985). These services are made available through a variety of traditional and nontraditional social work settings. EAP personnel, however, typically do not engage in this full range of roles and activities. In summary, occupational social work may be defined as a field of social work practice that includes a broad range of social and occupational welfare services intended to address the needs and to facilitate the biopsychosocial functioning of workers, their dependents, and their work organizations.

It sometimes is hard to maintain the distinction between occupational social work and employee assistance because the overwhelming majority of occupational social workers are employed in some type of EAP program. The other areas of occupational social work still are underdeveloped and have attracted relatively little attention in the literature of either social work or employee assistance. As professionals have struggled to achieve and sustain a foothold in employee assistance there has been little opportunity to speculate on other professional roles not directly related to EAPs or activities perceived as constituting unreasonable expectations for the individual EAP practitioner. For this reason, this book focuses on employee assistance as the most significant arena for occupational practice at this time. The terms *occupational social work* or *occupational social worker* should be understood to mean the social worker in an employee counseling program unless some other type of function is clearly specified or the field as a whole is being discussed.

THE CHANGING NATURE OF THE EAP FIELD

The "New" EAP Client

Originally EAP services were designed to address a single type of client with a chronic or late-stage drinking problem, someone who was in denial as to the nature of the problem and experiencing declining work performance. Workplace interventions were designed to make use of the work environment to break through the client's denial and precipitate a referral for treatment. Originally the only treatment providers available were AA and other 12-Step groups (De Rosa & Hickle, 1986) and possibly Veterans Administration hospitals. Later, as funding became available through demonstration grants and benefit packages, various alcoholism treatment centers became the standard treatment referral for alcoholic employees.

A few of the early EAPs had a different problem focus on workers experiencing fairly severe emotional problems (Weiner, Akabas, & Sommer, 1973). As with alcoholic employees, inpatient care followed by intensive outpatient therapy was the preferred form of treatment. Such seriously disturbed clients are still being referred to EAPs, and the techniques associated with getting help for them are still an important part of the work of the EAP practitioner. However, today more clients are receiving service for other social, emotional, and relationship issues, problems that do not reflect the same degree of severity as either the late-stage alcoholic or the severely emotionally disturbed (Leavitt, 1983; McClellan, 1987). These are more likely to be more universal problems in living that call for different techniques and models of assistance.

Another significant change in the profile of EAP clients is the change in patterns of substance abuse. As the scope and nature of chemical dependency have changed, the clear-cut late-stage alcoholic of 20 years ago has been replaced to a great extent by the cross-addicted employee who is using a combination of drugs, alcohol, and chemical substances that were not even being manufactured when the first EAPs were established. Cocaine, thought to be nonaddictive in the 1960s, has invaded all levels of work organizations and exhibits a pattern of addiction, recovery, and relapse different from that of alcohol abuse. Compulsive attachments to food, cigarettes, exercise, sex, and other human habits have broadened and confounded our definitions of addiction, and it is no longer possible to think of the treatment model so effective with alcoholics as generally applicable to all forms of chemical dependency or dysfunctional behavior. On the positive side, increased public awareness of problems of addiction and a greater acceptance of addictions as illnesses rather than moral or psychological deficits have had the effect of bringing people into treatment earlier and, increasingly more often, on a voluntary basis.

There has been a dramatic shift in the proportion of "involuntary" to voluntary clients in most programs. Actual numbers vary in response to general economic conditions, increases or decrease in a company's stress levels, different organizational cultures, and the treatment philosophy of the EAP director. However, in most EAPs the majority of employees seek help on their own without the intervention of their supervisors (Backer & O'Hara, 1991; Leavitt, 1983), and most are not exhibiting overt signs of declining work performance. These clients bring with them a mind-set about EAP services that is very different from that of the classic alcohol abusers or severely disturbed employees. They require different models of assessment and different forms of intervention. These altered realities also require different internal and external resource providers and different approaches to employee orientation and supervisory training.

Presenting Problems

Another change in EAPs today is the diversity of situations employees bring to EAPs ("Behavioral Benefits," 1991). Counselors frequently comment in describing this phenomenon, "You never know what's going to walk through that door!" The range of problems that come to EAPs is also unlike more traditional social work settings, where intake policies screen out many of the problems EAPs deal with routinely. Although alcohol and other addictions still account for approximately one third of the clients coming to work-based programs, as many or more, depending on the program, are seen for mental and emotional problems ranging from severe psychopathology to transitional crisis states. Some estimates identify marital problems as accounting for 40% to 50% of presenting problems in EAPs (Feldman, 1991). Recently, practitioners have been reporting an increase in problems associated with work-related pressures.

It is often suggested that the major reason for broadening EAPs to include other types of problems is to help identify larger numbers of chemically addicted employees. Quite often substance abuse problems become known not through declining work performance but as a result of marital or parent-child conflicts, financial or legal entanglements, or emotional symptoms of depression or anxiety. Under such circumstances an astute counselor can be of great help to an individual or family by identifying underlying problems of addiction and codependence. It would be a mistake, however, to classify most EAP clients in this way. Divorce, mental illness, parent-child conflicts, and other adjustment problems not associated with substance abuse also are costly to the employer, and they are being dealt with effectively through the more comprehensive "broad brush" EAPs. For both pragmatic and ethical reasons employees with such problems cannot be refused service, nor can they be relegated to a second-class status because they do not fit the traditional image of practice or the professional preferences of the counselor. Managers expect that EAPs address a broad range of problems experienced by their employees. If their workers cannot get this type of help from the EAP, most will not receive any help at all, and the EAP will lose credibility as a significant resource for the organization.

New Organizational Contexts

Two basic types of changes have occurred in the organizational contexts of EAP practice. The first has to do with the structure of the program models for EAP service provision, and the second is the altered nature of

corporations and unions that house these programs. There has been a proliferation of different types of EAPs as they have modified their designs to
reflect the changing needs of the workplace. In the past the typical
arrangement was for large companies or unions to hire their own staff to
provide assessment and referral services for employees or union members. Only the larger organizations could justify the expense of full-time
staff. A few large-scale EAP contractors existed. As hospitals mounted programs for their own employees, many of them also marketed their EAPs
to other local employers as a means of generating revenue or, in some
instances, filling beds in their chemical treatment or psychiatric wards.
The image of the in-house, management-based EAP still dominates much
of the thinking in the field, although more practitioners now are employed
by contracting firms. Increasingly, even large organizations may use a
combination of both in-house and contracted services as a way of addressing separate needs in different subunits or geographical regions.

The nature of EAP contractors has changed as well. Originally these
were often small groups of human service or mental health practitioners
who designed and marketed EAP services to local employers. Gradually
hospitals, community family service, mental health agencies, and other
not-for-profit groups entered the field. The most recent stage of development has been characterized by the absorption of EAP contractors into
large, for-profit, national and multinational firms, including insurance
companies or health-care providers. Although something of an endangered
species, individual EAP contractors continue to market and provide services to organizations, as do community-based agencies and consortia of
private practitioners. These developments have greatly complicated the
definition of the role of the EAP counselor. At one time an ethical question
facing these counselors was, "Who is my client: the employer or the
employee?" A more complex question arises for those practitioners who
must ask, "Where do my major loyalties lie: with my client, my client's
employer or my employer, or the benefits provider?" In some settings
professional decision making, in fact the very definition of what constitutes professional practice, is being undermined by others who have no
knowledge about troubled employees.

As employees of a new kind of service provider, practitioners are much
more directly affected by the dizzying pace of change in U.S. business
and the dramatic shifts in ownership, management, management styles,
economic recession, and expansion. With recurring cycles of development
and retrenchment, EAP staff have had to expand, merge, or redefine their
areas of expertise as they are being asked to assume responsibilities for

multiple new roles. In spite of efforts to standardize definitions of EAPs, it is becoming less likely that it will be possible for this to occur as business organizations try to adapt to socioeconomic changes through the "recycling" of their workforce. Trying to impose a single view of the function of the EAP or practitioner may be the best way to ensure the obsolescence of the EAP movement.

The New EAP Professional

As discussed earlier, the first OAPs and EAPs were run and staffed by recovering laypersons. These persons usually were employees of the company who assumed, often in addition to their regular salaried responsibilities, the tasks associated with helping other employees find help. Unfortunately, and probably inevitably, as the field has become more professional, conflict has emerged between the pioneers and those who came later with different experiences and different motivations. Professionalization has resulted in a broadening of efforts to deal with more troubled people than was possible in the original programs. The development of standards for education of EAP personnel and program operations contributes to increased accountability and protection for both employers and employees. On the other hand, the field is losing some of the clarity of vision, the dedication to what was once an unrecognized need and a depreciated clientele, and the creative energy and vigor typical of the first practitioners.

The two groups of professionals most identified with employee assistance are occupational social workers and addiction counselors. Each has made immeasurable contributions to the field. Each has something to learn from the other. The major contribution of addiction counselors to EAP practice has been their introduction of a broader and more optimistic view of the alcoholic and an approach to treatment that is effective not only in facilitating the recovery process but also in providing a means of helping people achieve both self-understanding and an altered approach to relationships that goes well beyond issues of addiction. Representatives from every other discipline who have sought entry into the EAP field have had to sit at the feet of addiction counselors and recovering substance abusers in order to better understand the behavior of chemically dependent employees and to learn how to constructively exploit the work environment to facilitate the treatment of addictions. Many service professionals from other fields were taught that alcoholism and other addictive patterns were symptomatic of either character deficits or other emotional or psychological stresses. The disease concept of alcoholism and the possibility of biochemical or genetic factors as playing a role in addictions characteristically were dismissed as uninformed or unprofessional. Such views fed into cultural and institutional denials regarding the prevalence of chemical dependency among so many other persons who did not fit presumed images of "the drunk" or "the addict." This view also helped to sustain the fiction that real or potential alcoholics were marginally functioning borderline individuals most likely to be found on skid row or in the caseloads of welfare agencies, community mental health clinics, and probation departments. Heads of corporations, doctors, society matrons, clergy, and professors did not become alcoholic. More current views of alcoholism challenged such easy assumptions. A next step in the evolution of our understanding of alcohol and drug use, one that owes a debt to both practitioners and researchers, is a multitheoretical understanding of chemical dependence and addictions that moves beyond the too simplistic polemic of either a psychologically or a genetically based model of addictions.

Social workers also have made major contributions to the evolution of employee assistance practice. When social workers began entering the ranks of EAP personnel, it was not unusual for them to be advised, "Whatever you do, don't tell the company you're a social worker." During that era social workers flocked to costly workshops on starting EAPs that usually included sessions on how to rewrite a résumé to disguise, not just modify, any information that suggested social work, as though this constituted clear evidence of an embarrassing lapse of good judgment on the part of the applicant. Fortunately, many social workers failed to take this advice and instead became among the most sought after professionals for employment in this field. Among the contributions they have made have been their expertise with a broad range of problems of human functioning other than addictions and a professionally honed and transmitted set of knowledge, values, and skills that has been tested over time in other settings. In contrast to that of other mental health professionals, their orientation is characterized by a person-in-situation perspective that emphasizes the need to understand the situational contexts of the problems people experience. Their understanding of intrapsychic and intrapersonal dynamics provides multiple bases for understanding the problems that occur between individuals and their systems. Other factors contributing to social work's acceptance in the workplace include existing standards for professional practice, a clear-cut code of ethics, an accountability structure through a national association, and a professional identity that already is recognized through state programs of licensing and certification.

FUTURE DIRECTIONS

In North America EAPs reflect the merging of both the EAP and the occupational social work traditions of practice. The EAP professional is expected to be able to demonstrate expertise in problems of chemical dependency as represented in the EAP movement and in the other types of problems in biopsychosocial functioning characteristic of social work. As there is growing acceptance of the fact that many different types of problems can impact on an employee's work behavior, the probability increases that comprehensive programs will become the standard model. On the other hand, though there has been a declining emphasis on substance abuse in recent years, it is likely that this may change in the United States in light of the 1988 Drug-Free Work Place Act (DFWA), which requires employers who have federal grants or contracts in excess of $25,000 annually to maintain a drug-free workplace through educational programs and policies and procedures that would provide services for addicted employees. Although EAP services are not mandated, they are recommended as a viable alternative in achieving the intent of the law. A key element in this act as compared with earlier federal initiatives is the strong emphasis on illegal drugs without specific attention to alcoholism, and the implicit need for practitioners to be more broadly informed about various patterns of drug abuse. Aside from the impact of the DFWA, it is clear that EAP practice will be greatly influenced by the continuing problems our society is experiencing with all types of drugs and the extent to which illegal drug trade itself is invading the workplace, introducing complicated legal and criminal considerations that practitioners may have to deal with.

An additional factor shaping the direction of EAP practice in the 1990s is the crisis of medical care in the United States and the related attempts by insurers and employers to protect themselves against the real and anticipated costs of providing health services to workers. Older models of EAP practice provided only assessment and referral services because of the expectation that external providers would furnish all treatment subsidized by benefit packages (Roman & Blum, 1987). This expectation is no longer relevant in an era of diminishing benefits and growing numbers of uninsured workers.

Managed care procedures have been introduced by employers and insurers as a means of dealing with escalating medical costs and assuring better service. Their effectiveness in meeting both objectives is hotly debated and EAP counselors can be found on both sides of the debate. Many see managed care reviews as addressing the problem only by cutting both the range and quality of treatment and the free choice of employees. Others are concerned about the inadequacy of the reviewers themselves to make decisions about chemically addicted or severely disturbed employees. Some EAPs have incorporated the managed care function as part of their services or have themselves been sold to managed care companies. Many argue that the expectation that employers continue to absorb the inflationary spiral in medical care is putting more and more employers at risk in terms of competitiveness and even their survival. The future of managed care and EAPs will be significantly influenced by the nature of President Clinton's new health-care initiatives and the willingness of Congress and the people it represents to accept these initiatives.

The absorption of EAP contractors into larger corporate entities creates many new issues for professionals who traditionally have been associated with public or philanthropic social welfare service delivery systems. Issues of identity, role definition, compatible or dystonic role assignments, and unanticipated ethical dilemmas are certain to arise. This does not mean occupational social workers should retreat to more familiar settings, nor should they deny their affiliation with the larger profession as they try to articulate a new professional persona. Social work professionals always have operated at the interface between individual and family welfare and the needs and expectations of the larger social system. This has been the source of much of social work's resiliency and relevance. The changing workplace is yet another opportunity to discover ways of operationalizing basic professional values related to concern for the person-situation perspective as both the persons and their situational contexts experience a changing reality.

Chapter 2

THE CONTEXTS OF PRACTICE

A number of human service professionals who made the transition from traditional settings to EAPs shared a fantasy about employee counseling at the workplace. They imagined carpeted offices with oak-paneled doors and engaging city views in major corporate settings. The occupational aspects of the fantasy included work with interesting and healthy employees, reasonable caseloads, markedly better salaries, and an organizational climate that valued what the professional had to offer. An implicit assumption was that EAPs were located in large for-profit settings, which, during the 1980s, were viewed by the popular culture as the place where most of the money, power, and action were located.

The reality of employee assistance has always been much more complex and less glamorous. In addition, EAPS have been intimately affected by the reversals of fortune that have engulfed corporate America since that time. EAPs are being bought, sold, and redefined as to their function by new corporate owners. EAP professionals are expected to deal with new contextual realities not envisioned just a few years ago. There is no reason to assume that the next decade will not see more variations in these arrangements.

In this chapter I examine several common program models as they exist in the 1990s, identify their special attributes, and investigate the tasks associated with their management. These include in-house, management-based programs; contracting groups that operate as external providers; union-based membership assistance programs; and various combinations of programs referred to here as "blended models" that involve a mix of both in-house and contracted services.

PROGRAM MODELS

In-House, Management-Based Programs

Corporate-based, in-house EAPs still exist, but they are a less standard format through which EAP services are offered. The original occupational alcoholism programs originated within corporate settings, which explains, in part, the persistence of this image of EAP practice in the minds of professionals both in and outside of the field. Indigenous recovering alcoholics effectively advocated in-house services directed toward helping other alcoholics, services that would also address the concerns of employers regarding the absenteeism, ineffectiveness, and unreliability of addicted workers. Currently, management-based EAPs exist in both for-profit and not-for-profit organizations of varying size including national and multinational corporations, federal and local governments, health-care settings, colleges and universities, and various service organizations. The type of setting will influence how the EAP is viewed and used by its constituency; however, several features tend to characterize management-based programs, some of which are rooted in the original alcoholism detection, assessment, and referral philosophies of the earliest programs.

Typically, an in-house program is an arm of human resources, either as a separate department or attached to health and wellness functions. It is rare for programs to be closely identified with the personnel function because of perceived threats to confidentiality or employee confusion about the nature of EAP services. In-house programs are most common in settings with large and geographically centralized employee populations, in which it is often more cost effective to operate an internal program than to contract for these services.

The most evident characteristic of in-house programs is that EAP staff are themselves employees of the organization they serve, a fact of professional life that contains both advantages and disadvantages for counselors and their clients. In-house EAPs are much more attuned to the unique culture of their settings and ongoing changes, potential problems, and shifting political coalitions. This provides an invaluable source of influence and information for EAP managers, who are able to assess needs and anticipate interventions on behalf of individual workers, subunits, or the overall system. This in turn contributes greatly to the credibility and increased use of the program. In-house managers have access to the formal and informal resource systems within organizations, and they may serve as client advocates in direct and indirect ways that are beyond the power of the average employee or external EAP provider.

The in-house location also may provide opportunities for organizational assistance that contribute to the evolution of more responsive work environments in general (see Chapter 9). The information, feedback, and intervention loops that on-site, in-house EAPs have access to produces a responsive and flexible program uniquely tailored to the host setting. Straussner's (1988) study of 23 in-house and contracted EAPs determined that top managers were less concerned with the types of services offered than with the program's adaptability to the needs of the organization. The in-house programs did, in fact, show greater flexibility regarding short-term or special needs of their companies than contracted services. In a survey of EAPs, one manager compared his technique of "working the organization" to that of an alderman having to "work the ward" in order to remain informed and effective (Cunningham, 1990).

There also are disadvantages to working in in-house programs. EAPs are not profit generating and may be vulnerable during periods of organizational change or mergers. Generally, however, the commitments of companies to their own programs have tended to be more enduring than contract agreements with external providers that are renegotiated over short terms. Another disadvantage is the possibility that in-house staff may be more subjective in their counseling simply because they share the same work environment. This is especially true when work-life factors may be contributing to a client's problems and the counselor is feeling many of the same stresses, such as when a company is downsizing. Also, if management is viewed very negatively by employees, the EAP's identification with it can undermine the program's credibility and its acceptance by employees. It is not always easy to remain clear about one's professional responsibilities to a company or a client if one's own stake in the fate of the organization is high.

In-house programs tend to be small with only a few staff, which means less division of responsibility and often a type of professional isolation that can be very difficult. The same person may be responsible for writing program policy, consulting with management, organizing and conducting employee orientation, developing resources, and seeing clients. Some practitioners see this as an advantage because the multiplicity of tasks can be challenging and stimulating. However, in such labor-intensive programs there is little opportunity for backup help and specialized roles. There is also limited opportunity for the professional sharing, consultation, and collegiality typical of traditional human service settings.

Because they are part of the middle management structure, EAP staff are expected to assume a management persona. This is not just a cosmetic, "dress for success" expectation. It is a pragmatic adaptation that helps EAP staff to communicate effectively with the decision makers and power brokers within any given organization. Especially in the corporate world, an economy of interaction occurs when managerial personnel readily understand the jargon, expectations, values, and assumptions of management (Kanter, 1977a). Managerial standing in a company requires the acceptance of certain values and behaviors necessary to the organization, and it is functional to adopt them as long as they do not compromise one's own professional values and the welfare of clients.

Corporate-based EAP staff also need to understand some of the givens of our economic structure, such as the reality that companies are in business to make a profit and most of the operations of the organization are directed toward that end. If EAP counselors see profit making as reprehensible or inevitably destructive of the workforce (Bakalinsky, 1980) then it is questionable that they can be of service to anyone. This is not to suggest that EAP staff must surrender their identity as human service professionals. It does mean that for those for whom the managerial image feels uncomfortable or dystonic, another type of EAP setting may be preferable.

Many in-house programs are located in organizations that are not corporate in nature, and different organizational issues and preferences will prevail. In government settings, for example, issues of civil service, patronage, and accountability to the taxpayer or political parties fuel much of the decision making and, consequently, the relationships between management and employees. In hospital or service settings, the well-being of the consumer of the services often determines EAP policy and what the counselor can or cannot do. Drug testing, for example, is mandated in certain government agencies or transit authorities, such as the Department of Transportation, and it is more common in hospital programs, where patients are in potential jeopardy from alcoholic or drug-using medical personnel.

Union-Based Member Assistance Programs (MAPs)

While recovering employees in companies were mobilizing efforts to help addicted coworkers, union members initiated similar efforts in their unions, the most notable of these being the United Auto Workers (Ogden, Hedges, Milstead, Sanders, & Mohler, 1977). These early volunteer efforts evolved gradually into union-based alcoholism programs and eventually into the broad-brush membership assistance programs of today (Antoniades,

1984; Masi, 1982; Molloy & Burmeister, 1990). During World War II, Bertha Reynolds, a social worker, started a service program for the Maritime Union intended to help its members deal with the personal and family problems generated by war, anxiety, and separation (Reynolds, 1951).[1] Although this effort was short-lived, its traditions of service to union members reappeared in the mid-1960s with the establishment of several social service programs in New York City trade unions (Kurzman, 1987; Weiner, Akabas, & Sommer, 1973; Yasser & Sommer, 1974). The development of membership assistance programs (MAPs) has been similar in many respects to that of EAPs in the corporate sector, but it has been neither as vigorous nor as widespread nationally.

Although MAPs often are very similar to EAPs, there is a resistance in some unions to the EAP movement, which is why different terms are used. Unions may view the EAP as antithetical to the interests of labor because of its preoccupation, at least in its marketing strategies, with worker productivity and cost-effectiveness, terms that union members interpret as supporting management efforts to get hourly employees to work harder for less money and fewer benefits. In addition, EAPs have been introduced into some companies as part of a strategy to discourage unionization. Unfortunately, as the union movement has lost ground the United States, many of the assistance programs that flowered in the late 1970s or early 1980s have been cut back or discontinued. Nevertheless, a range of services still are being offered through some unions.

The political analogy used earlier to express the need of EAP staff to "work the organization" may be even more relevant to unions. Union stewards and business agents constantly must demonstrate their ability to represent their workers in order to retain their posts, and turf issues can develop with MAPs that provide some of the services formerly negotiated by other union staff. Unions can vary in size and affluence, and the largest have internal administrative structures similar to management staff of any large organization. In such settings, the management persona referred to earlier may be totally appropriate. In other unions, however, such a persona could be highly suspect and a source of problems in communication and interaction.

Relationships between counselor and clients may be more egalitarian as members are more inclined to see the service as an entitlement. Unions often offer a greater range of services than management-based programs, services that may be offered through or coexist with MAPs. For example, for many years the Amalgamated Clothing and Textile Workers Union and

Joint Committee in Chicago provided true "cradle-to-grave" services to their members, including an outstanding day-care center; on-site medical, dental, and prescription services; legal services; social services; and a flourishing retiree center.

Unions in general have distinct cultural and political structures that are very different from those of the for-profit arena. In some respects the culture is more comfortable for many human service professionals who, like unions, identify with the provision of services and benefits to people who need them. The expressed concern is for the member, not the profit margin, and major accountability is to the membership, not the industry or employers.[2] Especially in trade unions, a sense of community exists among members, who share a historical tradition of the union operating as a reliable mutual support system in meeting the needs of its members (Antoniades, 1984).

Although few now remember the union wars in which men and women were injured or killed while demonstrating for their rights to unionize, this legacy is still fresh in the minds of committed unionists who continue to see evidence of the exploitation of workers not unlike that which existed earlier in the twentieth century. Union assistance programs should be aware of the significance of this culture and tradition and demonstrate respect for the philosophical roots of the union movement.

Perhaps the major disadvantage associated with MAPs currently is the ambiguous position of unions in our society. Although membership gains are occurring in some sectors, the blue-collar aristocrats of the post-World War II generation no longer have the power, influence, or funds to affect workplace events as was once the case. Unions must be as concerned about bottom-line issues as corporations, and it is not uncommon for members to be in competition with their unions for resources and benefits.

Contract Models

Most of the recent growth in EAPs and employment has occurred as a result of the development of contracting groups and external providers who supply fee-based services to employers. The model greatly facilitated the development of EAPs in branch locations of large organizations and especially in smaller companies that could not justify hiring separate professional EAP staff, although the cost per employee may actually be higher than in in-house programs (Straussner, 1988). Most contracted EAPs are broad brush in their focus, although it would be rare to find one that does not emphasize chemical dependency as an area of competence.

Many of the original contractors were hospital-based EAPs that marketed services to other employers as a way of generating income for the hospital. Family service agencies, mental health centers, and private practice coalitions of mental health and addiction counseling professionals also began to contract with employers, adding to the mix of patterns and services now available. Currently some contracting firms also offer a full range of other mental health, social work, or psychological services separate from their EAP functions. Others offer management-focused assistance in the form of organizational development, management consultation, managed care, or inservice staff training.

The contracting firm typically offers a package of services on a per capita basis, setting an annual fee per employee regardless of how many employees actually use the service. In return the employer receives a combination of specified services that can include assessment, referral, short-term counseling, management consultation, and job reentry counseling and follow-up. The package usually includes support functions of EAP awareness programs, employee orientation, and management training as to how to access the program. Contracting firms may offer several different levels of service with varying rate schedules that allow companies to purchase the exact combination of services they think they need.

Depending on the size of the contracting firm, EAP staff may be assigned one or several "accounts" for which they provide EAP counseling and related support services, sometimes on-site but typically at a detached location operated by the contracting firm. A clear-cut disadvantage of off-site locations and multiple accounts is the difficulty involved in interfacing with contract companies and their unique cultures in the same way that is possible in internal EAPs. Visibility and credibility often are more difficult to achieve, although off-site EAPs may be perceived as offering more protection and confidentiality to clients.

Contractors service large firms, but they are especially typical of smaller or geographically dispersed businesses. They often may include a wider range of other management services not directly associated with EAP functions. For example, large companies may have separate organizational development or training departments, but this is less often the case in the smaller establishments most typical of U.S. business. The EAP contracting firm may offer these smaller settings services such as general management training, staff development seminars, or managed care reviews in addition to employee counseling.

In contrast to in-house models, EAP contracting groups sometimes offer more limited or restricted EAP counseling services to their contract companies. Because the extent of EAP services is defined through contract agreements, there is less leeway for modification or individualizing of services for specific employee clients. The total number of interviews an employee may receive is specified, usually one to four, and the counselor may not have the option of extending that time even though it would be in the best interests of the client to do so. Although some contractors build in the option of more client contact based on the professional judgment of the counselor, this can become a point of contention in EAP contracting firms that are just as concerned with unit costs and bottom-line profits as are their client companies.

Whether for-profit or not-for-profit, contracting firms must function as small businesses themselves, with all the responsibilities associated with managing staff, marketing, maintaining employee and tax records, and developing operational strategies that allow them to remain competitive while protecting their own economic health (McClellan, 1987). The past decade has witnessed increasing competition among contractors, and increased investment of a firm's resources in the marketing function as a means of broadening the client base and increasing revenue. Sometimes the shift in resources to marketing can undermine the quality of services being rendered.

Contracting firms can offer the practitioner a collegiality that allows for inservice training, clinical and administrative consultation, and other types of professional experiences less available in internal EAPs. If the EAP contracting division is part of a private practice group or mental health center the counselor may have the options of working with non-employee client groups and of providing other types of clinical services not typical of EAPs. Larger contracting firms also may allow for a division of responsibilities and specialized functions that fit with the individual interests of staff, such as marketing, administration, or direct services.

Current issues for external providers include the growing size and sophistication of contracting groups and their absorption by existing for-profit health care, insurance, or benefit management firms. In large part this indicates the extent to which the corporate community has judged EAPs to be both effective and profit generating as well as profit enhancing. These developments also reflect trends in U.S. business that encourage "out-resourcing" of many functions once provided in-house as a means of reducing unit costs and improving bottom-line figures. This does, however, lend a sense of instability to the emerging status of EAPs as these services are combined with managed care, benefit management, and other formerly unrelated operations.

Blended Models

It is becoming more difficult to think in terms of "pure" EAPs that are solely in-house, union, or contract EAPs. The reality of the U.S. workplace is too complex, and as EAPs proliferate they take on this complexity. Perhaps most large employers now use various combinations of services, such as an in-house program in the primary facility and contract firms for smaller, dispersed units. In other organizations the management-employed EAP staff provide services to their own employees as well as marketing their services to other employers. In some workplaces an employee may have access both to a management-based EAP and to an MAP available through his or her union. Companies also may have internal EAP staff provide parts of the service while contracting for other parts, such as aftercare or follow-up, through an external provider.

The multiple options available probably are advantageous in view of the youth of the field, as they provide an opportunity to see the viability of different models over time. Blended arrangements offer employers a great deal of flexibility to meet changing organizational needs. However, if the different elements of the overall EAP service delivery system represent different practice approaches or if they are poorly coordinated, problems can develop. Political and other turf issues can arise, and, unfortunately, it is not unknown for one part of the network to undermine the work of another in order to expand its own sphere of operations.

In addition to the programs discussed above, there are joint union-management EAPs, which involve a high degree of collaboration between management and unions in the policies, procedures, and operation of the EAP. Such programs are not common, however, and are something of a misnomer as the EAP staff almost always are employed by the company and are part of its management staff. In most respects, except for their greater accountability and attention to union input, these tend to operate as management-based programs.

At one time in some parts of the country efforts were made to establish consortia of employers or unions that would share the costs and operation of an EAP for all of their members or employees. This model is difficult to bring about because of the inherent competitiveness among companies and unions. The increase in contracting options has made this a less needed or attractive alternative for many employers. However, this model does provide an option for some communities (Maiden, Kimble, & Sudtelgte, 1993).

PROGRAM ADMINISTRATION

Whatever the nature of the model or host organization, certain ‿‿. of EAP administration are more or less constant across programs. These include a strategy for organizational assessment that takes into consideration both an in-depth understanding of the organization and the special needs of its diverse elements as they change over time; the development of general program policies and operating procedures; "in-house marketing," or the need to keep all levels of staff informed about the EAP and its progress; and program evaluation.

Organizational Assessment

Organizations vary greatly in terms of their size; their employee profiles; varying ethnic, cultural, or gender distributions; their occupational tasks; and their administrative styles. They will actualize their needs and stresses in different ways, and it is essential for EAP staff to understand these differences and to individualize each employer. Both in well-established EAPs and certainly in newly developed ones it is essential to initiate and maintain a process that allows for continual appraisal of current and anticipated service needs in the light of changing organizational systems. An organizational assessment provides a formalized approach to identifying and documenting the nature of a specific workplace at a given time.

Organizational Structure

In a newly established EAP or in a prospective client company it is helpful to determine the basic organizational pattern, management style, decision-making rules, and communication flow of both the overall company and its subsystems. It is a truism that anyone wishing to have an in-depth understanding of a complex system needs to understand both the formal written organizational charts and the informal organizational tree, which often can be quite different and much closer to reality. Yet another dimension can be added: the "illusional" organizational structure, which is the way in which people in the system imagine the organization is run. Ingrained beliefs that the chief executive officer (CEO) is a wimp and his or her secretary runs the show, that the new ad executive is sleep- ing with the boss, or that promotion policies are or are not racist influence how workers live out their occupational lives in those systems regardless of the accuracy of these beliefs, and they contribute to yet a separate reality composed of both fact and supposition. These perceptions of reality are potent factors in determining what can or cannot be accomplished by a manager, a client employee, or an EAP.

Different systems within an organization develop their own subcultures, and it may be important for EAP staff to understand these differences and how they impact the life of the overall company and the EAP. In one organization for which I provided consultation services, a subsidiary firm operated with a degree of informality totally different from the major corporate headquarters. The CEO biked to work, involved all levels of staff in major decision making, and espoused a humanistic philosophy of management that placed human relationships first. His skepticism about EAPs was based upon what he viewed as their overriding concern with cost-effectiveness. Understanding such attitudes and how they differed from the norm was essential in helping the company establish its EAP services.

In developing a new EAP it is helpful to recognize that systems evolve their own ways of handling problems over time, which can be either very functional or very dysfunctional, and a good organizational assessment can help determine how problem resolution traditionally has been handled. Certain persons within the system may be indigenous problem solvers who have the respect of their coworkers and who can provide important information about the EAP through informal organizational channels. In other situations informal networks exist that are either very helpful or obstructionist of persons' efforts to get help. It is to everyone's advantage if the traditional means of handling problems can coexist with or facilitate the work of the EAP. If this is not likely or if the traditional approaches to problem resolution are damaging to the organization or employees it is important that EAP directors be aware of them so they can anticipate and hopefully neutralize their efforts in setting up and managing the program.

It also is important to keep in mind the constantly changing nature of most living organizations. Contracting or expanding companies, shifts in product lines or services, and major changes in employee profiles all contribute toward altered structures and relationships that affect EAP service delivery. Any one of these changing conditions may mean that new internal resources are available to the program's clients or that formerly reliable resources no longer exist. Such changes also may require a review of external providers and community-based resources. A striking example of this reality is the major shift occurring in the nature of employee benefits, which materially influence who can receive what type of care under what conditions. It is essential for EAP staff to have a thorough understanding of their organization's current and projected benefit structure in order to work effectively with clients.

It also is helpful, but not always practical, for EAP staff to participate in other aspects of organizational effort not strictly related to the EAP as a way of maintaining a continuing source of information about the life of an organization. In one municipal EAP, the program director monitored annual recruiting exercises for police and firefighters. In a large metropolitan bank, EAP staff participated in the work of the philanthropic arm of the institution by helping to set funding priorities. Decisions as to whether or not to participate in such activities should take into consideration the extent to which participation contributes to the credibility and acceptance of the EAP or, conversely, to a confusion as to its role or function.

Employee Profile

Basic to any organizational assessment is the need to have a grasp on the demographic distribution of the workforce in terms of gender, age, race, and ethnic factors. It is important, too, to know something about the job categories included in the employee profile and the physical locations and conditions where people work. It is likely that the nature of EAP services will be very different in an insurance company with 80% of its workforce consisting of young women a few years out of high school; for a hospital staff with a mix of professional, semi-skilled, and unskilled workers; and in an industrial firm with a heavily unionized workforce of skilled tradespeople.

Depending on the nature of the employee analysis, EAP staff may anticipate problems of discrimination directed toward certain groups of employees. High proportions of ethnic minorities may dictate the need for multilingual counselors. Certain types of work environments can be predictive of greater stress, physical illness, on-the-job accidents, or the need for a particular network of resources and external providers.

EAP Needs Assessment

New accounts or organizations in the process of setting up or redesigning EAPs require a determination of the needs the EAP is expected to address. In existing programs a continuing assessment of changing needs in the light of changing circumstances assures that the EAP remains relevant. In order to define or redefine the specific issues the EAP must address, a broad-based knowledge of how multiple levels of staff view the system and its human service needs is important, because there can be major differences between managers' perceptions and those of the rank and file employees (Grissom, Baldadian, & Swisher, 1988).

An understanding of these complexities is facilitated by involving all organizational staff in confidential written surveys, focused discussion groups, and feedback from program clients. Especially at the outset of a program it can be very helpful to conduct direct interviews with a series of company personnel selected because of their key positions in the system; because they represent a cross-section of staff levels in terms of gender, age, seniority, location, and work responsibilities; or on the basis of other criteria suggested by the nature of the company itself. As suggested by Clark (1993), in addition to the factual data such interviews generate, they are important because they help identify patterns of data across systems and subsystems and because the participation of staff in the assessment of needs gives them a realistic sense of ownership in the program and in the delivery of EAP services.

Sharing the results of the organizational assessment with key personnel facilitates this process even further and adds to the overall reliability and validity of the analysis (Clark, 1993). In addition, the assessment itself may identify situations that cannot be dealt with by the EAP alone. I conducted a needs assessment for a national company with a number of geographically dispersed subunits by using a stratified employee sample in an effort to obtain an accurate reflection of employee concerns and interests. One unit with a high percentage of women workers produced multiple complaints of sexual harassment, which required a broad-based effort on the part of the human resources, management development, and training departments to address.

Policies and Procedures

It is the responsibility of the EAP manager, along with critical personnel of the organization, to make basic decisions about the EAP: who will be seen, the types of problems to be addressed, the variety of services to be offered, the location of these services, and the funding. The organizational assessment is a primary source of information in making these decisions. In new programs, decisions also must be made as to staffing, implementation, and how the EAP will interface with existing structures within the organization. As these decisions are made, they typically are formalized into specific statements of policy and procedures governing the ongoing life of the program, including the full range of administrative practices and activities that help to guarantee the EAP's smooth operation. In addition to these general operational statements, it is necessary for the manager to produce a formal written policy announcement that is circulated to employees to inform them about the program and what it can and cannot do. Such statements share several basic elements:

A recognition that problems of a personal nature can occur that may or may not affect job performance, and that the program exists to help employees deal with these problems

A statement noting who is eligible for the services

A statement regarding the voluntary nature of the program

Assurance that all records and discussions of personal problems will be handled in a confidential manner and a statement as to how the term *confidential* is understood, including any exceptions to this policy

Assurance that use of these services will not jeopardize an employee's job security, promotional opportunities, or reputation and that all records will be kept separate from personnel files

Recognition of the roles of supervisors in those situations in which deteriorating job performance is an issue

A statement supporting self-referrals

Costs, if any, incurred by the employee through the use of the program

In addition to this broad policy statement, the EAP manager also must devise and keep current a set of administrative policies and procedures that guides the day-in, day-out operations of the EAP. These policies and procedures must be consistent with the broader policy statement, for example, by establishing methods for handling case records that guarantee client confidentiality. They also must be consistent with the administrative and management expectations of the larger organization. As an example, some companies require that the EAP manager construct and defend an annual budget; others do not.

In-House Marketing

Contracting firms, of course, always are involved in the process of expanding their client base through ongoing marketing efforts. In addition, all EAPs must be engaged in a process of internal marketing directed toward keeping all personnel aware of the services the program provides and how to access these services. Two of the most commonly cited administrative tasks of any EAP are employee orientation and management training.

Employee orientation addresses the need to keep all employees, especially new employees, informed about the policies and procedures of the EAP. The specifics of how this is done depend on the individual organization, existing orientation programs, the size and location of the workforce, and the rate of staff turnover. It is important to keep in mind that hearing about the EAP once does not ensure that employees will remember enough about it to use the service when a need arises. It is necessary for most EAPs to generate additional ways of communicating with employees, through posters, brochures, check enclosures, or articles in the corporation's news organs. It also is vital that efforts are made to keep family members or dependents of employees informed about the program and ways it can be of help, because the existence of a problem may be more apparent to them than to the employee.

Managerial or supervisory training is intended to communicate the same information about the program; however, it typically includes additional information on how managers can refer troubled employees to the EAP. At one time this aspect of training was of major importance, when the typical troubled employee was the late-stage, chronic alcoholic, in denial about his or her drinking, who was experiencing declines in work performance. Under these circumstances the supervisor or manager plays a vital role in helping to confront these employees with the concrete evidence of their inability to function adequately in their work. Early models of supervisory training focused almost exclusively on the techniques to be used by supervisors to document productivity failures instead of on making judgments about the person's mental or emotional health. Even though supervisors and managers might know of a person's drinking, smell alcohol on his or her breath, or be privy to reports of the person's irresponsible behavior off the job while drunk, this information could not be used as a basis for a referral, as this could be construed as "diagnosing" substance abuse by persons not qualified to make these judgments, putting both the manager and the company at risk for litigation. The distinction between documenting and diagnosing was, and still is, a difficult one to make, especially for managers not familiar with human services. The difficulty has resulted in confused double messages being communicated in training sessions, which in turn can reduce the rate of supervisory referrals. Although it still is important for managers to understand how to recognize and refer those clients who fit the profile of the nonvoluntary, chemically abusing worker, this scenario is descriptive of a shrinking proportion of employees who use EAPs. As stated earlier, the majority of clients come voluntarily, often without the knowledge of their supervisors, and often with no discernible or documentable declines in work performance. This new reality has made the role of the manager somewhat less central to the way in which employees make use of the program, and other personnel not in supervisory positions may be more crucial in steering troubled workers to the EAP.

McClellan (1987) refers to a shift from just supervisory training to "key person" training to capitalize on the significance of other staff in the organization's referral loop. The managerial role often is that of an advisor when and if a worker's problem becomes evident on the job or is shared voluntarily by the employee. Just as a supervisor might recommend that a person check with the medical or personnel department for other issues, he or she can recommend the EAP as a resource for dealing with personal issues. This new role for managers requires that they remain informed about company resources and their differentiated services to be of greatest help to employees.

For instances in which work performance is an issue and the employee is reluctant to consider an EAP referral, it is important to encourage managers to consult with EAP staff on a case-by-case basis to help them with the necessary steps to get help for the person without placing themselves, the employee, or the employer in jeopardy. Managerial training also can emphasize the consultative role of the EAP as a support to managers even when a referral is not likely.

Evaluation

Evaluation is acknowledged to be an important aspect of EAP management by most program directors; however, the reality of practice suggests that not much evaluation actually occurs (Jerrell & Rightmeyer, 1982; Steidinger, 1986). Generally, most evaluation studies are limited to determinations of the cost benefit or cost-effectiveness of the program. It is equally important, however, to evaluate the extent to which the program is meeting the needs it is intended to address and whether or not individual clients are being helped with their specific problems (Jerrell & Rightmeyer, 1982).

Many difficulties are associated with EAP evaluation. Initially at least, the program actually may increase a company's benefits costs if it is successful in moving clients into treatment. Program managers also are concerned about how regular and objective evaluations might constitute threats to confidentiality (Williams & Tramontana, 1977). A conundrum that many EAP managers face is the expense of mounting sophisticated and reliable evaluation analyses, an expense that can cancel out any gains in cost-effectiveness the studies might demonstrate.

Other factors affecting evaluation analysis are the inclusion of services directed toward problems other than alcoholism and the increased number of voluntary referrals. Most major evaluation studies have assumed an alcoholic client who is experiencing measurable declines in work performance (Edwards, 1975; Foote & Erfurt, 1978; Kurtz, Googins, & Howard, 1984; Trice, Beyer, & Hunt, 1978). It is more difficult to demonstrate that problems other than alcoholism are costing an employer significant sums of money if management is not involved in the referral, if there have been no discernible declines in on-the-job productivity, if absenteeism and turnover are less affected, and if no referrals have been made to inpatient treatment centers. This does not mean emotional problems, marital difficulties, or life crises and transitions do not also result in losses to an employer that can be contained through a good EAP. It does mean that demonstrating these facts is more difficult, and few EAPs have the time, staff, or budget to mount such evaluations.

Programs need to have a self-contained and protected computer capability that maintains aggregate information to be used as a basis for regular statistical reporting, which can provide a beginning database for other analyses. Several computer programs can help in these basic tasks; however, they often are very expensive. Smaller EAPs may find it more cost-effective to design their own evaluation program.

EAP managers also are responsible for determining whether the program is doing what it is mandated to do and whether clients are being helped with their presenting problems. Usage or penetration rates (the percent of the total number of employees in a company using the program in a given period) assessed periodically can help determine whether the EAP is experiencing patterns of referral that reflect positive growth and an ability to reach all parts of the organization. Whether or not a program can demonstrate its contribution to bottom-line figures, it should be able to demonstrate that the basic program objectives are being addressed in a systematic way and that managers and employees are, in fact, receiving service. Formal feedback from managers, all levels of employees, and program consumers helps determine how well the program is fulfilling these obligations and how responsive it is to changing organizational needs.

Determining how well individual clients are being helped with the problems that bring them to the EAP is essentially an evaluation of counseling effectiveness. Professionals routinely evaluate treatment outcomes on a case-by-case basis: what works, under what conditions, and with what types of clients and problems. Although usually informal, such reviews also constitute a type of evaluation that not only enhances the quality of services but also can alleviate cost concerns, establishing the credibility of the program in a variety of ways, and potentially adding to the fundamental knowledge base about clinical process in general.

In spite of the fact that hard evidence has been available for more than 20 years attesting to the effectiveness of psychotherapy and other forms of interpersonal helping (Bergin, 1971; Bergin & Lambert, 1978; Lambert, Shapiro, & Bergin, 1986; Meltzoff & Kornreich, 1970; Videka-Sherman, 1985), it still is not uncommon for counselors in all fields to assume that the effectiveness of treatment still is open to question. It is imperative that EAP practitioners not be equivocal in communicating with CEOs and major administrators about the effectiveness of clinicians and the demonstrated practical utility of the services offered. It is important to know and to convey with conviction that interpersonal counseling is effective with a wide range of problems, that the effects are durable, and that they can be documented (Lambert et al., 1986).

Advisory Boards

Many settings include an EAP advisory committee that contributes in various ways to the processes described above in addition to serving other functions. Its basic responsibility is to ensure that the EAP meets the needs of the organization and the employees. A representative advisory group that includes members from all parts and levels of the organization as well as external advisors can be a continuing source of communication between the EAP and the employees and an additional form of in-house marketing. It can help to depoliticize the EAP by setting it apart from existing systemic rivalries, and, in doing so, serve as a buffer between the EAP and organizational elements that could undermine the program's effectiveness. There is a risk that board members may represent their own political interests in such a way as to become a barrier to effective programing, which is why decisions about board composition are so important. In some settings the board may have the responsibility of conducting the ongoing evaluation of the EAP manager and program, a situation that can be either very positive or perilous, depending on the membership and representation.

Although it is generally recognized that an advisory board is important at the outset of a program, there is less agreement on its value on a continuing basis. The major benefit in retaining a board is the extent to which it allows EAP staff to remain in touch with both the internal organization and developments in the EAP field through a careful and well thought-out membership roster. A board that is well informed about the needs of the company and also the evolving nature of the EAP field possesses a high degree of expertise that can be capitalized into a type of power that helps protect the program and the employees from arbitrary changes, staff cutbacks, or policy mandates. Board members also may provide special areas of expertise that can enhance the work of EAP staff, such as on issues of program evaluation.

In this chapter I have identified a range of programmatic issues that are implicit in the operations of most EAPs, whether they are in-house or externally run. More than in many traditional forms of counseling, it is important for EAP practitioners to understand these programmatic and organizational realities in order to work effectively with the troubled employees who come to them for help. For many, this is the appeal of EAP work: to participate in direct and often intimate ways in the life of a large and complex society of individuals and to use their professional skills to make a difference in that organization. I talk more about the organizational aspects of EAP work in Chapter 9, and ways in which EAP counselors intervene in these systems to bring about positive change.

NOTES

1. During this same period the U.S. military greatly expanded its corps of mental health staff, including social workers, to provide similar services to military personnel and their families. This form of social service is considered by some writers to be a significant example of occupational social work (Masi, 1982; Teare, 1987).

2. Steve Haught, Regional Director of Personal Support Services for the American Federation of State and Municipal Employees in Chicago, IL, points out that in corporate settings EAP personnel must be concerned with two clients: the individual employee and the company. In unions that responsibility must be expanded to include the union as a third client.

Chapter 3

A THEORY BASE FOR EAP PRACTICE

In this chapter I identify a range of basic concepts concerning individual growth and behavior, family interaction, work systems, and addictions that can be useful for EAP practitioners in their daily work with clients. The discussion is deliberately general as I am assuming that readers have their own sources of related information based on their professional training and experience, which can be used to deepen their understanding of these concepts. The discussion is based, too, on a conviction that for the professional a well-grounded theoretical framework is a necessary tool in organizing and prioritizing the complex array of information available to us in our work with complicated human beings who are parts of complicated systems.

One factor that distinguishes the professional counselor from the lay volunteer is the probability that the professional is operating from a more explicit set of assumptions about how people function, grow, and come to grief. Although a caring, empathic, and resourceful layperson may be operating from a set of assumptions about human functioning and what constitutes "good advice," the professional usually has had a course of study that makes these assumptions more accessible to conscious examination and review. In addition, professional education typically exposes its neophytes to alternative theories, to criteria that can help in evaluating the effectiveness and applicability of that knowledge, and to a set of values and ethics that governs how that knowledge can and cannot be used. Two problems associated with the use of theory in professional practice are the tendency to underestimate the extent to which it plays a role in clinical interaction, or the reverse, overvaluing the significance of a given theory. In the first instance practitioners see themselves as drawing on instinct, intuition, or the pragmatics of the client situation rather than on theory, partly because their theoretical framework becomes such an integrated aspect of the "doing" it seems like simple "common sense." In consulting or supervision it sometimes is necessary to remind practitioners that words such as *differentiation, transference,* and *equifinality* were not a part of their adolescent vocabulary. Other professionals become strongly identified with a particular theoretical orientation that they apply in a rigid or noncritical manner. The theory becomes paramount, requiring defense and protection, rather than the clients being served. Under these circumstances any inadequacy in the theory's ability to explain or provide direction for practice results in a critique of the client rather than the theory.

The failure to place formal knowledge, theoretical systems, and paradigmatic models of practice in their proper place in the work of professional helping can lead to less than optimally functioning professionals who are insecure and uncertain about their own efforts. A more serious consequence is ineffective assistance to clients. It is important that human service professionals understand that theory is a tool to be used in providing the best help possible. It can be extremely potent in cutting through layers of problems, denial, and resistance. Like any tool it can become more functional with use in specific practice situations, which in turn fosters a more balanced and critical assessment of its advantages and limitations. Practitioners in occupational settings have the responsibility of determining which aspects of the general knowledge base about counseling troubled people are most relevant to their practice and specific employing organizations.

Before proceeding with a discussion of theoretical concepts underlying employee assistance counseling, it may be helpful to clarify the meaning of certain terms used in this discussion. The term *clinical* often is equated with a type of intensive psychotherapy that many recovering alcoholics have denounced as posing a threat to their sobriety (Brown, 1985). In addition, at one time a status distinction arose between *assessment* and *treatment* in EAP circles with assessment, especially the assessment of the chemically addicted, being viewed as the more complex, challenging endeavor requiring greater levels of expertise than treatment. Treatment as an activity often either was undervalued or was thought of as requiring specialized knowledge and expertise beyond the scope of most employee assistance counselors, such as the special skills needed to treat sexual dysfunction, incest survivors, or the more severe psychiatric disorders.

As used here, *clinical* is intended to refer to the direct professional interaction between the counselor and the employee client or the client system and those activities carried out on a client's behalf, which include efforts to bring about change in the person, his or her interactions with others, and his or her situation. It does not refer only to a particular form of individual therapy or a narrowed focus on personality modification. It does not assume that it is the client who has the problem or is necessarily the focus of change. *Treatment,* too, is used in a general sense to refer to any planned, purposeful, and professional activity intended to assist the client with whatever is causing distress. A call to the personnel office to help arrange for a shift change is treatment if it means, for example, that a single parent will be available when the children come home from school. Such an intervention may accomplish more for clients than intensive therapy because it adds to the parent's peace of mind and provides greater opportunity for family members to work out their relationships in a face-to-face context. Given these definitions, good assessment is just one aspect of overall treatment, and status distinctions between the two are professionally and pragmatically irrelevant.

The concept of *intervention* also may need clarification. In the treatment of substance abuse, it is used in a very specific sense to describe a particular form of confrontational interaction with chemically dependent persons. It is intended to penetrate the denial system using family, supervisors, or any significant others who can help repudiate the abuser's evasive tactics. My use of the term is more general, and refers to problem-solving interactions with a client, with others in his or her interpersonal network, or with his or her social and situational contexts that are intended to address the concerns the client is experiencing.

EXPLORING THE THEORY BASE

Ford and Urban (1963) make a distinction between *explanatory theory, change theory,* and *practice theory* in describing the knowledge base of psychotherapists. Siporin (1975, p. 94) makes a similar distinction, using the terms *foundation or behavioral theory* to refer to concepts that attempt to understand and explain why people and systems behave in the way they do, in contrast to practice theory, which is concerned with how to intervene professionally with clients. Explanatory theories usually contain assumptions and implicit predictions about how human behavior can be altered and changed, and these assumptions determine to a great extent how professionals approach the counseling task.

Professionals also operate from a related but often distinct set of concepts that is concerned primarily with proscriptive procedures for interacting with clients. *Practice theories* and *practice models* represent organized frameworks for identifying, categorizing, and intervening in client problems. In contrast to explanatory or behavior theories, which attempt to address the "why" question, practice models focus on the "what" question: "What should I do as a professional to help this client with this set of issues?" Most practice models are tied to one or more explanatory theories, but this is not necessarily the case. Often practice models serve as conceptual frameworks to help practitioners organize, evaluate, and select which set of explanatory ideas is most relevant to a specific case situation. Other practitioners, including many concerned with problems of alcohol addiction, are identified with a clear-cut and functional practice model that does not attempt to explain the etiology of the problem. The specific interventive strategies of documenting failures in functioning, encountering denial, using family members and significant others to assist in the process of confrontation, and the use of 12-Step recovery groups have been deemed effective without elaborate attention to issues of why people become alcoholic. Similarly, empirically based models of intervention (Tolson, 1988) retain a focus on what forms of clinical assistance can be documented as effective without the sometimes confounding effects of explanatory theory.

No claims can be made currently that any model or theory is superior to any other; practitioners from different disciplines and orientations seem to be equally effective (Lambert et al., 1986). The effectiveness literature does indicate, however, that having a theoretical orientation is important in helping clients, and that it may be one of the factors that cuts across all types of counseling and helps to explain the general effectiveness of most therapy when compared to untreated or placebo groups.

Most counselors are operating from a theory base whether or not they are aware of it. A practitioner's individualized theoretical orientation provides a mechanism for focusing attention on the client's complaint and a frame of reference for examining the dimensions of the problem in ways that often are unique and novel for clients. It also provides a basis for confirming that something can be done to ameliorate the distress the problem is causing, and for optimism that the client can regain control over the situation. A practitioner's conviction about his or her theoretical framework fosters credibility in ways that are not unlike those typical of the priest or shaman (Frank, 1974).

It is important to make the components of theoretical and practice frameworks conscious and accessible and to determine which concepts are especially useful to the EAP practitioner. EAP practitioners were asked about their theoretical orientation in my analysis of a group of 42 counselors (Cunningham, 1992). Their responses were typical of other human service professionals (Garfield & Bergin, 1986; Jayaratne, 1982) to the extent that almost without exception they identified an array of both explanatory and practice models that they used: They were eclectic rather than solely identified with any particular theory or model. Many made an interesting distinction between the primarily explanatory concepts they used during the process of assessment and those that governed their actual therapeutic interventions in a manner similar to the "technical eclecticism" referred to by Lazarus (1967) and Siporin (1985).

Most respondents identified various psychodynamic theories—ego psychology, theories of personality development—as providing a very usable set of insights that allowed them to pursue significant life history events, to make connections that clients found helpful between past and present problems, and to make assessments as to a client's general ability to function in his or her various life roles. However, these theoretical models were viewed as less directly relevant to their specific interventions with clients on a day-in, day-out basis. For these tasks counselors drew from a wide assortment of treatment techniques associated with many different practice models: problem solving, family systems theory, paradoxical techniques, neurolinguistic programming, relaxation therapy, behavioral modification, and guided imagery, among others. Their choices undoubtedly were linked to their personal educational and practice experiences and those clinical skills they found effective with clients.

These practitioners cited, as well, various forms of systems theory as providing an important means of understanding not only the problems clients brought to them, but also the complicated work environments in which clients were employed. Most of these respondents also identified addictions theory and emerging knowledge about dysfunctional families as central to their personal theoretical frame of reference, but their understanding of addictions theory varied. Some considered it to be an etiological, biogenetic explanation of alcoholism. Most saw it as a practice model that governed their interventive interactions with the chemically dependent. For many in this group issues of etiology were thought to be essentially irrelevant as long as the interventions worked. With these thoughts providing a background, I next examine areas of theoretical development that are important in working with employee clients.

THEORIES OF HUMAN BEHAVIOR

Personality Development

One advantage in the current proliferation of information about adult children of alcoholics and dysfunctional families is the way in which it has popularized and made palatable the concept that the problems we encounter in our current lives often are influenced by our experiences as children. Our culture has a deeply ingrained suspicion of psychoanalyzing. Satires ridiculing Freudian interpretations linking today's incipient ulcer with infantile eroticism have graced our dramas, literature, and comedy routines. Yet many men and women have recognized themselves in descriptions of behaviors and attitudes that children assume to protect themselves from the assaults of traumatic early experiences and that they may carry into adulthood (Black, 1982; Wegscheider, 1981; Woititz, 1983). It is perhaps this core understanding that is central to any theory of human development that makes it useful in treatment.

In addition, developmental theories typically include a set of explanatory concepts that attempt to decipher the combination of life events, particularly those factors in infancy, childhood, and adolescence, that more or less determine how a basic genetic endowment can be influenced and shaped as a person moves through the life cycle, and how the personality achieves a sense of form, constancy, and identity. Implicit in such explanations are ideas as to what constitutes normal and abnormal functioning within the dominant culture, and an understanding of the internal and external strategies and resources a person can draw upon to maintain a functional style of behavior.

Most personality theories acknowledge the obvious truth that humans do not always understand the bases of their behavior. Their motivations for doing what they do are not always rational or accessible to conscious control. Even the most desired change in functioning may not occur in spite of a person's best efforts to make it happen. Sometimes dysfunctional patterns are so ingrained that persons may not even be aware of how different they are from the ways in which others behave. Whether or not a counselor chooses to use classic Freudian concepts about the unconscious, there needs to be some acknowledgment that a vital part of clinical inter-action requires an understanding of how much of clients' feelings, beliefs, and attitudes are beyond their immediate grasp and perception. A corollary to this is that part of EAP counseling, even very brief contacts, may lie in the counselor's ability to enhance clients' awareness and understanding of what previously was inaccessible.

A limitation of some developmental theories is the inadequate attention given to issues of adult development and the extent to which early life phenomena can be altered for better or worse by subsequent relationships, traumas, stresses, or supports. Developmental theories that focus on adolescent and preadolescent stages of development may seem to suggest that how the person negotiates these stages can predict specific types of adult dysfunction, an assumption questioned by Stern (1985) and others. Yet another limitation is the extent to which some theories are concerned with pathology or dysfunction rather than with the recognition that everyone, even the most self-actualized, integrated, and evolved personalities, experience problems in functioning, disappointing relationships, and periods of apparent decompensation.

Psychodynamically oriented personality theories also are criticized for the extent to which they are based on assumptions of the normative nature of male development; any experiences of personal growth and development inconsistent with those seen as desirable for white men in our culture are viewed as unhealthy (Gilligan, 1982; Goldstein, 1980; Lowenstein, 1983; Young-Eisendrath, 1988). To the extent that such biases are implicit in the theories we use, practitioners run the risk of assessing women, people of color, or ethnic minorities as inherently immature, maladjusted, or imperfect. Because these groups are considered from the outset as representing something less than the normative model, their views of reality are questioned, their opinions and attitudes are disqualified, and their aspirations and objectives are not taken seriously (Young-Eisendrath, 1988). When such messages are communicated within the context of what is supposed to be a helping relationship with a credentialed expert, clients easily can come away from such an experience in worse shape than before they sought help.

In reaction to these perceived limitations, practitioners often choose to modify their theoretical framework by including concepts that help to explain a variety of human experience and cultural diversity. Theoretical frameworks can be further enriched by insights that acknowledge the open-ended nature of development; the extent to which one's experiences as a worker, spouse, parent, lover, or student can influence that development;

and an understanding of the reality that there is no end product of fully mature development, like a fully grown tooth, that we achieve or a single set of experiences that constitutes "good" or "bad" growth and maturation. Rather, the task for most people is to learn the skills involved in orchestrating the internal and external pressures in a way that maintains a functional balance at any given point and that sets the stage, it is hoped, for continued optimal growth and development.

Work and Personality: The Interface

One of the distinct advantages of workplace practice is the opportunity it provides for us to see and understand how adults function in one of their most significant life roles—as workers—and how the performance of work influences continuing development (Mortimer & Borman, 1988; Perlman, 1964, 1982; Smelser & Erikson, 1980). Personality theories often are underdeveloped in their analysis of adult behavior because of the absence of stage-specific biological markers during adulthood, except for menopause in women. Work, however, provides very significant life-event markers that both precipitate and terminate major life transitions such as entry into adult responsibilities, changes in the amount and complexity of those responsibilites, and retirement (Levinson, 1980). Work life also includes a number of challenges, barriers, and frustrations that influence ongoing adult development in diverse ways.

We are a society that values work. The hard-driving workaholic still is something of a folk hero in our culture, an acceptable model to emulate. On a very personal level work provides us with an identity source. People define themselves or are defined by others largely in terms of their occupational title. One of the first items of information men and women in our culture are apt to share with one another is the kind of work they do. When individuals are asked to talk about themselves, they most often will start with a description of their work. Our work locates us in the socioeconomic hierarchy and influences the value others place on us and their expectations for certain types of attributes or behavior.

We place a high value on those employed in the management of finance; some aspects of technology; certain forms of communication; extremely well-paid workers, such as athletes and entertainers; and any position that involves real or implied power over large numbers of people. Occupations associated with the powerless, the dependent, or the disadvantaged, such as teaching and human service, are considered low status and are penalized for being so with low salaries and inadequate benefits. Persons who do not work outside the home for pay are devalued regardless of their intent, motivation, or capacity to do so. We tend to ignore society's role in contributing to the deeply ingrained economic and social conditions that contribute to problems of unemployment and underemployment, and instead we punish the nonworker.

In addition, work provides us with a variety of opportunities for growth and development. It is through work that we come to know the larger world beyond our families, schools, and neighborhoods. It often provides the first experience young workers have with different cultures, races, attitudes, and values. It provides us with the chance to learn new tasks, to engage our problem-solving skills, and to experience a measure of success, all reinforced through that powerful motivator—a paycheck. It also acts as a regulator of behavior in which the worker must structure his or her time and performance in a way that meets the expectations of the employer and coworkers, a significant step in the direction of moving from the dependent position of being cared for toward that of suspending one's own needs temporarily in the interests of addressing the needs of the other (Perlman, 1964).

The workplace is for many an arena of intense and significant relationships that both challenge and frustrate the evolving capacity for human affiliation, separation, and individuation. Not only do most of us spend more of our waking hours with workmates than with immediate family, but also our tenure in work settings may be longer than our marriages, our lives as caretakers to our children, or the most engrossing sexual alliances. There is evidence to suggest that we can easily become the kind of person these relationships need us to be, or that the organizational hierarchy requires, whether or not we are aware of it and whether or not it is in our best interests as individuals (Kanter, 1977a). When work goes well it is a source of gratification, recognition, and enhanced self-esteem, which may compensate for earlier developmental deficits and failures.

But work does not always go well. For many it is a source of discouragement, depreciation, or entrapment into a life of diminishing opportunities, personally or economically. Lundberg (1974) suggests in her analysis of several studies that the kind of work required of people actually has the potential of putting a cap on their level of emotional development. Kohn's study (1980) indicates that intellectual ability, rather than being a stable personality characteristic, changes in relation to the complexity of work tasks, increasing if tasks are of sufficient complexity but slowing down or even reversing development when they are not. Work may provide a young person's first experience with sexism, racism, and exploitation.

Disturbed individuals in power positions contaminate the emotional health of others even while enhancing the economic health of the organization, and they can provoke the same types of symptomatic behavior in work groups as occur in dysfunctional families. Physically toxic conditions at the workplace can have profound effects on not just employees, but also their entire families (Stellman & Daum, 1973; *Work in America,* 1973).

For many people work can operate as a defense against threatening circumstances in other parts of their life. Parents who feel out of control in their interactions with their children can withdraw emotional investment from the family arena and direct it toward their work. The workaholic may be driven more by fear of the emotional risks associated with interpersonal relationships and a social life than by commitment to the job. For certain people who are relatively free to choose their work environments, their choices may be driven by the need to find a set of circumstances that will indulge their neuroses and hold them in place. For the average working person, such choices may be a luxury, and he or she must find a way to accommodate to even destructive work environments to survive at all. All of these factors are important to personality functioning and adult role performance; any can be operating with clients coming to an EAP.

Clinical practice at the workplace offers professionals an opportunity to broaden their understanding of these many facets of ongoing human development and change. Occupational practice clarifies some very traditional concepts that often are less evident in settings in which clients have diminished personal, interpersonal, and situational resources. As an example, many clinicians are committed to an emphasis on health rather than pathology, but this often is difficult to operationalize in professional settings that see only the most chronically ill and socially neglected, or that treat clients only at times of their most diminished performance.

In contrast, workplace clients exhibit a range of internal and external resources that facilitate treatment. Not only do they have the advantages conferred by income, benefits, job structure, and relationships; they also demonstrate the ability to organize themselves enough to meet the requirements of responsible task performance, decision making, collaboration with others, and problem solving over time. They demonstrate a diversity of flexible and creative coping behaviors that expands our understanding of human coping in general. The workplace also provides an arena to illustrate for clinicians the significance of the situational context in understanding problems in functioning and the extent to which situational interventions in the workplace can help not only to relieve stress, but also to stimulate and support healthy functioning.

Systems Theory

In addition to a basic understanding of the ability or disability of individuals to grow, learn, and mature, practitioners also need an informed basis on which to understand the interactions among people, organizations, and societies. Systems theory offers a helpful overall framework in understanding both the complex structures in which people carry out their work lives and the interactional patterns that exist in work groups. Ecological systems theory (Germain & Gitterman, 1980; Meyer, 1983) represents approaches to translating the basic insights provided by general systems theory into practice guidelines. A major advantage of a systems orientation in working with people is that it fosters an awareness of a person as a part of multiple levels of interaction with other individuals, groups, organizations, and institutions. In addition, we are helped to understand that these interacting forces are in a constant state of change over time as individuals influence and are affected by all of the elements in the system. A static view of a person at a single point is replaced by a dynamic appreciation of life in motion. Linear cause-effect relationships between variables are enriched by an understanding of patterns of action and interaction.

One area of practice that has been especially influenced by systems theory is the assessment of and intervention with families (Haley, 1976; Madanes & Haley, 1977; Minuchin, 1974). Currently a great deal of attention is being given to adult children of alcoholics and other dysfunctional families who are carrying into adulthood the consequences of early family disorganization including physical, emotional, and sexual abuse (Beattie, 1987; Black, 1982; Woititz, 1983). Family systems concepts allow us to organize the complex array of factors that may have contributed to the problem of dysfunctional families and to use this organizational framework as a basis for shaping intervention strategies.

For example, it is helpful to understand that families, like all systems, are made up of subsystems and that each of these units displays certain boundary characteristics that can be thought of as occurring on a continuum from very flexible to very rigid. The particular boundary arrangements typical of any one family determine to a great extent the capacity of its members to relate to one another within the family and to other external systems (Kantor & Lehr, 1975). No one style is inherently healthier than another; rather it is a question of what best serves the needs of the family as a group and those of its members at different points in the family life cycle. For example, at times of crisis or the loss of a family member, permeable boundaries allow for greater merger among family members, which in turn facilitates the grieving process and permits reintegration and realignment of roles. In contrast, as children develop and assume greater responsibility for their lives, well-defined and fixed boundaries help them to develop an identity that is unique and distinct from those of other family members.

Family systems also evolve idiosyncratic styles of communication and interaction that both shape and reveal internal power alignments, how decisions get made, and the range and quality of feelings that can or cannot be expressed (Hepworth & Larsen, 1990, 1993). Dysfunctional families are apt to organize themselves in relation to patterns of addiction or abuse that determine the thoughts, feelings, and interactions of everyone within the system (Steinglass, 1987). Acknowledged and unacknowledged family rules help determine the roles different family members play, who communicates what to whom under what circumstances, and both the long-term and short-term goals and expectations a family has for itself.

Communication patterns within families have come in for a great deal of attention for several decades (Bateson, Jackson, Haley, & Weakland, 1956; Laing, 1965; Lewis, Beavers, Gossett, & Phillips, 1976; Satir, 1967). All behavior is recognized as representing communication, and often the verbal and nonverbal messages we send and receive are incongruent. The potential of mystification, double-bind communication, family secrets, and myths to create cognitive disorientation and developmental arrests is recognized easily by EAP practitioners who daily encounter victims of such devastating family experiences. Adults who as children were told they were not seeing what they saw or feeling what they felt are victims of mystifying communication (Laing, 1965) in which their honest and accurate responses are disqualified and depreciated to keep the system from having to deal with an uncomfortable reality. Family myths abound in alcoholic families, as when clients must continue to describe a family member's addiction as a periodic "attack" of some other ailment or parental absences on binges as "business trips."

Clients often carry the self-destructive patterns they learned in their family into other systems and relationships. Although there is some danger in being too reductionist about the applicability of family systems concepts to other systems, it is easy to understand the dynamic that fosters a person's expectation, for example, that authority figures on the job will engage in the same power and control conflicts as did authority figures in his or her family of origin, or that asking questions, noticing too much, or forming trust relationships are dangerous undertakings. Persons who have learned to mistrust direct messages or who have become adept at conveying or deciphering dysfunctional communications can create havoc in a work unit almost as though different languages are being spoken. If the current or nuclear families provide little experience in effective problem solving, task performance, mutual respect, or positive rewards, work life can become a replication of dysfunctional interaction patterns that create barriers to more satisfying performance.

It is not just dysfunctional family patterns that are transferred to work systems. As Friedman (1985) noted, workers tend to recreate on the job the same types of arrangements that they have learned in their families because those are the only ones they know. Much of the maneuvering that occurs in work groups can be traced to attempts to reconcile different family-based expectations about relationships, problem solving, or communication. Some organizations identify and foster a family-like atmosphere, which can reinforce both the functional and the more problematic aspects of learned interpersonal interaction.

As discussed in more detail in Chapter 8, all family members are influenced by the scheduling, economic, and interpersonal experiences encountered at the workplace, and when all adults in a family are wage earners, it is much more difficult for a family system to ensure that the needs of all family members are being dealt with. The need for multiple salaries is contributing to dramatic changes in the style and structure of family life as employees look toward alternative arrangements to supplement their own efforts. For example, permanent or a constantly changing series of child-care workers become significant members of the family system, exchanging their own patterns of functional or dysfunctional behavior with the other family members and influencing in the process the development of the children they care for. A systems perspective allows us to remain sensitive to the multiple ways in which work and family realities interact and often compete with one another for the time, energy, and attention of the employee.

Addictions Theory

A major aspect of the work in virtually all EAPs involves the identification, assessment, and referral of chemically addicted employees or their family members. Professionals entering the field must have these skills, and often new EAP practitioners are socialized into an understanding and endorsement of the medical/disease model that argues that addictions are hereditary diseases rather than psychiatric labels or moral weaknesses.

Frequently the disease concept is contrasted with traditional psycho-dynamic explanations of addiction, and hot debates ensue as to which position best explains the etiology of chemical dependency.

The perspective presented here is grounded in the belief that the current state of our knowledge of chemical dependency makes clear that no single causal explanation is tenable, and only a multifactored understanding of the etiology of alcoholism and drug abuse is possible. It is my position, too, that a general understanding of the etiology of addictions is important not just to the researcher and theoretician, but to the practitioner as well, because understanding something about the general causes of substance abuse directly affects their approaches to assessment and intervention with specific clients. This is not to say that a practitioner working with an individual client needs to construct a treatment strategy aimed at discovering the cause of the addiction. It does mean that a multifaceted understanding of the factors that create addiction or hold it in place is essential in directing assessment, knowing what questions to ask, anticipating what elements are likely to contribute to relapse, and facilitating recovery for all clients.

Throughout much of the twentieth century, mental health professionals and others attempted to explain addictions on the basis of the emerging theories of personality development or a range of other psychological variables. Although the predominant theoretical explanations changed over time,[1] common, related themes included images of alcoholics and addicts as (a) emotionally immature, unstructured, or character-disordered beings who lacked the internal controls or moral will to refrain from drugs or drinking; (b) someone who had experienced severe trauma during very early, pregenital stages of personality development that generated an addictive personality and addictive behavior in adulthood; or (c) a person with a drug or alcohol addiction that was symptomatic of other repressed psychological trauma (Blum, 1966; Nathan, 1987). These etiological assumptions led to treatment approaches that emphasized as an objective major restructuring of the personality or a search for the underlying psychological conflict or developmental deficit that, if discovered, would lead to the cessation or control of the addictive behaviors.

Such treatment simply was beyond the reach of most substance abusers, and an unintended consequence of this approach was to provide excuses for the chemically dependent to continue the use of drugs or drinking. If there was some unknown "X" factor that explained the patient's behavior, then there was nothing he or she could do about it until "it" was uncovered in treatment. The therapist became an enabler, creating conditions that fed into the denial systems of abusers and supported their attempts to minimize the amount of their abuse, which in turn helped to reinforce their life-threatening behaviors. This theoretical orientation was supported in part by early studies done with biased samples of low-functioning male alcoholics recruited from shelters, skid row, and the caseloads of chronic Veterans Administration patients and correctional institutions. Over time, the accumulation of both research and practice evidence (Ausubel, 1980; Cox, 1985; Marlatt & Baer, 1988; Nathan, 1987) failed to demonstrate the utility of only psychodynamic explanations of alcoholism unless addictive behavior was used as a criterion for personality classifications.

The disease concept of alcoholism gained strength among practitioners partly in reaction to the psychodynamic theories, which were seen as actually life-threatening to the person trying to gain some understanding of his or her behavior (Brown, 1985; Freeman, 1992b; Watts, 1981). Although Benjamin A. Rush defined alcoholism as a disease as early as 1794 (Miller, 1991; National Institute on Alcohol Abuse and Alcoholism, 1990), much of the credit for our current use of the term belongs to Alcoholics Anonymous (AA) and other 12-Step groups. The AA movement, which began in the 1930s, was in touch with a different group of alcoholics who represented a much wider array of backgrounds, personality types, and life experiences than those under investigation by mental health professionals. The disease metaphor stated that alcoholism was an illness that its victims neither caused nor could cure on their own. Being restored to health required acknowledging one's powerlessness over alcohol and calling upon a higher power and the continuing support of companion sufferers to modify one's behavior enough to permanently avoid the use of alcohol. Thinking of alcoholism as a disease helped reduce societal and self-stigmatization of alcoholics as being morally weak, a shift in attitude that most certainly aided in recovery. More recently the disease concept has been used in at least three different ways:

As a statement about etiology, that is, an assumption that most or all substance abuse and addiction is caused by biochemical or genetic factors that have been only partially identified

As a practice model guiding processes of assessment and treatment based on a recognition of the importance of denial, confrontive interventions, and inpatient or outpatient addictions treatment combined with regular attendance at 12-Step recovery groups

As a philosophical approach to treatment that says that addictions need to be understood as primary conditions and not as merely symptomatic or secondary to other psychological states and that priority must be given to the treatment of the chemical abuse before other issues are attended to, as the addictions are life-threatening in and of themselves

Unfortunately, identification with the disease concept of alcoholism is used cynically by some as a political statement, almost a separate "credential" intended to facilitate entry into the tight world of EAP practice. Because it was the dominant model during the early years of the EAP movement, neophytes learned that espousing this position—whatever their real beliefs about addictions might be—would facilitate their acceptance by the leaders in the field and potential mentors.

Not recognizing that the term has different shades of meaning to different people contributes to pointless confusion and misunderstandings that can undermine honest attempts to deal with afflicted clients. The extreme etiologic view argues that all addictions are genetic or physiological in origin, with allergies or diabetes commonly cited as metaphors, and, as such, that they need to be understood as being beyond the control of the sufferer. This perspective gains credence with the growing body of research that points to a variety of genetic, neurological, and biochemical factors that may be implicated in the cross-generational transmission of alcoholism (Moss, Blackstone, Martin, & Tarter, 1989; Schuckit, 1987; Tabakoff et al., 1988). Ongoing research generally is supportive of the concept of the presence of genetic and biochemical elements as causative factors in some forms of addictions; however, the results vary for different substances, and we do not yet know all the ways in which these factors operate in different populations and under different conditions. Further, too many examples of alcohol-addicted patients do not fit this diagnostic protocol. Most of the evidence that does exist relates to alcoholism, and the assumption cannot be made by practitioners that anything true of alcoholism must be true of all forms of addictions. All chemical addictions involve physiological components, but there is accumulating evidence that emotional and environmental factors also precipitate the onset of substance abuse and the eventual development of chemical dependence (National Institute on Alcohol Abuse and Alcoholism, 1990). In addition, emotional and environmental factors may moderate the effects of genetic predisposition to alcoholism (Windle & Searles, 1990).

This does not mean physiological factors are not present in the development of abuse or addiction. They are, and they need to be understood by clinicians in order for clinicians to do a responsible job of assessment and treatment. Nor does the diversity of research evidence refute the fact that vulnerability to some forms of alcoholism and possibly some drug addictions is transmitted across generations. It does mean the cutting edge of knowledge development for the coming decade is the need to more fully understand the interactive effects of physiological, psychological, and environmental factors in explaining why some persons who are genetically predisposed to alcoholism do not develop the disease and others who are not genetically predisposed do, and to translate that understanding into more effective models of practice (Cloninger, 1987; National Institute on Alcohol Abuse and Alcoholism, 1990; Tarter, Alterman, & Edwards, 1985; Zucker & Gomberg, 1986).

The expectation that there is a biogenetic X factor that eventually will explain all or most forms of substance abuse is as unwarranted as a psychodynamic X factor. At the very least we have to come to an understanding that alcohol and drug addictions are not unitary phenomena, and that the insights that help us understand one group of abusers may have much less relevance to another.

I am proposing here as part of my theoretical framework a modified definition of alcoholism as outlined in the *Seventh Special Report to the Congress on Alcohol and Health* (National Institute on Alcohol Abuse and Alcoholism, 1990), which states that like other somatic illnesses—such as hypertension, diabetes, and coronary artery disease—alcohol dependence is characterized by biological and physiological processes in which a possible genetic predisposition is activated and/or maintained by an array of psychosocial factors. Like other diseases, alcohol dependence is identifiable by a cluster of symptoms that predict the course and outcome of the disease, including increased tolerance of alcohol, physiologically consistent withdrawal symptoms, and predictable biological effects on other bodily systems that give rise to secondary disease processes. Included in this statement is an awareness that not all persons who may be genetically predisposed will become alcoholic, and that not all alcohol-dependent drinkers come from backgrounds that point to genetic transmission of a vulnerability to alcoholism.

There exists less empirical evidence on which to make a similar statement about drug abuse, at least in terms of genetic predisposition, but, like alcohol dependence, drug addiction is recognizable through a cluster of physical and psychological symptoms and predictable paths of biomedical deterioration that can be differentiated to some extent by the substance being abused. Also like alcohol dependence, drug abuse entails side effects that contribute to other types of medical problems that can become severely debilitating when the drug use is prolonged. In the case of controlled substances any use other than by prescription is abuse because it is illegal.

In addition, emerging research evidence links eating disorders to a range of contributory elements including genetic and biochemical factors (Burrows, 1992). However, other apparently addictive behaviors, such as sex, gambling, or compulsive abusive relationships, which are characterized primarily through social and behavioral symptoms, require other explanatory paradigms upon which to base assessment and intervention (Quadland, 1988). Under these circumstances the use of the disease concept of addiction as a philosophy of treatment may be more functional than trying to assume a comparable etiological base to alcohol or drug addiction. For example, such a philosophy would dictate that the clinician must treat the problem as a primary condition or "disease" and as the focus of assessment and intervention, and not as secondary to an undiagnosed primary illness. It would recognize the overwhelming power of addictions, whatever their source, over vulnerable persons, whatever their circumstances, and that labeling, stigmatizing, or moralizing with the victim is destructive (Lesieur & Custer, 1984).

This disorganized array of information puts a greater burden on practitioners to become and to remain informed about the nature of addictions as an essential ingredient in the accurate assessment of clients and for purposes of treatment planning. Even more important is the need to individualize each client as a basis for determining what unique mix of biological, psychological, and environmental factors are operative in his or her addiction and which must be addressed in treatment. Failure to do so increases the probability of relapse and treatment failures.

NOTE

1. In the 1930s and 1940s the cause of alcoholism was thought to be an "oral stage deficiency" indicating that in infancy the alcoholic had not received adequate oral gratification. Later theorists speculated that the opposite might be the case: that the cause was oral overstimulation during this period.

Chapter 4

INITIATING SERVICES
AND GENERAL ASSESSMENT

Up to this point I have examined the programmatic and organizational aspects of employee assistance and the types of professional knowledge and information the EAP practitioner must have to perform in a credible and responsible manner. The core element of employee assistance, however, is the troubled employee who is in need of some sort of help to function more successfully in one or several life roles.

In this chapter I look at the circumstances that bring the employee and the counselor together, including the practice implications of management referrals and self-referrals, special issues governing the nature of the counseling relationship, and the general content areas typically covered in EAP assessments. These consist of (a) analysis of the presenting problem; (b) in-depth understanding of the client as an individual, including current status, mental, emotional, and physical health, and religious or spiritual orientation; and (c) a review of the client's significant life systems, including family, work, and social systems. Chapter 5 covers the special and increasingly more complex issues associated with the assessment of chemical dependency and substance abuse.

REFERRALS TO THE EAP

Rarely is there a separate intake function in work-based programs, unlike traditional counseling agencies. Some employees seek assistance with problems not within the purview of the EAP, and these may need to be redirected to the personnel office, the business agent, the union steward, or the medical department. Generally, however, the only determination of eligibility is whether the person is a company employee or a dependent or family member of an employee. As one counselor phrased it, "There is no rigmarole, no forms to fill out; I can usually see the person within 48 hours."

The extraordinary diversity of EAP clients means the next person seeking help may need only basic information about elder care, or may be a major corporate decision maker whose errors, made while drunk or hungover, are costing the firm millions of dollars, or may be a depressed single parent too overwhelmed to cope with multiple and conflicting role expectations. All employees, however serious or mundane their needs, are entitled to a patient hearing and a professional assessment of the significance of whatever circumstances are troubling them. The helping process begins with the first phone call, as the interaction is directed toward establishing some clarity about the nature of the presenting problem and a framework for working together to do something about it. A primary consideration in initiating help is the type of referral to the EAP service— either management based or self-referral—and the implications these two different processes have for action by the EAP.

Management Referrals

Although the number of supervisory referrals has declined in most programs, EAPs still place an especially high priority on being able to respond quickly to requests for help from management. Prompt action may be necessary because an employee's behavior has undermined the productivity of an entire department. The worker's job may be at risk or his or her behavior may pose a threat to others. Management referrals often include some of the most serious and intractable problems of substance abuse or emotional illness. Technically such clients are "voluntary" in the sense that no one can be forced to make use of EAP services.[1] In fact, such an employee may understand that few other options are available unless job performance improves. In rare instances the employee may be too out of control or emotionally distraught to make a voluntary decision and the EAP staff may be called in on an emergency basis. Yet another scenario is the management referral based not on job performance problems but on the manager's awareness that a worker is encountering personal problems that might be relieved through the EAP.

Most EAPs include as a part of their services some form of management training directed toward keeping supervisors and other key personnel informed about the types of services the EAP provides, the situations that suggest that an employee needs such services, and the types of information required from a manager to support such a referral (see Chapter 2). However, it usually is not until a problem arises that the manager really will be able to attend to and understand this information. Most managers require individual consultative help from the EAP to actually implement a referral, especially for the first time. This personalized consultation helps to establish the basis for the manager's concern, the steps necessary to bring about a referral, and any attitudes or personal issues the manager may have about making the referral.

As indicated in Chapter 2, the distinction between referring someone to the EAP because of personal problems while refraining from actually diagnosing what those problems are is a complicated one. Even EAP counselors have difficulty interpreting the difference, especially in companies in which performance standards are vague or inexact, lines of accountability are not clear, or the nature of work assignments does not lend itself to clear-cut criteria for determining when the job is being done well or poorly. Whenever possible, it is important to determine the manager's view of the normative expectations of job performance even if these expectations are not spelled out in written job performance evaluations. This provides the manager with a frame of reference for assessing the degree to which a particular employee's behavior constitutes a genuine deviation from the employee's typical behavior and that of the work group. It also is important to determine how informed the manager is about performance standards that exist within the company and whether or not those standards would apply in this situation.

Mrs. B. supervised the checkout clerks at several suburban supermarkets. She called the external EAP counselor in reference to a long-term older employee who was missing more days than usual, two or three each month for the past several months. The worker seemed unhappy and withdrawn and was garnering complaints from both customers and coworkers because of her slowness in handling orders. During the phone conversation with the EAP counselor, it was suggested that Mrs. B. consult the performance appraisals conducted regularly on all employees. Mrs. B. determined that the employee's performance still was within the acceptable range but that it had shown a marked decline from the very high standards this worker had maintained for most of her career with the company.

On the basis of her consultation with the EAP, Mrs. B. temporarily rearranged her work schedule to spend more time at the store where this employee worked. Over time she observed some tense interracial interaction between the employee and the young African-American, part-time students who worked as baggers on weekends. There were clear-cut problems of communication, teasing on the part of the students, and racial slurs from the employee in question. Mrs. B. decided to try to talk to the employee informally without reference to the EAP, and the situation was more or less resolved with a change in work schedule for the employee.

For situations in which performance declines are more clear-cut and better documented, it may be necessary for the manager to meet with the employee in one or more sessions to communicate the nature of these declines and their implications for the employee. These confrontations often are difficult even for very experienced managers, and supportive coaching from the EAP may be helpful. Such coaching may include identification of enabling attitudes on the part of the manager or other employees that are making it difficult for the troubled worker get the help he or she may need. The manager can be helped to remain focused on job performance, what is not being done, and what needs to occur in the future. If there is indication on the basis of the employee's behavior or the discussion about this behavior that other problems are affecting work performance, then the EAP can be identified as a resource for possibly resolving such problems. When the behavior is grossly inappropriate, is upsetting emotionally or physically to others, or interferes with the productivity of the work group overall, then consideration needs to be given to other resources within the company that may have to be called in to help managers deal with the situation, such as security, medical personnel, or upper-level management.

When management refers an employee, the EAP must be clear about the extent to which the practitioner is accountable to the referring source while still protecting the privacy and confidentiality of the client. Differences in policy exist among EAPs as to how much or how little information can be shared with the manager. Generally, however, EAP program directors will inform the referring manager that an employee has followed through with the referral. In some programs, counselors also let referring supervisors know the employee's degree of cooperation with the treatment plan. Any other information, except for exemptions stipulated in federal and state statutes concerning privacy rights, can be discussed with the supervisor only with the written consent of the employee. The actual content of counseling sessions rarely is shared. Whatever the policy, managers need to understand what feedback they can expect from the counselor and the extent of any further responsibility they have to the employee or the program regarding the referral.

Yet another aspect of supervisory referral is the need at times to help the manager or referring source deal with his or her own emotions about initiating the referral. It is not uncommon for managers to feel they have failed in their responsibilities to the company or the employee because they are not able to handle the problem on their own. The counselor provides a genuine service by taking the time to explore such attitudes and to offer reality-based reassurances that they are unfounded. At times the troubled employees whom managers bring to the EAP and the evocative discussions surrounding them remind managers of similar problems in their own lives, and counselors may find that they are consulting in reference to two sets of personal problems: the employee's and the manager's. When this occurs it is important to help the manager maintain a clear distinction between her or his own issues and the employee's, while at the same time offering relevant help to the manager about whatever is of concern, up to and including a self-referral for his or her own problems.

Self-Referrals

Most EAP clients seek assistance voluntarily without intervention by managers. They may have talked about their problems with supervisors, business agents, or shop stewards who suggested the EAP, but the decision to follow through is their own. In these instances no contact with others in the organization is possible without written client consent, except, as noted above, for legally determined exceptions to the various confidentiality statutes.[2] This sometimes is confusing if a supervisor has been instrumental in facilitating a self-referral and genuinely is concerned about the client's well-being. Well-designed and clearly stated EAP policy statements concerning what can and cannot be shared need to be communicated to all levels of staff on a regular basis to help deal with such confusion.

In the 1990s, many EAPs are experiencing an increase in self-referrals that are directly related to on-the-job stresses (Miller, Jones, & Miller, 1992). As companies are downsizing, becoming "leaner and meaner," and searching for ways to increase productivity without adding to their employee base, employees at every level are faced with mounting responsibilities, reduced salaries, fewer benefits, and fewer options for finding another job. Such circumstances can raise difficult issues in working with an employee about the types of interventions that may be necessary to bring about changes but that also might compromise the confidentiality of the employee. These problems can be addressed through various organizational interventions (discussed in Chapter 9). The point is that when an employee brings such issues to the EAP, his or her right to confidentiality still is paramount. It may seem logical to contact others in the company regarding the problem, but nothing can be done that would identify the client without informed written consent from the client and full client understanding of the implications of any organizational intervention.

INITIATING THE HELPING RELATIONSHIP

A complex challenge facing EAP counselors is the management of the clinical relationship. They must, on the one hand, communicate interest, concern, and professional credibility to clients, but, on the other hand, not encourage the kind of dependency that will make either a referral to another resource or self-help difficult. Relationship issues are further complicated by ambiguity about the nature or length of the association between the counselor and the client. The counselor's defined responsibility may include fairly long term and intense follow-up with hospitalized or vulnerable clients, sometimes extending beyond the client's termination with external resources. In on-site programs, clients may continue to request help for new issues over long periods of time.[3] Whatever the pattern of use, the professional relationship endures in some form for as long as the counselor and the client continue to work within the same system, even if contacts are no more than casual encounters in the cafeteria line. Under such circumstances there is no such thing as terminating with clients in the same sense as in traditional practice settings.

Several points are important in determining how to structure the beginning relationships with clients. Most clients respond to a positive, supportive, and informative relationship style that protects their autonomy as individuals and fosters a conviction that they can assume responsibility for working on whatever issues are of concern to them. It is important that clients not be allowed to become too dependent on the counselor in ways that can impede their transitions to other providers if this becomes necessary and that expectations not be raised about long-term relationships with EAP counselors. At times, however, these guidelines can be applied too rigidly to the extent that EAP counselors actually inhibit an effective referral and the client's motivation to get help.

One of the features that sets professional EAP programs apart from more routinized and automatic EAP information and referral services is the skill of the professional counselor that goes beyond affixing diagnostic labels and matchmaking with resources. Diagnostic understanding and sensitivity also include an ability to arrive at an individualized perception of the client's relationship needs at the point of contact. A client in crisis has different relationship needs than one who is locked into a long-term codependent relationship and is confused about the source of his or her chronic depression. A client who is defensive and wary because of a management referral requires different approaches than someone asking for routine information about child-care options or a person lost in grief over a drug-abusing adolescent child. In some instances it may be more productive to allow a degree of dependency initially to help marshal the client's internal resources and external supports so he or she can move on to other forms of help.

One area in which EAP clients may differ from agency clients is their lack of familiarity with either existing social resources or the concept of counseling. As a result a central feature of initiating service often is the need to educate the client about the nature and purpose of the assessment and the benefits and mutual expectations of counseling, whether offered in-house or through an external provider. Traditional agency clients are more likely to have had other episodes of service with helping resources, and most private practice clients have at least a basic understanding of the nature of therapy. In contrast, EAP clients typically have a limited understanding of interpersonal therapies. This is as true of well-educated and socially sophisticated employees as it is of those with limited education or life experiences. Preparing these clients for the counseling experience is achieved both through straightforward education and information about the process and through the modeling of clinical behavior within an EAP relationship that is respectful, client centered, confidential, and productive. This process of socialization assumes major importance in the event of a referral to an external provider, as very often the success of continuing help depends upon the quality of the interaction that occurs with EAP staff.

Clients may balk at the idea of a referral to an external provider, especially if they have had a difficult time making the decision to come to the EAP in the first place. This simply may be because they have found the EAP relationship supportive and gratifying. In other situations the client's motivation and commitment to changing his or her circumstances may be unclear, and the counselor may need more information about presenting problems or the person's capacity to make use of an alternative resource before a referral can be made. EAP counselors may allow a more dependent relationship to develop to help clients examine their reluctance to move on or to let them experience what a counseling relationship is like within the relative safety of the EAP. At times, circumstances surrounding the referral to the EAP are so devastating that remedial help must be undertaken at once before "next steps" even can be considered, and this help requires a more sustained and supportive relationship at the outset. This is especially true of clients in crisis when immediate intervention is necessary simply to keep them functioning.[4]

It also is not uncommon for normally well defended clients to experience significant insights and profound emotions as a result of the assessment process itself, no matter how brief it may be. For example, recognition that the protective behaviors learned as a child in an abusive family are ruining his or her marriage, or that he or she has had no opportunity to grieve for a deceased parent, can explode into awareness within the first interview. Sometimes this can be anticipated and controlled by the EAP counselor until the person is in a longer term therapeutic relationship, but human behavior is too unpredictable to guarantee that this always will be possible or that it even is desirable to delay dealing with such emotions.

Such awakenings on the part of clients need to be viewed as opportunities for interventions, opportunities that may not recur in any other context. At the very least the EAP counselor needs to offer support, understanding, perhaps limited interpretation, and an opportunity to neutralize some of the client's emotional trauma. The decision to move any further clinically is a professional one that has to be made on the basis of the total situation affecting the client, including the ability of another resource to deal effectively with the issues that have surfaced. The advice, based in practice wisdom, that the EAP counselor cannot become too involved relationally with clients is sound in most instances, especially when a referral clearly is in order. The point being made, however, is that there are exceptions that need to be taken into consideration and that require a depth of clinical understanding of people, their problems, and the nature of clinical interaction.

GENERAL EAP ASSESSMENT

At one time in most counseling and psychotherapy practices, long-term treatment was presumed to be the norm, and clinicians conducted in-depth assessments in six to eight interviews upon which treatment objectives were based. Once the diagnosis and treatment goals were established, "real treatment" could begin. Recent practice has changed significantly as the pervasiveness and effectiveness of short-term treatment models are acknowledged more generally (Lambert et al., 1986), and as it has become more apparent that long-term treatment is the exception and not the norm in most agencies, clinics, and private practices (Budman & Gurman, 1988; Koss & Butcher, 1986). One effect of this trend has been to alter clinical assessments, because the total course of treatment may be no more than six or eight interviews. The focus of assessment also has changed toward an emphasis on current presenting problems with comparatively less attention being paid to developmental history, personality analysis, or those areas of the client's life not directly affected by the presenting problems. A somewhat different reality prevails in the way in which EAP counselors approach the task of diagnostic assessment, one that combines the short-term emphasis on current problems with a detailed analysis of the client's background, depending on the nature of the presenting problem.

Most EAP practitioners possess a high level of diagnostic skill that facilitates thorough and accurate assessments of clients' problems in a timely fashion—a central feature of any effective EAP. In workplace programs managers and employees expect that immediate attention will be given to their service requests and that a reliable plan of intervention will be initiated as quickly as possible. EAPs market their services with assurances that they will provide a quick and effective response to problems. There is less tolerance for the waiting lists and delayed decision making that characterize much of traditional clinic or agency practice. EAP counselors do not have the luxury of trial-and-error decision making or postponed diagnosis. As one counselor commented, "We can't wait around for issues to emerge; we have to learn to ask difficult questions like, 'Have you ever tried to kill yourself?' "

On the other hand, assessments need to be as thorough as possible so a determination can be made about the problem and client motivation as a basis for generating either one or a series of referral options. EAP counselors frequently conduct in-depth, sometimes wide-ranging, explorations into other aspects of the client's life not necessarily considered to be problematic by the client, such as screening for chemical dependency, asking about general physical health, inquiring into work life and other life systems including religious practices, and requesting past generational family data. Conditioned by their work with the chemically dependent and an understanding of the dynamics of denial, EAP counselors do not automatically assume that the client is totally aware of all the elements of his or her current difficulty, although client input is highly respected.

The combination of workplace expectations for prompt action and a broad-brush, comprehensive approach to data gathering and assessment fosters an intense, thorough, dynamic assessment style. This style requires a sophisticated knowledge of human and organizational functioning and of a breadth of theory, in addition to the ability to engage clients quickly in a cooperative alliance in their own behalf.

Conducting the Assessment

Clinical assessment in any setting rarely involves a straight-line process from problem identification to remedy. Clinicians routinely deal with complex individuals in complex circumstances. Our explanatory theories still are not adequate enough to allow us to decipher this complexity easily, much less to provide unerring proscriptions as to how to help people with their problems. All professionals can hope for is that their knowledge and experience will decrease the margin of error involved in giving help. The process of assessment requires a continual set of professional decisions based on the unfolding of information provided by the client and what the counselor knows about people in general and persons with the same types of problems. Practitioners must make judgments based on their explanatory theories and expertise as to what areas of information are more or less important and what questions they need to ask to inform their subsequent decisions. The following case situation illustrates this back-and-forth process, including some of the private thoughts of the counselor as she structures the assessment process.

A 46-year-old plant worker, Mr. C., comes to the EAP complaining about his loss of energy, sleeplessness, and uncharacteristic episodes of crying. The EAP counselor, Mrs. Wendt, sifts through her accumulated knowledge and determines that she needs to assess the possible presence of depression, medical problems, or substance abuse. Mr. C.'s answers to her preliminary questions do not suggest a diagnosis of substance abuse, but they alert Mrs. Wendt to a series of problems he is having on the job, at home, and financially. She wonders about compulsive spending or the possibility of accumulated stresses contributing to acute depression, and she asks several questions to establish whether his complaints are long term or recent in nature. Either possibility suggests its own series of further inquiries.

She discovers that the behavioral symptoms can be linked in time with a hospitalization for a mild heart attack the year before, which prompts additional questions about medication, its side effects, and the extent to which Mr. C. had access to or participated in follow-up cardiac care. Mr. C. is not taking his medication regularly, partly because of the cost, which is in excess of $150 a month. He clearly is overweight and chain-smokes throughout the interview.

Mrs. Wendt asks whether he knows about lifestyle changes that could affect his long-term prognosis. Has he had the chance to ask questions about risk factors or physical activity after heart attacks? A review of Mr. C.'s medical plan raises the option of referral to a cardiac rehabilitation program. Her systems theory orientation influences her to go further, however. Mrs. Wendt knows that family members and other significant people in the client's life probably have been affected by the illness, and she explores with him the reactions of family members to his disability, the extent to which their fears are contributing to family stresses, and whether they are in need of help and more information about his condition. He is astonished when she asks whether he has been experiencing problems with impotence; he has, and is relieved to know this is not uncommon with heart patients and usually is remediable.

Additional questions point to other major changes in Mr. C.'s patterns of socialization and work life. His job responsibilities have been altered because of his illness with a resultant decrease of income through loss of overtime hours. He is doing work for which he was poorly trained and that provides limited opportunities for advancement. Most of his friends participate in sports and work out at a neighborhood park. Mr. C. says he is unable to compete any more and has avoided contact with them. He becomes aware of how restricted his life has been since his hospitalization, and he starts to cry.

Mrs. Wendt explains that even the crying is an understandable reaction to the major life changes he has been through, and she inquires further about problems in relation to loss, identity, and self-esteem. They discuss a possible referral for longer-term counseling. They decide it might help, too, if she contacted, with his permission, the personnel department or his supervisors to work out a better job assignment. She also tells him that his health benefits will partially reimburse medication costs. This is the first time Mr. C. has been seriously ill and he was unaware of this provision.

The issue of alcohol use is revisited as he acknowledges that he has been drinking more to deal with his stress and is afraid to mix his medications with the alcohol. Mrs. Wendt makes an immediate intervention, on the one hand validating his caution but on the other hand emphasizing the self-destructive nature of both the drinking and the discontinuation of life-saving medication. It becomes clear that anyone providing long-term treatment for this client should be knowledgeable about both depression and addictions, and ideally should have a basic understanding of pharmacological effects of medications. It occurs to Mrs. Wendt that perhaps the facility offering cardiac rehab also would be able to provide outpatient psychotherapy. She recommends that Mr. C. contact AA as a way of becoming more informed about alcohol abuse and to determine whether or not his drinking may have reached unmanageable proportions for him. He says he will think about going to an open meeting.

The next question in Mrs. Wendt's mind is, "What about the family?" Would they be interested in one or two sessions with the EAP counselor to help identify their concerns? Would services be available for them through the rehab facility? As Mr. C. details their probable unwillingness to see a "head shrinker," his own ambivalence about psychotherapy becomes clearer. Although he demonstrates motivation to follow through on the cardiac rehab referral, he is much less convinced about other options. He accepts another appointment to get some help with filling out the claims for his medication, but also to give him time to think about the implications of the other elements of the proposed treatment plan. In the time remaining, Mrs. Wendt calls the medical center where Mr. C. was hospitalized for his heart condition, as well as several other centers, to determine availability of and the client's eligibility for cardiac rehab services. Mr. C. agrees to make an appointment with the cardiologist for a checkup and to see about initiating this referral process.

During a telephone evaluation of the EAP several months later, Mr. C. was asked to comment on the help he received, and he provided the following information. He had several phone conversations with the counselor in relation to the medical referrals, but he could not find the time to get back for another in-person appointment. Nevertheless, he was surprised at how much it helped just to talk and to get rid of some of the feelings he was having; he thought he was going crazy. He remembers that first interview with Mrs. Wendt as being both somber and reassuring. She took everything he said very seriously, and she helped him see that he was thinking the way most people do after a heart attack. He eventually realized that he was not facing up to either the facts about his drinking or the seriousness of his health problems. She helped him reach a better understanding of his medical condition and the degree to which he has at least some control over his physical health. She also made him feel that he could do other things to change his life for the better. He went to the cardiac rehab and is in a support group for heart patients that sustains the lifestyle changes he made, including abstinence from both cigarettes and alcohol. He is working out again with his friends, and even though he is limited in what he can do, both the physical and social benefits have him feeling better about himself. This, along with a change in medication, has lessened the problems of impotency.

He has not gone to AA or for psychotherapy as he does not see a real need. He and his wife are thinking about calling Mrs. Wendt, however, about family counseling because the stresses in their marriage have continued. He still is working on the same job and still is unhappy about it. A change in assignment is unlikely because the company is downsizing. He definitely would recommend the EAP to other employees. It may have saved his life.

As this example points out, the exact character of the assessment will vary depending on the nature of the issues the client brings, the experience and theoretical breadth of the counselor, and the client's motivation and capacity to collaborate in problem solving. Most counselors, however, will try to assess certain core features about clients and their problems, as discussed below. These include a basic understanding of the nature of the presenting problem as understood by the employee and significant people in his or her environment, knowledge of the employee's overall functioning across several areas of performance, and information about the major life systems the employee encounters and how these may contribute to the problem or provide resources for problem solution. Not all of the questions and comments contained in the outline will be appropriate to all clients. How extensively a counselor pursues any given area is determined by the mix of personal and systemic issues of greatest relevance to a particular client.

EAP directors have evolved a number of different forms and procedures for obtaining information about their clients. A general format developed by the U.S. Department of Health and Human Servicces is included in the appendix.

Understanding the Presenting Problem

Whether a client is self-referred or management referred, the starting place for most counselors in conducting an assessment is the client's view of his or her problem. Two seemingly contradictory views condition how EAP practitioners relate to the client's perception of the presenting problem. One places a high priority on the importance of taking the client's view very seriously for both ethical and clinical reasons, and the other, which is rooted in work with addicted patients, acknowledges that, in spite of their best intentions to be honest and open, many clients are in denial about the true nature of their difficulties, and it is the counselor's responsibility to wade through layers of verbal subterfuge in order to accurately assess the problem. Clinicians themselves do not have a total grasp on all the multiple factors that motivate their own behavior; it is no less difficult for clients to arrive at this understanding. One reason people ask for help is because of a recognition that an impartial opinion can clarify aspects of a situation that were out of their awareness. The counselor must make a decision as to the clinical significance of the client's perspective about the problem on the basis of evolving diagnostic information.

As reflected in the example of Mr. C. above, the assessment process is one in which both the counselor and the client pool their respective areas of expertise as a way of coming to a shared understanding of what is operating and how things can change for the better. Clients, in most respects, are experts on their own problems, the unique ways in which they are experiencing those problems, what they have tried to do about the situation, what has worked and what has not, and what they would like to be different. The counselor contributes his or her professional expertise, including insights about how most people react to similar problems, about issues of mental and emotional health or illness, about supportive or destructive systems, and about problem-solving options and resources. Denial is accepted as behavior representing a continuum from functional to pathological that has to be understood in context and sometimes confronted in the client's interest. But the starting place is the client's rendition of what has occurred.

If a management referral is involved the counselor often is faced with two very different versions of the client's behavior, the impact it is having on the work group, and how the problem can be resolved. As one person put it:

> When I worked [at an outpatient psychiatric clinic] all we had to think about was the client's perception of reality. It wasn't necessary to concern ourselves with how others viewed the problem; it was just the client's perception that counted in treatment. Now I have to think about how the supervisor or other people at work see the problem and deal with that, too. It's very different. (Cunningham, 1990, p. 41)

Family members often see yet a different reality. The counselor's responsibilities go beyond just determining the real "truth" of the situation. Each person's version of the truth has meaning to him or her and influences what can be done to remedy the situation. If the supervisor sees only an unreliable drunk who lacks the willpower to change, recovery and reentry back into the job will be much more complicated. A client's belief that everyone is exaggerating how much he or she drinks increases the probability of relapse. A spouse who is dealing with her own emotional trauma over having been physically abused while the client was drunk cannot be a support to him in recovery until and unless her own needs are taken seriously. Assessment, therefore, may require interventions with significant others in the forms of education, patient listening, reassurance as to the validity of their feelings, and discussion about other ways of looking at the situation.

It should be understood that "the problem" is not a static set of elements; it changes as clients, counselors, and significant others share their points of view. Simply discussing the difficulty for the first time often alters the client's awareness of what has occurred. Putting it into words, giving one's fears a name, or learning that certain troubling thoughts are normal and not an indication of "craziness" allows the person to reframe the problem so as to render it manageable and solvable. The very process of the assessment becomes a source of enhanced perception that can significantly modify clients' understanding of themselves and their circumstances. To make connections between one's current state and recent or distant events can stimulate powerful insights that not only revise one's view of the problem, but also actually contribute to its resolution. Part of the real "therapy" of EAP work lies in the opportunity it provides clients to articulate their concerns with a supportive, informed, nonjudgmental, and respectful professional. One of the reasons that short-term treatment in general, and especially in EAP settings, is so effective may be because of the healing and restorative effects of being listened to fully for once, being understood, and being valued by the counselor.

Understanding the Employee

The Employee's Current Situation

It is important to know something of the person's current situation beyond those issues that relate directly to the presenting problem. Where does the person live and with whom? Who are the people he or she interacts with in a typical day at home or on the job? Is this a young single parent or a widower close to retirement? Is this the first time the person has been to the EAP, or have there been other contacts in relation to similar or other issues? How does the employee look or act physically and emotionally? Does he or she relate appropriately? Such questions provide the initial information that helps the counselor formulate basic hypotheses about the nature of the problem and areas needing more attention.

It also is important to assess the client's readiness and ability to initiate the changes in his or her life that will help relieve his or her distress. Any major change, whether self-initiated or imposed by another, is difficult; it challenges fundamental beliefs persons have about themselves and often requires both new ways of viewing the world and adopting unfamiliar, untested behaviors. It should not be assumed that employees referred by management lack motivation or that self-referred clients possess motivation in abundance. Some involuntary clients actually may be more motivated to work toward changes because their long-term denial of the existence of any problems has been penetrated, and the consequences of not altering their behavior are clear. On the other hand, some voluntary clients may want things to be different but may be unable to see their role in perpetuating their problems. Others may be quite clear about changes they want to undertake, but they are locked into repetitive patterns of self-destructive actions that they seem powerless to control. A continuing task in almost any type of interpersonal assistance is the need for the clinician to identify, enhance, and sustain client motivation because of its importance to positive treatment outcomes.

Mental and Emotional Health

Whatever the nature of the problem, the counselor usually makes an initial determination of how well the client appears to be functioning emotionally. In Chapter 3, I identified a number of concepts that can be helpful in making this assessment. With a few clients, a quick decision needs to be made as to any behavior that signals that they may be in serious emotional distress, out of control, or a threat to themselves or others. A certain amount of anxiety, wariness, and even resistance on the part of the client can be understood as appropriate to the counseling situation, especially if it is an employee's first exposure to the experience. Other behaviors may be totally appropriate to the nature of the problems, such as when a client is in crisis or deep grief (Golan, 1978). The counselor needs to ask the questions that will help determine whether the employee's affects are consistent with the emerging assessment picture.

In assessing general functioning it is useful to attend to or to elicit behavioral descriptions that help determine clients' intellectual performance and cognitive and perceptual styles. One counselor noted that her EAP clients, construction workers and engineers, differed from her former agency clients in their tendency to think visually rather than verbally. They could draw diagrams illustrating dysfunctional family interactions that they could not describe in words. Other concepts to include in this part of the assessment are the clients' capacity to learn from their mistakes, to draw conclusions from the consequences of their behavior, and to make sensible judgments about such behavior and those around them. Does the client give indications of an ability to see reality more or less as others do, or is his or her reality testing flawed in some way?

A key feature of anyone's overall functioning is his or her ability to relate to others in more or less nonconflictual, consistent, and productive ways. Regular problems in relationships extending over fairly long periods of time raise questions as to a client's basic relationship capacity, an issue that can be very significant in assessing a client's ability to make use of counseling help. Problematic attachments to persons, things, or experiences can alert the counselor to the possibility of compulsive disorders, nonchemical addictions, or codependent behavior. Any apparent inability on the part of the client to empathize with or even recognize the legitimate needs or distresses of significant people in his or her life can be symptomatic of other forms of personality disorders suggesting emotional immaturity and problematic or traumatic developmental experiences. More severe, repeated, disturbing behaviors—such as extreme mood swings, disassociative states when the person may appear to be out of contact with reality, or unprovoked violent or self-destructive behavior—suggest the possibility of psychotic states or serious personality disorders usually requiring additional diagnostic input.

In addition to knowing about how clients relate to others, it is equally important to understand their view of themselves: the extent to which their self-perception is or is not accurately reflective of their abilities, failings, hopes, and aspirations. Do they see themselves as separate, autonomous individuals or as inextricably bound to others emotionally? Are their lives organized around their own realistic goals or those of others? Are their attitudes, behaviors, and beliefs based on an image of themselves as unworthy, undeserving, inadequate imposters or as competent and worthwhile, fallible perhaps, but deserving love and attention? Whatever other problems clients may be struggling with, their fundamental views of themselves are key aspects of how well they can accept and make use of any help that is offered. When these self-perceptions are impaired, alteration of their beliefs about themselves is likely to become one of the objectives of treatment.

A word of caution is indicated in applying these or any criteria for assessing behavior. To a great extent these criteria reflect certain biases as to what constitutes norms for healthy functioning under different circumstances. Increasingly, companies are having to deal with the reality of a culturally diverse workforce that challenges old assumptions about normal and abnormal functioning. Failure to remain sensitive to such differences in cultural attitudes undermines the accuracy of assessment and sets the stage for irrelevant or even harmful interventions that can make the situation worse (Hepworth & Larsen, 1993).

Diagnostic Classification

In order for most employees to receive insurance reimbursement it is necessary to indicate in the application process the category of disorder being treated. Some EAPs apply the *Diagnostic and Statistical Manual of Mental Disorders* (DSM-III-R) (American Psychiatric Association, 1987) or the *International Classification of Disease* (ICD-9) (World Health Organization, 1978) to all EAP clients who seek assistance for anything more complicated than a simple request for information, whether or not a referral or insurance claim is involved. For most EAP counselors knowledge of one or both of these systems of diagnostic classification is essential.[5]

Many professionals react negatively to the expectation that they must pigeonhole people or use flawed descriptive criteria to explain very complex conditions. Like any tool, the classification schemes often are applied improperly, and no perfect system exists that captures all the nuances of behavior in the context of changing circumstances. It is important to keep in mind what the classification schemes can do and not expect anything more. They provide a disciplined way of thinking about disturbed clients and a more or less common and recognizable language for certain types of mental and emotional disturbances, which enhances communication among professionals. These classifications are better at identifying more serious forms of disturbance than the ordinary problems of living most clients are concerned about, a feature that tends to pathologize what essentially are minor or transitory difficulties. Freeman and Landesman (1992) make a significant point about the importance of identifying a person's strengths as well as deficits when it comes to the clinical assessment of mental and emotional functioning. This appeared to be a notable quality of the counselors I interviewed who identified their ability to operate from a strength perspective as a factor in their success with clients. Classification models that emphasize the deficiencies of clients' performances need to be applied carefully and with understanding as to the one-sided nature of the evidence they generate.

Another limitation is that these schemata offer no insight about the noxious circumstances some human beings face, which constitute the actual "illness." Clients frequently have to contend with disabling conditions over which they have no control. Their problematic behavior may, in fact, represent a "healthy" response to such situations or environments, and if counselors are not alert to these aspects of a client's life they may become part of the problem. In summary, classification models such as the DSM-III-R and the ICD-9 are essential for certain aspects of EAP work and very helpful in other areas when properly used, but they provide only part of the total picture necessary for a balanced and integrated assessment.

Physical Health

A feature of most EAP assessment is screening for physical as well as emotional problems. This aspect of assessment owes its origins in part to the occupational alcoholism programs, as problems of addiction not recognized or acknowledged by clients often manifest themselves in a series of medical problems and physical symptoms. A primary reason for physical screening is the need to identify or rule out the possibility that chemical abuse or dependence are either at the core of a client's difficulties or complicating them in some way. Specifics of drug and alcohol screening are dealt with in detail in Chapter 5, but counselors routinely make such inquiries not just to screen for chemical use but also to determine whether other types of chronic or acute physical symptoms may be of diagnostic significance. Problems of insomnia, weight fluctuations, or minor or disturbing aches or pains are uncovered in such reviews, and part of the treatment plan may include referral to in-house medical staff or private physicians. The information also helps the counselor understand in a more complete way how the physical condition of a client may be causing or be worsened by other aspects of his or her problematic person-situation interaction, and how attention to physical complaints can be an important aspect of treatment.

Another health concern of special significance to the work-based counselor is the effect of work environments on the physical well-being of employees and their families. The research linking the work environment to emotional and mental illness is not conclusive; however, the evidence that many work sites are contributing to the physical illness of workers, and in some instances that of their family members, is conclusive and growing (Stellman & Daum, 1973; *Work in America,* 1973). It has been estimated that more than 100,000 U.S. workers die each year from occupationally related illnesses and accidents. Although work-related accidents are relatively easy to document, work-related illnesses often are impossible to establish for a variety of reasons. For one, it may take years for the effects of the toxic conditions existing in some plants and industries to produce diagnosable symptoms. Nevertheless, the growing body of information concerning the effects of certain materials on the physiological health of human beings can be incorporated into an assessment profile. It is important for counselors to be informed about the general features of their occupational settings, including information about possible work-based health hazards, how such hazards impact on employee health, and the appropriate safety precautions that need to be observed. Often exposure to such hazards creates physiological effects that mimic psychological symptoms such as depression or other affective states, and an astute EAP clinician can recognize when a referral to a good occupational health resource rather than a psychotherapist may be indicated.

This is a sensitive area for EAP personnel as employers often are guarded about releasing information concerning potential hazards out of concern for lawsuits and Workers' Compensation claims. It is not improbable that the counselor may be in a position of having to provide services to an occupationally impaired employee that could be interpreted as undermining the best interests of the company. Counselors can debate the ethics of their interventions from multiple perspectives: their responsibility to the employee, the employer, or themselves. For social workers, however, the Social Work Code of Ethics (National Association of Social Workers, 1980) is clear about the primacy of the individual client in such conflicts of interest.

Spiritual Life and Religious Participation

A facet of personal behavior more likely to be covered in EAP assessments than in general clinical practice is the religious belief systems of clients and the significance of such beliefs to workers and their families. This is another assessment emphasis that has its roots in the classic EAP alcoholism detection programs. Most EAP counselors are highly identified with the various 12-Step recovery groups (such as AA, Al-Anon, and Narcotics Anonymous) and the reliance of such groups on a concept of a Higher Power as an ally in recovery. Most psychotherapy tends to underestimate the significance of religious and spiritual factors as supports in gaining and maintaining mental health, although these attitudes are changing (Cornett, 1992; Peck, 1978).

Just as reliance on a Higher Power can be a support in recovery, it can be a support during illness, divorce, or periods of confusion and lost direction, or even in fully integrating the joy of the positive events of one's life. The structure, fellowship, and validation of one's own values and beliefs provided by regular religious participation can be powerful assets when other aspects of life seem out of control. Ritual of any kind can give meaning and significance to events that are beyond comprehension. Issues of shame and guilt can be dealt with more successfully within a belief system that includes a forgiving and loving deity.

Spiritual beliefs, practices, and affiliations can have negative consequences as well. If the deity is punishing rather than forgiving, or if the spiritual fellowship reinforces rigid, self-destructive, or harmful attitudes and behaviors, then this can be contributing to the client's problems or frustrating their resolution. Affiliation with certain religious or spiritual groups can generate suspicion or prejudice in observers, including counselors, because of their minority status. Because our Judeo-Christian culture still is not totally accepting of other types of religious expression such as Islamic, Asian, or Native American rituals, members of these and other groups can experience discrimination as a consequence of their religious identification. Whatever the nature of a client's spiritual life, it is an aspect of human performance that can be instrumental in understanding and helping clients. Failing to learn about a client's spiritual attitudes and experiences may represent a failure in fully knowing that person at all.

Understanding the Systems

The Family System

Yet another area of assessment influenced by the EAP's concern with issues of alcohol and drugs is the attention paid to a client's current nuclear family and the family of origin. Systems theory tells us that we all are affected by the behavior of the ecological systems of which we are a part and that of the individuals who share those systems with us. Addiction theory identifies alcoholism and other substance abuse as "family diseases" that take their toll on all members of a family, whose individual and collective well-being are compromised by the chemical substance abuse. Clinical assumptions that flow from these overlapping bodies of knowledge tell us that we cannot truly understand a person unless we know something about the real or surrogate family relationships he or she is a part of. Second, especially if addictions are involved, all members who have been affected by the illness need to participate in the recovery and healing if the client is to recover.

In Chapter 3, I identified several sets of concepts especially relevant to the assessment of family systems. Many of these concepts are elaborated upon in Chapter 8. Here I draw your attention to some general areas of inquiry to cover during initial assessment interviews. Hepworth and Larsen (1993) suggest a framework for assessing family functioning that is useful to the general practitioner who, unlike family therapists, may not have a firsthand view of family interaction. Factors to be assessed include both internal and outer boundaries of the family and its subsystems; its power structure and decision-making processes; how feelings are allowed expression; family goals; role assignments; a family's strengths; the communication styles of family members, including family myths and secrets; and the family life cycle (Hepworth & Larsen, 1993, pp. 310-311, 320).

Hepworth and Larsen suggest that when these interactional patterns cannot be observed directly, it is important to explore with the client various critical incidents that illustrate problematic family interactions and the sequence of events surrounding them. In using this technique the clinician asks the client to give detailed, even verbatim accounts about the behaviors of different family members during such incidents as a means of achieving a more total picture of what occurred (Hepworth & Larsen, 1993, p. 288). In reviewing the framework identified by Hepworth and Larsen it is easy to recognize how these elements can be affected by work-life considerations. For example, power alignments in families are very sensitive to who works, the status of each person's job, and the extent to which that employment links them to external systems (Perlman, 1964). Both formal and informal role expectations can be compromised or enhanced by the demands on family members made by an employer in terms of time, energy, and emotional investment (Kanter, 1977b). Family life cycle events reflect changing work realities—such as in situations of promotion, the "glass ceiling," retirement, or job loss—and such events influence how the client interacts with family members.

Of special interest are not only how the family of origin and current family function as a whole, but also how these processes impact on the formation and maintenance of the individual client's personality. Consider which elements of these family structures contribute toward a stable, integrated, consistent sense of self and which have fostered personal disorganization. What features of the current family situation provide supports for continuing growth and development and which foster instead dysfunctional and self-defeating attitudes and behaviors?

Addiction theory is becoming more substantially grounded in data that indicate that at least some forms of addictions are influenced genetically. For this reason, counselors attempting to determine the probability of a client's vulnerability to substance abuse often elicit detailed family histories, perhaps using ecomaps and genograms covering several generations (Hartman, 1978). The process itself has been valuable not only for clients who may be genetically predisposed to addictions. Many clients can make use of this process to identify other destructive family and interpersonal patterns of behavior not necessarily linked to addictions, and to recognize the multiple ways in which past events influence current behaviors and how personal and family interactions are influenced by larger system realities.

The Work System

At one time it was assumed that all clients were referred to EAPs because of declining work performance. Even when most programs became broad brush in their orientations, a continuing assumption was that emotional difficulties and interpersonal conflicts would impact on work performance in much the same way as do problems of substance abuse. At least one study indicated that more time is lost on the job due to emotional and family problems than to alcoholism (Weaver, 1979). However, as indicated earlier, increasingly the EAP client is coming for help voluntarily. The problems that these men and women bring may be severe, but for the most part their difficulties have not resulted in documented declines in work performance or productivity. Nevertheless, the work environment may be having a major impact on clients in ways that are significant for assessment. One obvious and fairly pervasive consequence of the workplace context is the fact that it fosters in practitioners an understanding of the significance of employment roles and experiences in the lives of adult clients, which in turn fosters an acute awareness in EAP diagnosticians of the significance of systems interactions in general, not just at the workplace. EAP counselors cannot ignore issues of work; they are continually exposed to this major institutional reality in the lives of their clients.

For EAP counselors to remain alert to potential work system factors in their clients' problems, it is necessary for them to have a dynamic understanding of the employing organization—its structure, policies, personnel, and current stresses and how these fit into some historical perspective. A client's depression can be better understood if it is occurring during a work stoppage or a period of organizational retrenchment. It is essential to know the kinds of benefits the workplace provides for its employees and any significant gaps in benefits that exist. What concrete or other types of barriers exist in the work environment that hamper the delivery of services including EAP services? It also is important to know something about the specific nature of this particular employee's work setting: the physical reality, interpersonal factors, role expectations—latent and overt—and the services or products being produced. Who are the significant others with whom the client interacts for so many hours each day? Is there anything significant about the employee's history with the company or past employers?

In Chapter 3, I identified many of the ways in which work influences the past, current, and future emotional health of clients. Our culture socializes people into a degree of guardedness about sharing their feelings in general, and their feelings about their work life in particular. Although it is accepted that one can gripe about the job with workmates up to a point, or complain about work to family members under some circumstances, we learn that it may not be in our best interests to acknowledge all of our feelings about our work. We assume that we are supposed to be able to handle whatever stresses or imbalances work generates, and that to admit feeling dissatisfied or overwhelmed by our job means we are failing to perform adequately in this significant adult life role.

Consequently, it is important to ask how the client actually experiences his or her work, and to be prepared to probe beyond superficial statements that everything is okay. How much stress or gratification does the job entail? Ask whether his or her job performance provides gratification or a sense of competence, effectiveness, and accomplishment, even if only linked to concrete advantages such as salary or benefits. What is important here is the employee's perception of these issues, not the counselor's, and possibly the perception of referring supervisors as well.

We can understand more about a client's current emotional state and the circumstances affecting it if we know the extent to which work life contributes to an internalized set of boundaries or, instead, to emotional diffusion and disorganization. If responsibilities are unspecified, directives are contradictory, and supervision is unpredictable or unduly intrusive, the emotional health of employees will be affected. This is not to suggest that the causes of all problems of personal identity and diffusion lie in the workplace. However, if someone is already struggling with these issues, whatever the cause, his or her task will be more difficult under the circumstances described above. Even relatively high-functioning persons may find their coping strategies less successful if the worksite itself is dysfunctional. A worker's internal states are influenced by the extent to which he or she is accepted by peers, is given recognition by supervisors, or is engaged in job responsibilities that contribute to his or her sense of worth and self-esteem.

Employment often supplies the signposts of major life transitions, traumas, and conflicts that are highly significant marker events in adult functioning and development. It may be important to determine what special life-cycle transitions a client is experiencing and how they are tied into the person's work life. What role conflicts do these transitions create? What new roles must be added? What new role behaviors are required and how can the person learn them?

Inquiries about a client's work performance provide the counselor with an opportunity to assess various aspects of the client's reality testing, judgment, ability to maintain drive regulation and control, and capacity for object relations, as well as the nature of the client's coping abilities and defensive functioning. Employees who cannot make it to work on time or who put in excessive overtime are communicating information about basic ego functioning as it is played out in this setting. Work also can serve as a defensive or coping strategy in the sense that total commitment to the job becomes a rationale for avoiding the discomfort associated with learning how to manage social contacts, family responsibilities, or even leisure time.

An especially important advantage of having access to information about employees' work behavior is the opportunity it provides to contrast that behavior across systems. If clients are experiencing problems in both their personal life and their work life, that leads to different diagnostic conclusions than if problems occur only at work, only with a spouse, or in some other confined area of their life. On the one hand, when problematic transactions are generalized across systems, counselors may need to explore the client's personality, behavior patterns, or possibly a series of multiple stresses in all areas of life. On the other hand, if problems are localized to work, family, or social relationships, this suggests that practitioners need to look more closely at stress factors that might be operating in that specific area of functioning. This is not to say that external stress or situational factors never are operating when problems are generalized across systems. Nor is it a question of personality factors not being relevant when only one area of functioning is affected. It is a question of making decisions as to which aspects of a client's life should take priority in assessment, and which ones are more likely to provide the counselor and the client with some rapid insight and understanding as to the elements involved in the client's distress.

PUTTING IT ALL TOGETHER

Obviously there is a purpose for collecting all this information. It is not the facts alone that are important, but how those data are combined to produce a holistic picture of a unique human being. In EAP work the general objective is to obtain an in-depth and individualized understanding of a troubled employee in order to generate one or more realistic courses of action to help resolve or reduce the employee's problems. These options are not prepackaged, all-purpose, "cookie cutter" treatment plans keyed to specific diagnostic classifications. Rather, they represent a sensitive appreciation of both the unique and the multifaceted realities of a life in motion that intersects with the lives of other equally complex individuals and groups. Assessment information is compared, weighed, and prioritized on the basis of its relevance to this person and his or her needs at this time. It is this process of weighing, comparing, and deciding which aspects of information provide the most dynamic and authentic view of the client that constitutes the art of diagnostic assessment and that moves the clinical interaction from simply identifying the problem to doing something about it. The process provides a focus for ongoing work and direction as to what combination of resources and interventions is most likely to be of help.

In addition to providing a basis for individualized referral and treatment, the assessment process also is therapeutic in and of itself, whether or not counselors care to refer to it as treatment. The opportunity to talk about problems decreases their immobilizing impact. The experience of acknowledging feelings and defusing their power to intimidate is self-enhancing. Becoming informed about problem-solving options is empowering, and the experience of recognizing patterns of behavior in oneself or others provides an entirely new lens through which future experiences can be examined and understood. Most assessment also provides clients with a type of "case theory," a set of assumptions or hypotheses about the course of their lives that can become a cognitive anchor in the midst of confusion. For example, for a client to recognize as a result of the assessment not only that he or she has developed a lifetime pattern of forming self-depreciating relationships, but also that this pattern may be influencing his or her ability to advance professionally can be a powerful motivator to reorganize his or her life. Such insights can set into motion a range of subtle alterations in behavior that in turn have a catalytic effect in producing profound change.

NOTES

1. There may be some exceptions to this in organizations having drug-testing and "fitness for duty" policies.

2. These are usually exceptions to confidentiality statutes concerning threats of homicide, suicide, or incidents of child abuse. State and federal statutes affecting confidentiality are becoming more complex and it is important to have legal counsel review them as they apply to the different jurisdictions in which a company does business as well as those jurisdictions of external providers used by the EAP, such as an out-of-state treatment facility. A major resource is Nye and Kaiser (1991).

3. One long-standing program in the Chicago area has been able to document several hundred requests for service from a single employee during her 19 years of employment with the company.

4. Several of the counselors interviewed in my survey (Cunningham, 1990) indicated that they were becoming more accepting of such practices as, in their experience, they actually increased the probability of the client following through with a new resource.

5. Both classification systems are in the process of revision. The DSM-IV is expected to be available in 1994.

Chapter 5

DIAGNOSTIC ASSESSMENT
Substance Abuse and Chemical Dependence

In EAPs, the assessment of the presence of drug or alcohol problems typically is part of a broader process of data gathering and analysis, as described in the preceding chapter. In this chapter I examine in greater detail
problems of substance use and abuse. The focus is on chemical addictions,
meaning alcohol and drugs; I do not include here other presenting problems
such as compulsive attachments to gambling, abusive relationships, shop-
ping, or sex, which mimic chemical addictions behaviorally but cannot be
totally understood or explained using those criteria that apply to drug or
alcohol abuse.

   In today's EAPs, employee clients who are experiencing problems of
abuse and addiction generally come to the attention of the EAP in one
of three ways: (a) they are referred by others within the company either
for documented declines in work performance, due to failed drug tests, or
because of other behavioral symptoms of abuse occurring on the job; (b)
they are concerned about their drinking or drug use patterns and they want
more information or help; or (c) they are experiencing other problems that,
upon investigation, point to the possibility of a drug or alcohol problem.
A feature of EAP practice is a recognized responsibility on the part of
counselors to identify possible misuse of drugs and alcohol regardless of
the nature of the referral. Even in situations in which no connection is
apparent between the service request and chemical dependency, the EAP
counselor can identify for the client warning signs that point to future

difficulties, and in this sense make an important contribution to the prevention of drug dependence.

There are several differences in how the EAP counselor engages in the assessment process compared to the clinician at a drug or alcohol treatment center, where there has been a preliminary identification of substance use or abuse. Because of the broad-brush focus of most EAPs the counselor is not necessarily aware at the outset that a client is having a drug problem. Even when the possibility of abuse or dependence is clear to the counselor, the problem may be totally out of the awareness of the client. In such situations, a type of spiraling process is used, in which the counselor may include several basic, general questions as part of obtaining a health history. These questions inquire about patterns of use of nicotine, prescription and other drugs, or alcohol either as a way of ruling out the possibility of abuse or as a basis for deciding to conduct a more comprehensive drug screening. As the assessment continues and data support the presence of problematic use of chemicals, more detailed and specific information is taken, and eventually the client may be asked to cooperate in a drug or alcohol screening test.

The primary objectives of screening for chemical dependency or abuse within the EAP are to obtain as accurate a picture as possible of the patterns of use demonstrated by the client, the most salient factors that contributed to the development and maintenance of the disease, and the extent to which such patterns play a role in other problems in functioning encountered by the employee or those with whom he or she interacts at home or on the job. In most instances EAP staff make informed but preliminary diagnoses about the probable presence or absence of a drug or alcohol problem. Final and more thorough assessments and diagnoses can be made at the treatment facilities, which have additional time and testing resources at their disposal. However, not all clients have access to such resources, and for them the EAP counselor is the one professional who can provide accurate information and assessment of their behavior.

In Chapter 3, I indicated that both practitioner experience and current research support a view of chemical dependency that acknowledges that individuals succumb to chemical dependence and addiction for different reasons and often because of a complex mix of genetic, biochemical, psychological, and environmental factors that are, for the most part, only partially understood by clinicians and researchers. This perspective was endorsed simultaneously by the American Society of Addiction Medicine (ASAM) and the National Council on Addiction and Drug Dependence (NCADD) in their revised definition of alcoholism, which gives greater consideration to the psychosocial and environmental components of the disease (Christner, 1991). Although these factors are not always causative in the strict sense of the word, they often serve to hold the illness in place once the processes of abuse and dependence have begun and also to frustrate attempts at recovery. This knowledge makes the tasks of assessment and treatment more difficult, as substance users are demonstrating patterns of abuse that are complex and difficult to unravel. Comprehensive assessment involves more than the determination of dependency or abuse, or the most accurate diagnostic classification.

To be an effective helper the counselor must arrive at a holistic understanding of the individual, the significant interactive contexts affecting that person, and any other factors that may be contributing to or arising from problems of abuse. What events are implicated in the development of substance abuse and who else in the relationship system requires attention whether or not they are included in the assessment process? How is the chemical use affecting other areas of the person's life? Understanding the unique set of circumstances that applies to each employee client can result in more effective treatment and cost savings to the employer (Freeman, 1990, 1992a; Schuckit, Irwin, Howard, & Smith, 1988).

Different subgroups within our society experience diverse patterns of expectation and stigmatization in connection with drug use, patterns that are related to both the genesis of addiction and rates of recovery. Membership in different cultural groups also can determine which drugs are used and under what circumstances, the availability of treatment resources, and the probability of recovery. The counselor must be aware of the systematic differences that exist both in patterns of substance use or abuse and in available treatment options based on ethnicity and race (Bell & Evans, 1981; Brisbane & Womble, 1985; Freeman & Landesman, 1992; Gunther, Jolly, & Wedel, 1985; Ziter, 1987), gender (Christner, 1991; Freeman & Landesman, 1992; Inciardi, Lockwood, & Pottieger, 1993; Turnbull, 1988; Van Den Bergh, 1991), and age (Blackmon, 1985; Christner, 1991; Kurtz, 1992), all of which are important in assessment and treatment. Not very long ago it was almost heresy in some professional circles to talk about the special needs of women alcoholics, teens, Native Americans, Hispanics, or African Americans because the basic treatment model, directed toward confronting denial and then achieving surrender, recovery, and relapse prevention, was believed to be universally applicable. Although this still can be a controversial topic, there currently is more acceptance of the insights arising from research and practice that point to differential patterns for distinct groups of people.

Assistance is likely to require not only referral to an appropriate treatment facility but also some attention to how family members, the workplace, and other systems will react to the referral. Successful aftercare and relapse prevention may well be dependent on how effectively social, interpersonal, and environmental concerns are addressed and planned for (Billings & Moos, 1983; Donovan, 1988). In the increasingly competitive world of EAP contracting, some firms have severely limited for cost-effectiveness reasons the degree of the EAP counselor's involvement with employee clients beyond making a referral. In the real world of client service, however, practitioners are aware of the extent to which the recovery process of chemically dependent clients is jeopardized by treatment plans that fail to anticipate and prepare for the inevitable personal and system failures that will occur.

GENERAL ASSESSMENT CONSIDERATIONS

DSM-III-R and ICD-9 Classifications

The two classification systems most used by practitioners in arriving at a diagnosis of chemical abuse or dependency are the *Revised Diagnostic and Statistical Manual of Mental Disorders* (DSM-III-R) (American Psychiatric Association, 1987) and the *International Classification of Diseases* (ICD-9) (World Health Organization, 1978). Both provide standardized definitions and a set of diagnostic criteria to aid in the process of assessment, and each classification now makes a distinction between the concepts of *abuse* and *dependence*. This distinction is based on the belief that a recognizable difference exists between (a) the use of substances by nondependent or nonaddicted persons that does, however, lead to serious medical, social, and emotional problems in functioning and (b) the use of chemicals more characterized by psychophysiological manifestations of addiction—craving, increased tolerance, and withdrawal symptoms.[1]

Indicators of abuse include patterns of chemical use that have caused social, psychological, physical, or work-related problems or that have placed the person at risk for physical or mental damage. These patterns either have lasted for at least a month or have recurred regularly over time, and they may be transitory or recurrent. Clients who might be included in this category do not yet manifest additional symptoms of dependence. Some never do manifest such symptoms, whereas others move along a continuum toward total dependence.

Indicators of dependence include reliance on alcohol in ways intended to maintain high blood-alcohol levels; a compulsion to use the substance and loss of control over how much is used; increased tolerance, which is the need for larger amounts of the substance to obtain the same mood-altering effects; the experience of withdrawal symptoms; and cycles of relapse after abstinence. With dependence, the sufferer becomes increasingly committed to the pursuit of the substance to the exclusion of other life roles or obligations. In contrast to abuse patterns, dependence patterns are chronic and not transitory or periodic.

These definitions of abuse and dependence include a focus on psychological and social events that occur with continued use of the substance as well as on the physical and medical criteria associated with tolerance and withdrawal. One implication of this broadening definition is a blurring of the distinction between physical and psychological dependence or physical and psychological addiction, which need to be understood as different aspects of the same phenomenon rather than distinct processes. One involves physiological processes and the other involves a range of emotional, psychological, and affective states that may precede and set the stage for physical dependence or that may occur as a consequence of physical dependence (Johns, 1990). In addition, social and environmental cues can elicit both psychological and physiological reactions that reinforce dependence or threaten abstinence. In short, each of these sets of facts can be so inextricably bound up with one another that distinctions among them serve no valid clinical purpose.

For purposes of general EAP assessment it also may be useful to add a third category of substance use. Neither abuse nor dependence may be present, but the uninformed legal use of alcohol or the legal or illegal use of controlled substances often can lead to other difficulties. A principal role for EAP staff is the prevention of problems through education and the early detection of future individual, family, or organizational problems. The use of alcohol, nicotine, or prescription drugs, for example, can have serious consequences for pregnant women. The illicit use or possession of controlled substances has legal as well as biopsychosocial implications for both employees and the companies they work for, implications that are more significant since the onset of the Drug-Free Workplace Act. In addition, some research evidence suggests that minimal inquiries about alcohol- and drug-use behaviors combined with basic education about their effects can influence for the better subsequent drinking patterns, before any problems manifest themselves (National Institute on Alcohol Abuse and Alcoholism, 1990).

A major complicating factor in addictions screening is the polydrug user, who may be dependent upon or using more than one substance. The relatively straightforward diagnostic tasks associated with the late-stage, chronic alcoholic of 30 years ago are submerged by the need to unravel presenting problems that involve use of a mix of substances that produce more serious and lethal mental and physical consequences and that confound efforts to arrive at a treatment plan. Patterns of polydrug use include a progression from one substance to another in order to obtain greater "highs"; the use of multiple drugs simultaneously for the same purpose; the use of some substances to counter the effects of others; or an unplanned, disorganized use of whatever is available (Gupta, 1990). A key concern for the client who is using multiple drugs is the need to determine current or potential health problems associated with the mix of substances. When polydrug use is suspected it is especially important for the clinician to obtain more detailed information about which substances are being used or have been used in the past, the particular patterns of use evidenced by the client, and the use or abuse behaviors of family members and associates. Sometimes reliable answers to these questions may have to wait until after detoxification, or they may require information from family and friends.

Dual Diagnosis

The past decade has brought an increased awareness of the incidence of both substance abuse or dependence and psychiatric illness in the same patients. For purposes of this discussion, I am using the term *dual diagnosis* to refer to the current coexistence of both a mental disorder as defined in the DSM-III-R or ICD-9 and either chemical abuse or dependency. Research is underway to identify the major interactive patterns between various drugs and psychiatric disorders (Drake, Osher, & Wallach, 1989; Helzer & Pryzbeck, 1988).[2] Common factors are emerging that indicate that substance-abusing samples usually have higher rates of psychiatric illness in every category of psychiatric disorder when compared with studies of the general population. Separate studies of psychiatric patients indicate that they have higher rates of substance abuse than the overall population (Brown, Ridgely, Pepper, Levine, & Ryglewicz, 1989; Buckstein, Brent, & Kaminer, 1989; Galanter, Castenda & Freeman, 1988). Although samples of substances abusers have more of every type of mental disorder, they are most apt to evidence higher rates of anxiety, affective disorder, and personality disorders. Depression is the most common of the affective disorders associated with substance abuse; antisocial personality is the most common personality disorder. Nonopiate polydrug users are more psychiatrically impaired than persons using a single substance (National Institute on Drug Abuse, 1991). Gender effects may be operating in the association between alcoholism and depression and prognosis, with alcoholic women who have had a major depressive episode more likely to experience better outcomes than male patients with the same characteristics (Rounsaville, Dolinsky, Babor, & Meyer, 1987). The treatment of one aspect of the dually diagnosed patient does not necessarily contribute to the improvement of the other; however, failure to treat both contributes to higher rates of relapse.

Issues of dual diagnosis are of special importance to the EAP clinician because of the many problems associated with errors in judgment and referral of such patients. The EAP counselor often is the first person to assess the possibility that both chemical abuse and psychiatric disorders exist simultaneously, but it typically is a very difficult diagnosis to make without special testing and consultation. The counselor needs the type of professional training and experience that include at least a basic understanding of the major psychiatric disorders, their characteristic manifestations, and how they differ from symptoms of chemical dependency. The counselor must be able to ask appropriate questions that will help determine, for example, whether a client's memory lapses are symptomatic of drug-induced blackouts or mental decompensation.

The broadly based psychosocial assessment discussed in Chapter 4 can help make some of these distinctions (O'Hare, 1992). Multigenerational family patterns of both substance abuse and mental illness might emerge that clarify diagnoses. Inquiries about personal and family history can help determine when either disorder first became apparent. Some authors suggest it is helpful to identify the earliest onset of either condition as the primary disease and the preferred treatment focus (Freeman & Landesman, 1992; Schuckit et al., 1988; Turnbull, 1988). However, other factors may have to be taken into consideration in determining whether the addictions or the psychiatric symptoms need immediate attention, such as the ways in which the client's symptoms or different treatment options affect other people in his or her social systems.

If the client currently is using substances, a major consideration in arriving at a diagnosis is the need to arrange for detoxification because of the extent to which symptoms of drug abuse and withdrawal may mimic psychiatric syndromes. For example, patients often exhibit symptoms of major depression or anxiety disorder that diminish markedly from the point at which they actively are using a substance through extended periods of abstinence (Blankfield, 1986; Brown & Schuckit, 1988; Dorus, Kennedy, Gibbons, & Ravi, 1987). These symptoms may continue to manifest themselves for as long as 6 months after detoxification before disappearing completely (DeSoto, O'Donnell, Allred, & Lopes, 1985). Finally, counselors should have access to a consultant or consultants who have experience with both types of illnesses, who can evaluate the significance of assessment data obtained and help determine the next steps to be taken either to clarify the diagnosis or to plan for treatment.

Although there has been major improvement in the detection and treatment of dual disorders, they still are frequently unrecognized by general medical staff or professionals trained in either drug treatment or psychiatric care. It still is difficult to find treatment resources willing or professionally able to address both types of problems. Unfortunately, the fact that a facility claims to provide dual diagnosis services does not guarantee that they do it well. Further, it is increasingly difficult to justify to insurance providers the added expenses associated with the treatment of dually diagnosed clients.

CATEGORIES OF ABUSED SUBSTANCES

Human beings are stunningly creative in their ability to find new ways of altering their moods, and the range of addictive substances seems to increase steadily. There is not sufficient space here for detailed discussion of all of the different substances people ingest or inject themselves with, so I deal with those most commonly encountered in EAPs.[3] Two sources of special interest to EAP personnel are the *Drug Abuse Curriculum for EAP Professionals,* (available through the U.S. Department of Health and Human Services, Alcohol, Drug Abuse, and Mental Health Administration, Office of Workplace Initiatives, National Institute on Drug Abuse, Rockville, Maryland) and Gilman, Goodman, Rall, and Murad (1985), *The Pharmacological Basis of Therapeutics,* which provides detailed but accessible information about the range of substances, their effects, and both trade names and street names.

Alcohol and Other Sedatives

Alcohol

The substance most abused in our culture and most familiar to EAP professionals is alcohol. Although small amounts of alcohol can have a stimulating impact, the major effect on the central nervous system is a sedative reaction similar to that associated with other sedatives described below. Although most people who drink may never experience any of the consequences associated with alcohol abuse or dependence, the thrust of the research on the effects of even moderate drinking suggests that many more people are at risk for negative consequences than we may be aware of because of the impaired judgment that occurs under the influence of alcohol, the combined effects of alcohol and other substances, or preexisting medical or emotional problems.

Chronic alcohol abuse has a major deleterious effect on most systems of the human body. A factor in the severity of the medical consequences of alcohol abuse and the progressive nature of the disease is the fact that, compared to other drugs, alcohol is less effective in producing or sustaining the euphoric high of intoxication, and larger and larger amounts of alcohol are needed to achieve some effect. Common physiological effects involve the liver in the form of cirrhosis and hepatitis. The gastrointestinal tract is subject to esophagitis, chronic pancreatitis, and esophageal cancer. Chronic drinking contributes disproportionately to morbidity rates associated with diseases of the cardiovascular system. Prolonged patterns of drinking create severe neurological symptoms including hallucinations, dementia, seizures, and blackouts. Emotionally, alcohol use, abuse, or dependence can trigger or complicate severe emotional states of anxiety and depression and also can increase the probability of "acting out" and self-destructive behavior. The tragic effects of alcohol on the fetus still are being investigated, but we do know that fetal alcoholism syndrome (FAS) is one of the leading causes of mental retardation in developed countries and that fetal alcoholism effects (FAE) compromises other children in a variety of ways (National Institute on Alcohol Abuse and Alcoholism, 1990).

Although most of the medical consequences of alcohol consumption are associated with chronic abuse, other consequences may develop with moderate use. Negative psychological, social, and economic repercussions happen either as the result of the mood-altering properties of the substance or because of the extent to which it prevents the person from meeting the normal responsibilities of living. Even a single drinking event can result in an intoxicated driver killing someone while driving an automobile. Family violence, unwanted pregnancies, victimization by street criminals, and economic loss all can occur while a person is intoxicated, even if "getting stoned" is not a common event for the person involved. Alcohol consumption is significantly associated with other types of life-threatening events including falls, burns, and suicides. In addition, other people in the drinker's orbit are placed at risk for equally serious medical, social, emotional, and economic consequences—consequences that may bring these people to the EAP counselor.

Sedatives and Antianxiety Agents

A feature that sedatives, barbiturates, antianxiety agents, and alcohol have in common is their depressive effect on the central nervous system, resulting in detectable symptoms of drowsiness and impaired motor coordination. All these substances are available through legal means and all have a potential for misuse and abuse. Sedatives, because of their calming effect, are used to treat anxiety and panic attacks, seizures, convulsions, muscle spasms, insomnia, minor emotional problems, and alcohol withdrawal. Both the abuse of and dependence upon sedatives can occur. Withdrawal can be severe and life threatening and requires medical monitoring because of the potential for seizures and convulsions. Among the more common trade names for sedatives are phenobarbital, Nembutal, Seconal, and Amytal. These are less used now since the introduction of benzodiazepine "tranquilizing" drugs in the 1960s, which are more effective and specific in treating anxiety and insomnia without the more generalized side effects of sedatives.

Benzodiazepines are sold under the trade names Ativan, Xanax, Halcion, and Valium, among others. Their legal use has declined also as medical personnel have become more aware of their potential for abuse.[4] Prescriptions are written more conservatively and for shorter terms, but it still is remarkably easy for a credible patient to obtain such prescriptions from unsuspecting or unethical doctors almost on request. Abuse is more likely to be associated with attempts to self-prescribe and self-medicate for problems of insomnia, fear, and anxiety, but it also can occur in other ways, such as through overdosing to moderate the effects of withdrawal from other substances, and in combination with other drugs, especially alcohol and cocaine (Hartog & Tusel, 1987). The use of benzodiazepines with other drugs usually is an attempt to boost their effects or to lessen withdrawal symptoms. There is less potential for overdosing than with sedatives because it would require extremely large quantities of pills to achieve that effect. However, the combined use of benzodiazepines with alcohol, even in relatively moderate amounts, can be life threatening. They are less likely to be used as recreational drugs than are stimulants, as they do not produce anything approaching the same degree of euphoria or "rush."

Withdrawal from benzodiazepines can include insomnia, excitability, nausea and gastrointestinal problems, and at times sensitivity to light and sound (Paolino, 1991a).

Stimulants

Drugs of abuse in this category either are derived from natural sources, such as cocaine, khat, nicotine, and caffeine, or are produced synthetically, such as amphetamines. The overall number of compounds present in these drugs is quite large, which means many of their effects are specific to the drug, the dose, and the psychosocial factors associated with their use. All stimulants, however, produce a general arousal of the nervous system that includes mental alertness, euphoria, hyperactivity, increases in blood pressure, insomnia, and loss of appetite.

Cocaine

Although the experience of the human race with the leaf of the coca shrub and its extracts is centuries old, relatively little confirmed knowledge exists about its effects physically and emotionally, nor is there a reliable set of procedures in place to help those who have become its victims. As recently as 20 years ago, inservice training seminars for drug treatment professionals could not document that cocaine use was addicting, a fact that may have contributed to its spread among other drug users trying to mitigate withdrawal symptoms from heroin or amphetamines. Cocaine did not fit the then prevailing definitions of addiction derived from diagnoses of alcoholism or opiate use and characterized by more clearcut signs of dependence or severe withdrawal symptoms. In addition, cocaine abuse and dependence occur in persons who do not fit the stereotypical image of addicts. Men and women who by most measures are reasonably stable, are well integrated, and have no history of preexisting psychiatric illness or criminal behavior can become victims of cocaine abuse (Washton, Stone, & Hendrickson, 1988).

We now know that dependence on cocaine occurs readily and is common, and that increased tolerance and dependence can occur in just a few weeks. Broadened definitions of dependence that include behavioral factors such as loss of control, craving, compulsion, and continued use despite adverse consequences clearly describe cocaine's effects (Paolino, 1991b). A feature associated with cocaine that reinforces its addictive and toxic effects is that the euphoria it produces often includes a craving for more cocaine, unlike heroin and alcohol, which produce a level of satiation;

craving with these drugs comes during withdrawal (Jaffe, Cascella, Kumor, & Sherer, 1989). Emerging data on brain chemistry suggest that cocaine stimulates neural pathways in the brain's basic "reward" centers that produce this biologically based craving for the drug (Gold, Washton, & Dackis, 1985). Currently, the manufacture and sale of cocaine is a multibillion-dollar industry, international in scope and intricately bound up with other aspects of commerce, trade, political coalitions, and world events. The cocaine industry is ranked as comparable to the fifth largest Fortune 500 company (Paolino, 1991a). In addition, it no longer is the drug for only the affluent, as new ways of modifying the basic compound have both decreased its cost and broadened its markets to include all ages and classes of people.

The basic form of cocaine is hydrochloride salt, which is water soluble and therefore easily injected, swallowed, or snorted. "Freebasing" cocaine, which involves "freeing" the cocaine from its hydrochloride or sulphate salts so it can be smoked, was a costly, time-consuming, and dangerous process until a new procedure was introduced, changing the hydrochloride salt into crystal-like pellets. This produces "crack," an inexpensive and easily obtainable version of the drug that is ready for smoking with no further processing (National Institute on Drug Abuse, 1991). Street myths exist to the effect that snorting or smoking are less addicting than injecting cocaine; however, current evidence suggests that all are equally addicting.

Another factor in cocaine abuse is that the rush experienced after using the drug is intense but relatively short term. The initial effects of cocaine occur within 3 to 5 minutes. Peak effects can last anywhere from 15 to 45 minutes with a rapid decline in impact as the drug is quickly metabolized in the body. Withdrawal effects are less dramatic than with other drugs, a characteristic that contributed to the belief that cocaine was a relatively benign intoxicant. The stages of withdrawal are characterized by an initial depressive "crash" lasting for several hours followed by a period of sleeping and dysphoria that can last for days. In the following stage of up to 10 weeks, the abuser is apt to experience life as joyless, pain filled, and oppressive in contrast to the brief high experienced after administering the drug. This sets the stage for repeated use if there is no form of effective intervention. The pleasurable effects induced by the drug lessen as frequency of use and dependence increase. The mental alertness, sexual arousal, and high energy originally experienced after taking cocaine are replaced by loss of energy and sexual drive, apathy, and social and emotional withdrawal (Washton et al., 1988). Practice wisdom circulating among those who treat cocaine addicts describes the intractibility of the denial of its users, a phenomenon usually described as being far more intense and prolonged than in alcoholics.

Cocaine's toxic effects are especially associated with the cardiovascular system and include blockages in blood flow, strokes, irregular heart rhythms, and cardiac arrest even in persons with no history of cardiovascular disease. Tolerance increases rapidly and users can move quickly to dosages that would have been lethal initially. Even occasional use can kill (National Institute on Drug Abuse, 1991). The drug also causes fetal damage and contributes to a range of neurological and medical problems in babies of cocaine-abusing women.

A belief persists among some professionals that women are especially prone to cocaine addiction. However, a number of authors question this assumption, seeing it as more indicative of societal stereotypes about women than of empirical information about drug use (Erickson & Murray, 1989; Inciardi et al., 1993). A problem in trying to arrive at a better understanding of this and other issues of drug abuse and treatment is the extent to which women have been underrepresented in much of the research conducted in this field (Inciardi et al., 1993).

Amphetamines and Related Drugs

This group of stimulants includes a number of chemically related drugs that have stimulant effects on the central nervous system causing symptoms of hyperalertness, euphoria, increased physical endurance, impaired judgment and reality testing, and an elevation in feelings of confidence and self-esteem. These drugs include amphetamines (Benzadrine), dextroamphetamine (Dexedrine or "speed"), methylamphetamine (methadrine), and methylphenidate (Ritalin). Many were developed for legitimate medical uses, but they have found their way into the stream of the illegal drug trade. As the medical profession has become more conservative in the use of these drugs, illegal laboratories have increased production. The chemical manufacture of these substances makes it possible to produce variations with slightly different components that are not yet legally restricted, as in the case of MDMA ("Ecstasy"), which is reputed to be similar to LSD or cocaine in its effects (National Institute on Drug Abuse, 1991).

The drugs in this category are taken orally in pill form, snorted, or injected. The euphoric effect of most stimulants takes longer to develop than that of cocaine, and it lasts much longer: 3 to 4 hours when injected and 8 to 12 hours if taken orally. Their abuse leads to chronic irritability, anxiety, sleep disturbances, and violence in the form of suicidal gestures.

In situations of chronic intoxication, users may experience convulsions, coma, death, or a form of psychosis characterized by paranoid delusions; auditory, visual, or tactical hallucinations; and aggression. Both increased tolerance and physical dependence are features of the abuse of these stimulants, and abrupt withdrawal can precipitate depression, anxiety, diminished mental functioning, and extreme fatigue or lassitude. It often is difficult to detect abuse because much of the use of these drugs is periodic and recreational, or the abuser may have started using them as part of a medically supervised course of treatment for legitimate medical complaints. It is not unusual for EAP counselors to encounter clients who are totally unaware that they are, in fact, physically dependent on prescriptions they have taken innocently for long periods of time. Women are believed to be more at risk for amphetamine abuse. Doctors are more inclined to prescribe them for women than men, and the rate of emergency room admissions for complications of their use is greater for women than men (Inciardi et al., 1993; Prather & Minkow, 1991).

Opiates

The drugs in this grouping either are derived from opium, which is harvested from the poppy plant, or they are synthesized in other ways. Opium contains both morphine and codeine, and heroin was developed as a variant from morphine, originally for the purpose of treating morphine addiction. Similarly, methadone (Dolophine) was first manufactured to assist in the withdrawal of heroin addiction because it can suppress withdrawal symptoms for up to two days in addition to nullifying the effects of any other drug taken during that period, but it since has become a drug of abuse. Other substances in this category with less powerful addiction potential are codeine and paregoric. Opioid drugs exert an inhibitory effect on the nervous system. The resultant calming effects, including the suppression of pain, makes them important agents in the legitimate and common treatment of numerous medical disorders, which means, too, they are more accessible to large numbers of people and therefore their potential for abuse is great.

These drugs are taken orally in pill or liquid form, and some can be smoked. The most intense and immediate effects occur through intravenous injection. Overuse or abuse of the drug can lead to tolerance and withdrawal symptoms. Madden (1990) describes characteristic heroin and methadone withdrawal as lasting about a week for heroin and as less intense but more prolonged for methadone. Withdrawal symptoms include anxiety, restlessness, insomnia, anorexia, nausea, diarrhea, and pains in the muscles and joints. An increase in nasal secretions results in a runny nose and tearing of the eyes. These effects generally are severe enough to interfere with a person's ability to perform work or family functions adequately, to the extent that he or she often can be detected during screening assessments. In addition to the threats of increased tolerance and withdrawal, the risk for overdosing by injection is high. Abusers also experience higher rates of immune system disturbances than nonusers, including venereal disease, viral hepatitis, and HIV infection. It had been assumed that such infections occurred solely because of shared use of needles and diminished responsibility for personal care and conduct while under the effects of the drug. However, the accumulated evidence of the past 25 years now indicates that in addition to these risk factors, the prolonged use of heroin, in and of itself, has detrimental effects on the immune system that increase the overall vulnerability to a range of serious infections (National Institute on Drug Abuse, 1991).

Marijuana and Nicotine

The use of marijuana and cannaboids in the United States have declined regularly since the mid-1970s as the potential and actual negative consequences of their use are more generally perceived (National Institute on Drug Abuse, 1991). Minorities tend to have higher rates of nicotine use and women under 23 are reported to have the fastest growing rates of cigarette use (Moncher, Schinke, & Holden, 1992). Marijuana still is the most widely used of the illegal drugs, however, and the potency of the drug being sold on the streets has increased, a factor that also may increase the severity of reactions to its use. In general, the likelihood of physical or psychological dependence is low for the occasional adult user, and reports of complicated withdrawal in general are rare. There is, nonetheless, increasing concern about the physiological effects of heavy or prolonged use as well as possible effects on children and adolescents. For heavy users increased tolerance may occur. Animal studies suggest the possibility of negative effects on the immune system and fetal development. Studies of infants born to human drug-addicted mothers detected delta-9-tetrahydrocannabinol (THC), the principal active ingredient in marijuana, in the babies' intestinal content even when it was not evident in blood samples of either mother or child (Osterea, Subramanian, & Abel, 1988, as cited in National Institute on Drug Abuse, 1991, p. 134). The significance of this fact is not yet understood, but it raises concern about other effects of marijuana use on the fetus that have yet to be determined. The U.S. Surgeon General's Office campaign to educate the public about the serious and costly consequences of cigarette smoking has resulted in changing cultural attitudes and reduced patterns of use among some groups. In spite of advertisements by tobacco manufacturers that continue to link cigarette smoking with glamorous, affluent, and sophisticated lifestyles, in some settings smokers are experiencing a kind of stigmatization once reserved for publicly obnoxious alcoholics. In its most recent report to Congress, the Department of Health and Human Services summarizes current research evidence on nicotine use that continues to support and amplify the evidence of its negative physical repercussions (*National Institute on Drug Abuse,* 1990). A summary of the finding reaffirms that, like other psychoactive agents, nicotine, the active ingredient in cigarettes, is characterized by patterns of increased tolerance, addiction, abuse, and dependence. Attempts to discontinue its use precipitate predictable and sometimes severe withdrawal symptoms that can vary considerably from one person to another.

Long-term or heavy use of nicotine is a recognized risk factor in cardiovascular illness; in cancer of the lungs, mouth, and throat; and, increasingly, to the fetus of nicotine-abusing mothers. Some consequences of fetal exposure to the nicotine inhaled by the mother include more miscarriages and birth complications, lower average birthrates, slower development even a year after birth, and possibly greater susceptibility to other addictive drugs. One study reported in *National Institute on Drug Abuse* (1990) detected effects from maternal smoking that were more pronounced than those produced by the mother's use of alcohol, marijuana, or other abused drugs (O'Connell & Fried, 1987). Nicotine use is highly associated with the abuse of other drugs and apparently is a "gateway" drug in the sense that it is highly predictive of later onset of other forms of drug use or abuse.

The weight of the evidence as to the serious medical consequences both on smokers and of second-hand smoke on nonsmoking workers has convinced many employers to initiate smoking cessation campaigns that often involve input from EAPs. In addition, workers come to EAPs voluntarily for help and information about their cigarette addiction, and many of the same considerations that apply to other forms of drug use are relevant to work on these issues as well. Such employees, like other addicted personnel, need help with denial as to the seriousness of the consequences on themselves and others. They need information, education, and resource materials as to medical and behavioral aids in achieving abstinence. It even may be necessary to intervene with family members, as the support of significant others is a major predictor of recovery. As the environments that allow cigarette smoking decrease, nicotine addicts will be experiencing increasing pressures and stresses associated with the reality of their compulsion that can be addressed in an EAP context.

SOURCES OF ASSESSMENT INFORMATION

I spoke earlier of a spiraling process of assessment, which implies that the inquiry involves repeated analysis of data as new information is gathered. It often is necessary to direct the exploration of facts and incidents in a person's life back and forth between present and past, between drug-use behaviors and family reactions, and between workplace concerns and personal functioning. The point of assessment is not simply to determine the presence or absence of a drug problem, but to obtain a holistic understanding of a person with a problem that is in most instances affecting and affected by multiple systems including but not limited to the workplace.

Freeman and Landesman (1992) argue for a differential approach to assessment that individualizes the client and provides a basis for determining whether the drug or alcohol use is a primary or secondary problem, the extent to which the abuse is chronic or acute, and the ways in which the person's functioning has been affected, with consideration being given to both failures and strengths in functioning. This information lays a basis for constructing a treatment plan that is responsive to individual case needs and that offers an appropriate mix of resources to support the strengths of the individual and his or her systems.

The EAP counselor has several sources of information available to make an assessment. These include (a) the direct, face-to-face clinical interview with the client and with significant others; (b) paper-and-pencil screening tests; and (c) laboratory tests.

The Clinical Interview

The clinical interview is directed toward eliciting information concerning the history and patterns of use including information as to what substances are used, in what combination, how frequently, in what amounts, and something about the onset and duration of these patterns. Determining whether dependence is present requires exploring additional information regarding loss of control, increased tolerance, evidence of complicated withdrawal, a medical problem suggesting long-term use, and an inability to discontinue use. Finally, the counselor must determine what additional psychosocial problems may have developed as a result of the abuse or dependence. The misuse of chemicals can result in a series of physical, social, and behavioral consequences that can be detected through the exploration of a client's work performance, general health, family matters, and social and behavioral functioning, as discussed in Chapter 4.

Clients themselves may provide reasonably accurate self-reports about their substance use if they are sober and not otherwise symptomatic, if they are aware that other sources are being used, and if they are assured of confidentiality (National Institute on Alcohol Abuse and Alcoholism, 1990). However, clients, especially cocaine users, may be less reliable in reporting the social and emotional problems their use of chemicals may be causing. The accuracy of self-reports can be enhanced through the use of a well-structured and nonjudgmental interview process. Family members, coworkers, and supervisors can add important information to amplify or correct the user's impression of the facts of his or her use of drugs or alcohol within the bounds of the confidentiality and privacy provisions that apply.

The significance of denial has been well established in working with alcoholics and, as mentioned earlier, is even more intransigent in cocaine abusers. It exists in varying degrees in patterns of abuse of other drugs. Denial is a complicated phenomenon that represents an attempt on the part of many abusers to deal with the erosion of their fundamental image of themselves and their ability to cope with the consequences of chemical abuse and dependence. As discussed by Brown (1985) most persons at the onset of their addictive careers have a concept of themselves, first of all, as something other than an alcoholic or an addict and, second, as someone who has control his or her life including the use of drugs or alcohol. As the consequences of their drinking or drug use undermine these beliefs, abusers must invest more energy into protecting their deeply valued images of themselves. This involves a variety of psychosocial mechanisms that filter out those aspects of reality dystonic to their self-concept. They become more selective as to what they allow themselves and others close to them to see, hear, or believe. As their ability to function normally becomes compromised, they must manipulate events and people to compensate for failures in performance.

It is important to understand that the processes involved are not merely stubborn refusals to acknowledge the obvious; the processes largely are unconscious and out of awareness because they touch on core identity issues developed over a lifetime. The psychological shock that occurs when the denial is penetrated—the "hitting bottom" of AA wisdom—attests to the profound psychic trauma involved in not only having failed at being able to maintain a preferred image of oneself, but also losing any sense of self at all.

How the clinician deals with such denial needs to be determined on the basis of an individualized assessment of the person and his or her history and likely reaction to different approaches. Some clients may respond to the hard-nosed, straightforward counseling style in which the substance abuser's minimizing of his or her problems and rationalizations are consistently challenged and rejected. Other emotionally vulnerable clients can experience this as abusive and possibly a repetition of earlier abuse experience. It may be possible to conduct an intervention with the employee using the counselor, supervisor staff, or coworkers and family members to penetrate the person's rigid defense against admitting the nature and extent of his or her problems.

Pencil-and-Paper Screening Tests

EAP counselors commonly use one or more pen-and-paper screening tests, either incorporated in the clinical interview or self-administered by clients, to help determine the presence of chemical dependency problems. These instruments are effective in assessing the social and psychological factors associated with substance use and can remind clinicians of areas of client behaviors that are diagnostically significant. However, they may be less reliable for women and minority clients. Among the most frequently used are the Michigan Alcoholism Screening Test (MAST) (Selzer, 1971) (originally designed for face-to-face interviews) and its variations: the 25-item self-administered questionnaire, the 13-item Short MAST (SMAST) (Selzer, Vinokur, & van Rooijen, 1975), and the 10-item Brief MAST (Pokorny, Miller, & Kaplan, 1972). The Drug Abuse Screening Test (DAST) (Skinner, 1982) deals with nonalcohol drug abuse and is available as a self-administered questionnaire (DAST-20) (see Appendix) or in a shorter version (DAST-10).[5] Its content is similar to that of the MAST.

Washton and colleagues (1988) have developed the Cocaine Abuse Assessment Profile: Addiction/Dependency Self-Test, which is similar to the MAST and DAST but more detailed and specific to cocaine use. Some programs may use additional assessment tools administered by the counselor. The Addiction Severity Index (Cacciola, Griffith, & McLellan, 1985;

McClellan, Luborsky, Woody, & O'Brien 1980) is designed to determine the presence of both alcohol and drug use in addition to the interactive effects of a variety of environmental factors. It is administered by the clinician.

A subscale of the Minnesota Multiphasic Personality Inventory (MMPI), the McAndrew Alcoholism Scale (MAC), is able to identify alcoholics with a family history of alcoholism and to differentiate alcoholics from mentally ill persons who do not abuse drugs.

Laboratory Tests

Depending on the size of the company or its network of resources, some EAPs may have access to laboratory tests that can indicate recent and possibly even longer-term use of alcohol and drugs. Drug testing in one form or another is becoming standard for many large employers and has grown dramatically during the past decade (Axel, 1991). Such tests usually are in relation to preemployment processing, but the impetus provided by the Drug-Free Workplace Act (DFWA) of 1988 has spurred the development of "for-cause" testing whenever an employee's behavior is thought to be suspicious or places the worker or others at risk. Random testing still is uncommon because of the ethical and legal challenges it has generated.[6]

Generally EAPs are not involved in either managing or processing such tests, and the practice wisdom in the field cautions against this kind of involvement. Not only can the punitive and disciplinary aspects of drug testing compromise the EAP's primary role of helping to provide counseling and assistance to the user, but it also can implicate the EAP staff in a range of complex legal issues, union-management battles, and murky interpretations of rights and responsibilities that just now are being identified. It is important, however, that the counselor be aware of some of the basics of testing in order to be of most help to clients and their employers and to understand the contexts in which the findings need to be evaluated.

The basis of drug testing is the chemical analysis of bodily substances, usually breath, blood, or urine, to determine the presence of one or more substances being used. More relevant information about recent use and other impairment is obtained from blood samples. Increased challenges by unions and employees regarding the accuracy of drug testing now require that the level of scientific certainty meet legal or forensic standards of being "beyond a reasonable doubt" (Willette, 1991) to protect both employees and the organizations they work for. Most drug testing, therefore, involves a two-step procedure requiring an initial immunoassay analysis using one form of chemical analysis followed by a gas chromatography/mass spectrometry (GC/MS) involving another. This combination of tests can detect recent use of a range of different substances and the quantity of the substance present in the system. Drug-testing firms offer different options to companies as to the range of substances to be screened. For example, a company may choose an option dealing specifically with drugs that would include marijuana, cocaine, amphetamines, opiates, PCP, and barbiturates. Others, depending on the nature of their workforce, might add methadone, benzodiazepines, or other substances (Willette, 1991).

Potential problems in evaluating the outcomes of testing can occur because of falsification of results by employees, poor-quality testing, and manipulation of the processes or results of drug-testing programs by employers. Individual and organized approaches to thwarting drug-testing procedures increasingly are a part of the street lore of users. Coombs and West (1991) describe black-market entrepreneurs who sell "clean" urine for as much as $50 a vial and the "Urine King," who markets powdered samples and a booklet on how to beat urine tests (p. xix). As employment-based drug testing expands, these new industries are likely to proliferate.

On the other hand, there is growing concern among unions and other employee associations that fraudulent drug-screening practices are used by employers to harass or to rid themselves of "difficult" employees (Walsh & Trumble, 1991), including "whistle blowers." In addition, although laboratory tests are highly reliable when conducted under experimental test conditions, in practice their reliability may be compromised by inadequately trained or overstressed technicians, poorly organized tracking procedures, inappropriate storage or handling, and other lapses in quality control. The implications of these factors for EAP counselors are that the results of drug testing can provide important confirmatory information about the extent and nature of drug use, but they are subject to error and misinterpretation, and are most valuable within the context of a broader assessment.

TREATMENT PLANNING

Beyond the assessment itself, the EAP counselor has a number of tasks and responsibilities to the client and his or her interpersonal systems, the exact nature of which are determined by the results of the assessment process. Most immediate is the need to make decisions about referral options for treating the drug-abuse problem. These decisions, however, need to be made within a much broader context than that of chemical dependence alone, a context that takes into consideration both immediate and long-term planning for the employee, the employee's family and work life, and the ongoing role of the EAP counselor in the process. Before any referral can be made, much clinical work is required to assess and intensify the client's readiness and motivation to get help, to anticipate what this will mean in terms of disruption of other life roles, and to lay the foundation for a recovery process that will minimize enabling on the part of others and optimize supports. Depending on the nature of the specific case situation, some of these tasks can be performed better by treatment center personnel, but when the client's benefits or the treatment resources are limited, this may not be possible. The importance of the EAP counselor extends beyond preliminary assessment and referral. A more accurate description of the role includes elements of advocacy, mediation, and case management, and a view of the EAP counselor as a treatment team member who is in a position to perform specific functions related to the workplace better than anyone else. The assessment process, therefore, needs to generate the type of information that can support these multiple responsibilities of the counselor over time.

As suggested above, chemical dependency assessment and treatment planning are being influenced in profound ways by changes in our health-care system that are contributing to a two-tier system of service: one for those who can afford adequate health insurance and another for those who cannot. Insurance contracts, changing benefit structures, and cost-containment strategies are playing increasingly decisive roles in determining the quality, effectiveness, and appropriateness of treatment plans for EAP clients, especially the chemically dependent or mentally ill. The growth in the numbers of both EAPs and addiction treatment centers has been directly related to the availability of benefit funds to pay for the type of care deemed effective for alcohol or drug abusers. With a declining proportion of our workforce having any health-care coverage and with an increasingly adversarial relationship between insurers and claimants, the EAP counselor often is in the position of having to wage advocacy battles with employers and benefit providers to ensure that the level of care an employee needs will be available. However accurate the diagnosis, treatment planning often must be based on what is possible, not necessarily what is best. Whatever the benefit picture may be for a given client, the counselor still has the responsibility of trying to generate a treatment plan that offers some hope of assistance and recovery.

NOTES

1. For an interesting and useful comparison of the DSM-III-R, now under consideration for DSM-IV, and the proposed ICD-10 classification schemes, see Chapter 7, "Diagnosis and Assessment of Alcohol Use Disorders," *Alcohol and Health: Seventh Special Report to the U.S. Congress* (U.S. Department of Health and Human Services, 1990).

2. Some definitions include persons who have been diagnosed as having a psychiatric disorder at any point in their lifetime even if there is no evidence of its presence currently.

3. There may be some variations in different geographical areas as to the preponderance of certain drugs of choice. Until recently, for example, Chicago was the only major city in the United States without a major crack/cocaine problem. Phencyclidine (PCP) use has declined generally but still is a problem in Washington, D.C.

4. Legal prescription of benzodiazepines reached its peak in 1975, at 90 million. By 1985 the number of legal prescriptions dropped to 81 million (National Institute on Drug Abuse, 1991).

5. Permission for the use of the DAST is required from the Addiction Research Foundation, 33 Russell St., Toronto, Ontario, Canada M5S 2S1.

6. See Angarola (1991) and Lo (1990) for excellent summaries of both the legal and the ethical issues, respectively, of drug testing in the workplace.

Chapter 6

REFERRAL TO EXTERNAL PROVIDERS

Both managers and employee clients expect EAP staff to be especially adept in matching an employee's needs with resources that provide prompt and effective intervention. The depth and thoroughness of the assessment become a means of increasing the probability that key problems are identified and prioritized accurately and that help will begin quickly. Failure to meet these expectations can adversely affect the credibility of the EAP and the long-term life of the program. As a result most EAPs devote a significant part of program resources to locating, evaluating, and updating their network of providers. The "referral out" function is distinct from the procedures governing internal referral to the EAP. Referring out is the process of locating one or more providers external to the employing organization to supply the ongoing services required to deal with clients' major concerns. These external resources may assume responsibility for all of a client's needs or they may be ancillary to the continuing work being done in-house by the EAP counselor.

Several key aspects are involved in ensuring that both the company and the client are well served in the referral process, including (a) the development of a network of reliable, competent, and cost-effective resources; (b) timely and sensitive clinical work with clients to facilitate their transition to the resources; and (c) ongoing monitoring of the resources collectively or in behalf of specific case situations to ensure that client and company needs are being addressed. Most EAP counselors are in general agreement about the importance of the first two of these areas. Not all share the same opinion about the last. In addition to discussing these issues in this chapter,

I devote some special attention to the use of self-help groups as a referral resource.

DEVELOPING AND MAINTAINING A RESOURCE BASE

Programs vary as to the proportion of EAP clients referred to an external resource. In my study of 26 programs (Cunningham, 1990) counselor estimates ranged from a low of 10% up to 100% with modal norms between 70% and 90%. Referral rates are influenced by how the EAP defines its service, the particular service orientation of EAP staff, and the availability of benefits that can be used to help subsidize continuing service through external referrals. In programs that service a high proportion of chemical dependency or serious psychiatric problems, referrals for both inpatient and outpatient care are likely to be high. If program staff are able to provide short-term counseling for a range of presenting problems, fewer referrals are made. In organizations with a high proportion of "working poor," or low-salaried employees, referral options are more limited and EAP staff must find other ways of helping clients.

Commonly used resources for EAPs include inpatient and outpatient chemical dependency treatment centers, community-based mental health or family service agencies, private therapists, and self-help groups. Generally, a high priority is placed on making sure that only the best and most reliable resources are used and that the referral procedure constitutes as smooth as possible a transition from the EAP to the service provider. This process is becoming more difficult as referral decisions must take into consideration the costs involved and managed care reviews. Recently there has been a flurry of controversy concerning the relative effectiveness of inpatient and outpatient treatment, partial hospitalization, and day-clinic settings for the chemically dependent based on studies that suggest comparable results (National Institute on Alcohol Abuse and Alcoholism, 1990; U.S. Department of Health and Human Services, 1987) among these different treatment options. In addition, EAP practitioners note that in many instances outpatient care can be as helpful to selected clients as inpatient while creating less disruption of the client's employment or family life (Christner, 1991). As a result of the controversy, health insurers are more reluctant to fund inpatient treatment, or they may limit inpatient care to only those patients who have failed in one or more courses of outpatient care.

It is a matter of growing concern in the EAP field that decisions that materially affect the health and recovery potential for clients are being made by persons with no knowledge of either the client or clinical treatment. This reality greatly complicates the referral responsibilities of EAP counselors, who must become more advocacy oriented to ensure that their clients receive the best treatment available. To advocate effectively counselors must demonstrate that they have done a thorough job of assessment and that they are knowledgeable about the various treatment options in the community. At times this may mean taking the situation to others in the organization and making the case for a more costly resource if it is what the client needs and if it gives more promise of providing enduring results.

Counselors need to be cautious and thorough in reviewing and selecting potential resources. A common method of developing a resource base is to rely on recommendations of other EAP professionals in a given area. Such recommendations need to be further evaluated, however, to ensure that they meet the specific needs of each company and its employee group. A common practice is for EAP staff to make site visits to a prospective resource whenever possible to appraise the facilities, support staff, and general ambience, especially for inpatient treatment programs. Some EAPs have developed structured forms or checklists outlining their criteria to aid in this process. When resource marketers or private practitioners are being evaluated, they can be invited to an interview with EAP staff and asked about their theoretical orientation, their handling of hypothetical or actual case situations, and their understanding of self-help and 12-Step groups. Potential providers should be able to provide copies of their résumés and licensing or accreditation credentials.

Some EAPs make a practice of recommending three or more likely resources to a client, who is then free to choose the one he or she feels most comfortable with. Not only does this practice promote client autonomy, but it also may protect the company from legal liability in the event of a treatment failure (Backer & O'Hara, 1991). Multiple options are easier to generate in resource-rich locations, but providing several choices may not be realistic in smaller communities, when the client's benefits are limited, or when a highly specialized resource is indicated.

A complicating feature of many case situations is the fact that clients often are dealing with not just one but several interrelated problems that require a series or "package" of resources directed at the multiple needs of clients and their family members. It often is necessary for counselors to orchestrate this mix of services over time or to function as case managers to ensure that the external resources are all delivering the proper care.

Regional Resources

A number of EAPs serve client companies with many different locations in the United States and abroad, so that client assessment and referral must be handled through telephone conversations with the employee and potential resources. Resource development under these circumstances requires creativity and innovation and a talent for professional networking. Many communities have resource directories or community service organizations that provide information about local health and welfare resources. Human resource personnel within a client company may provide useful recommendations. State chapters of professional organizations such as the National Association of Social Workers have information about both local agencies and private practitioners. Local members of the Employee Assistance Professionals Association (EAPA) and the Employee Assistance Society of North America (EASNA) can provide additional information. Current information about resources for chemical dependency may be available through local AA and NA groups. A common source of information used to identify regional resources is personal recommendation by EAP colleagues. Once an EAP program has established positive working relationships with several private or institutional resources in an area, these resources then become the source for further information about other resource needs that may arise.

Creating Resources

Some situations require that counselors create a resource that does not exist in any formal way. In one instance, a young woman, only a year into sobriety, had to return to live with her family to care for a dying parent. Concerned about the fragile state of her own recovery, she was not certain she could survive in an abusive home situation in which her parent and a brother still were alcohol dependent. With some help from her AA sponsor she was able to identify an older recovering couple who "fostered" her by providing a physical and emotional refuge whenever the stress of her own family life seemed too threatening.

There are other ways in which the resource requirement often is idiosyncratic to the needs of the client. If, for example, the clinical assessment points to an unhealthy or too circumscribed lifestyle, the counselor may recommend a health club or recreational resources that address some of the client's gaps in knowledge or experience. In a hospital that provided limited benefits, a creative EAP counselor initiated an extensive series of education and information groups for employees focused on client issues that she could neither deal with on a one-to-one basis nor refer out (Cunningham, 1990). By enlisting the help of other members of the hospital's training and clinical staff, she provided information to hundreds of employees on issues of parenting, elder care, depression, and chemical dependency. These meetings were not seen as substitutes for individual treatment; however, they impacted on many employees in the organization in ways that otherwise would not have been possible.

Ethical Considerations

Finally, it is necessary to speak to the issue of the selection and use of resources on the basis of bribes or fee splitting or exclusive preoccupation with bottom-line issues. Unfortunately, it is not unknown for external providers to offer various inducements to EAP personnel as a way of filling beds in treatment centers or ensuring a steady supply of clients covered by generous benefit plans. It also is not unknown for EAP contracting firms to encourage their staff to refer EAP clients to the parent organization for continuing services such as inpatient treatment. Even though the client may receive adequate care, the process is questionable, placing the client, the company, the EAP program, and the counselor in jeopardy. Of even greater concern are situations such as those described in an article in the *Dallas Morning News* in which Texas-based women marketers of psychiatric hospital care allegedly were being asked to provide sex to EAP managers in exchange for an increased flow of referrals ("Marketers Complain of Sex Offers," 1992).

EAPs experienced their greatest growth during the business boom of the 1980s, when situational ethics evolved into a "greed is good" mentality. Not only did ethical and responsible behavior become unfashionable; slick deal making and quasi-corrupt practices also achieved a glamor and status similar in some respects to the allure of the cocaine dealer in urban ghettos. Social workers and other human service professionals interested in making the shift to business settings were covertly advised that they had to shed their values about professional interaction along with their polyester suits and Timex watches. Lack of sophistication about how the business world operated was viewed as the only serious personal failing. These attitudes may be changing in our overall society, but they still are widespread and prevalent in many parts of the business world as organizations try to find ways to survive national and international economic uncertainty.

The time is at hand when, individually and collectively through their membership organizations, EAP professionals must reaffirm the professional and ethical bases for work in this field. EAP staff must recognize their obligations to those whom they are contracted to serve and to one another when colleagues are being victimized by illegal or amoral practices. Beyond this, professionals also need to start blowing the whistle on those providers or EAPs who compromise client service, their client companies, and the profession as a whole by resorting to psychopathic tactics.

CLINICAL ISSUES IN CLIENT REFERRAL

In Chapter 4, I identified several sets of circumstances that determine when and whether a referral is made and the problems some clients experience in starting over with a new person. Several practice principles facilitate client transitions from the EAP to the external provider. These include starting with an individualized treatment plan, involving the client as much as possible in the referral planning, educating clients as to reasonable expectations about providers, and following though with the client long enough to make sure both the client and the external provider are prepared to work together on whatever issues need attention.

Individualized Referral Planning

It is tempting to rely primarily on a handful of easily accessible resources that have provided good service in the past, or to operate on the assumption that standard referral packages apply to all clients having the same problem. If the person is alcoholic, for example, he or she must need inpatient detoxification and treatment, aftercare, AA, and maybe an Adult Children of Alcoholics (ACOA) group. However, one of the major points of conducting in-depth assessments is to understand what is unique about how this person is experiencing his or her problem (Freeman & Landesman, 1992). This sense of being understood as an individual and not as a problem type is a potent factor in the client's acceptance of a treatment plan. If, on the other hand, the client senses that he or she is viewed as "a case" to be handled in a standard, routinized fashion, not only is the referral less likely to occur, but also the EAP can lose credibility in the process. In some case situations, genuinely individualized assessment and referral planning might demonstrate that an external provider is not indicated or that the client has sufficient personal and environmental resources to deal effectively with his or her concerns without outside help (Kurtz, 1992).

As is true in other aspects of employee assistance, referrals must be handled with sensitivity to issues of gender, culture, and race or ethnicity. Although the situation has improved with respect to specialized treatment programs for women, counselors need to be aware of the extent to which certain resources not only are not helpful to women substance abusers but also actually are detrimental to their recovery efforts. The literature is replete with information about the problems women encounter in coeducational treatment programs including lack of attention to female patterns of substance abuse (Corrigan, 1980; Fewell, 1985; Kurtz, 1992), sexual harassment and exploitation (Eldred & Washington, 1975; Inciardi et al., 1993; Levy & Doyle, 1974), and the need for treatment centers that take into consideration the unique aspects of women's addictions (Beschner & Thompson, 1981; Smith, 1991).

Similar concerns must govern resource development and referral of older, minority, or handicapped clients or those who do not speak English well. It is extraordinarily difficult, for example, to find resources with Spanish-speaking counselors even in areas with large Hispanic populations. In some treatment programs minorities may experience racism from staff or other patients (Brisbane & Womble, 1985; Kurtz, 1992). Such categories of clients may need a broader range of ancillary services—including medical, social, and psychological—especially if the basic programs of local treatment centers are based on assumptions of chemical dependency most typical of white, Anglo-Saxon men. If clients are subjected to inappropriate and harmful treatment experiences because of careless or mechanized referral planning, not only are company benefit dollars being misused, but lives also may be lost.

A sentiment expressed by some counselors (Cunningham, 1990) suggests that the compliance rate for referred clients may be increased if more time is spent exploring their feelings about the referral and their emotional readiness to make the transfer. This is supported in part by the findings of a study of 120 EAP clients, 60 "compliers" and 60 "noncompliers," who were referred to external providers (Fizek & Zare, 1988). These findings indicated significant correlations between high compliance rates and the number of preparatory sessions conducted by the EAP counselor. To some extent this runs counter to the prevailing belief that it is easier on the client to make the referral as soon as possible to avoid the trauma of disengaging from a relationship with the EAP counselor and then having to reengage with someone else. Although this situation might be problematic for some clients (and counselors), these difficulties can be minimized by using the additional time to enhance the probability that the client will make the best use of external referrals. Interviewing techniques can be structured to allow clients to make independent decisions, when indicated, about the need for further treatment; to assess and strengthen motivation to continue treatment; to deal with the understandable anxiety the referral can precipitate, especially when inpatient care is recommended; and to demonstrate within the EAP counselor/client relationship what is unique and healing about therapeutic relationships.

At times the best and most individualized resource for a client is not a treatment center or private therapist but one within his or her own personal network. EAP counselors place a high priority on empowering clients to act in their own interests, and one way of accomplishing this is helping clients recognize the personal strengths they bring to a situation in terms of intelligence, motivation to effect changes in their lives, and demonstrated coping and problem-solving abilities. In addition, they may have a strong support group at work, an empathetic extended family member, a religious connection, or a social outlet that can assist in the change process.

Marian, age 62, referred herself to the EAP 2 years before because of her growing dependence on alcohol. The onset of the drinking coincided with her mother's terminal illness and her own recovery from a mastectomy. She subsequently was diagnosed as cross-addicted to alcohol and amphetamines. During an aftercare interview following a course of intensive outpatient treatment, Marian talked about a rediscovered spirituality that highlighted a missing dimension in her life. At one time she was active in her church's religious and social life, but she "lost the faith" when the priest/pastor left the church to marry. She responded to the counselor's suggestion that she consider what this or some other church might offer her at this point in her life. She reported later that her original parish had changed greatly, but so had she. Both she and the parish were less judgmental. She found a new niche for herself in its vigorous spiritual life.

Other types of personal resource development also can be effective. Bibliotherapy can provide a source of new understanding for many clients. Added skill training within the context of EAP sessions supports client self-esteem. These resource recommendations need to be as professionally based as any other, with attention to the unique needs of the client, likely consequences, and their possible ineffectiveness. When judiciously made, these recommendations have important advantages over more formal resource referrals. They involve no eligibility requirements, fees, or managed care reviews. Personal resources usually are accessible and lasting, and they have the potential of forging personal relationships and fostering coping strategies that the client can apply to all types of problems throughout his or her life. They also carry no risk of pathologizing difficulties that may be essentially normal problems of living.

Mutual Referral Planning

Generally during the assessment process multiple factors emerge that either contribute to the client's presenting problem or hold it in place, and specific treatment needs become apparent to both the counselor and the client. Clients should be involved in making decisions about which problems are most pressing; which are of most concern to them and their families; and which kinds of intervention, including external referrals, are realistic in terms of their time, money, belief systems, and energy. Considerable sensitivity and expertise are required to help clients make timely and informed choices, but this does not mean the counselor is a passive participant in the process. Counselors can be firm and persuasive in their professionally based recommendations concerning a plan of treatment, but the ultimate decisions about making use of a resource are the client's. Attempts to coerce or manipulate clients into a course of action they cannot understand or agree with is apt to backfire, with the result that clients reject both the referral and any further help from the EAP.

Counselors have the responsibility to provide their clients with accurate information about the likely choices available and any positives and negatives associated with their use, such as costs, location, and probable length of service. Counselors also should be able to inform clients about what steps are necessary to make the connection, whether or not their benefit plan will cover some or all of the costs, eligibility requirements, and when service can begin. Clients need to be encouraged to express their reactions and to raise any questions they may have about the provider or the processes involved in making use of the service.

Most counselors make a prior contact with a resource. This is especially true when a new or unfamiliar provider is involved. As one counselor expressed it, "[Clients] are often buffeted by all kinds of environmental demands; if we don't . . . pave the way for them and make sure initially that it's a good connection, we set them up for another failure" (Cunningham, 1990, p. 29). Making the first contact provides an opportunity to ensure that the resource is prepared to provide the required service in a way that takes into consideration the client's special needs and any questions or reservations the client might have. It also guarantees that the client will not encounter any surprises that may make the transition more difficult, such as a new fee structure, waiting lists, or an inaccessible location. Client consent is required if the client's identity and specific problems are discussed with a potential referral source, and it may be helpful for the client if that initial contact occurs while the client is present. Doing so makes clear to everyone why the referral is being made and what the mutual expectations are for all concerned. Even if client consent is not available, the counselor still can call a resource to obtain updated general information about the types of services available and procedures for accessing them.

In those instances in which family members or others are directly involved in bringing about changes in the client's circumstances, then they, too, need to be involved in joint or separate discussions about the use of service providers. Their issues, questions, concerns, and readiness for the transition need to be taken into consideration. In situations that require inpatient treatment for a family member it is essential that the rest of the family be helped to understand the purpose of treatment as well as some of the emotional effects and pragmatic problems, such treatment is likely to create. For women clients especially, additional resources may be required to deal with issues of child care or other family responsibilities. Family members also may need help with issues of reentry once the client returns home.

Client Education

Most employees are not well informed about treatment programs, private psychotherapy, community agencies, or even self-help groups. EAP counselors must educate them about available services, their relative benefits, and how these resources are viewed in the professional community. In addition, clients often need to be encouraged to assume a consumer orientation regarding potential referral sources. Having to apply for any kind of help is intimidating, and it is difficult for the uninitiated to recognize appropriate or inappropriate requirements or behaviors. As one counselor put it, the unprepared client will use more care in selecting a TV repairman than a psychotherapist (Cunningham, 1990). Clients need advice as to the kinds of questions they should ask and the types of responses they have a right to expect. Clients also should be told that if they decide a resource is not acceptable they can return to the EAP for a further discussion of options.

If psychotherapy is recommended it may be useful for the counselor to make the point that the assessment sessions they are having in the EAP are similar to therapy sessions in other settings. All good treatment offers the client a special relationship in which his or her needs and concerns are paramount—a relationship that is caring, confidential, noncompetitive, and nonexploitative. The very uniqueness of the EAP relationship can become the basis upon which clients find the courage to continue treatment with someone else. If the client has a good expectation of what the new service provider will be like and can anticipate and plan for the types of information that need to be exchanged, the more likely it is that the referral will "take" and the employee client's request for assistance can be satisfactorily addressed.

Yet another aspect of client education is important in the referral process. The very process of negotiating the referral can provide clients with a real-life experience in how to analyze pressing personal problems and how to take action to do something about them. As counselors described this process, "People [expect] to be told what to do, but I encourage them to make their own decisions. . . . I let them hear themselves making the decisions and they learn they can do it"; "I give them the basis for making informed decisions and empower them to solve their own problems or at least to move on to the next step" (Cunningham, 1990, p. 39). Clients can learn about their rights as citizens of a community, how to untangle mystifying policies and procedures of bureaucracies, and how to intervene in their own systems to make them more responsive. For employees with chronic or acute symptoms of powerlessness and low self-esteem, the very event of taking an action that helps to relieve their distress can be therapeutic.

Follow-Through

EAPs differ regarding their degree of involvement with clients and external providers once a referral is made and accepted. Some counselors feel that any follow-up beyond confirmation that a referral was completed is a needless intrusion into the client's relationship with someone else and serves no clinical purpose. Others have a more protective and advocacy-oriented attitude, requiring that the external provider keep the EAP informed of any major changes in treatment, subsequent referrals, and termination. To a great extent such differences of opinion are a function of dissimilarities in an organization's workforce, counselor-to-employee ratios, or the specific services the company has arranged for with the EAP contracting firm.

In most programs, however, counselors remain involved in at least the initial stages of the referral, particularly when inpatient treatment is required. In these situations counselors visit hospitalized clients, participate in discharge planning sessions, and even include a client's manager in treatment planning if the supervisor made the referral to the EAP or if the client gives consent. One of the decisions made during such discharge planning sessions can be the extent to which the EAP counselor should remain a part of postdischarge treatment as a collaborating member of a treatment team. The counselor often can provide important information about work-related stresses or supports that can influence recovery.

The clinical rationale for this degree of involvement in the treatment process is that most clients will be returning to work and the EAP probably will have ongoing responsibility to support both the reentry to employment and the client's recovery from chemical dependence or physical or mental illness as part of the EAP's aftercare services. The counselor is more effective if he or she participates in the discharge and outpatient treatment planning. Signals of distress, potential relapse, or dramatic changes in the client's life can be dealt with more effectively if the counselor knows something about what has been occurring in treatment. Also, for an increasing number of clients, outpatient care options may be limited and eventually the EAP counselor may be the only professional to whom troubled employees can turn at times of crisis.

Responsible follow-through with clients involves staying with them until there is an indication that they have some means of dealing with their problem, even if there appears to be no resource that can provide them with help. In some situations this may mean a course of short-term treatment in-house; for others it might require detailed discussion about the reason for the paucity of formal resources and ways in which the client can draw on his or her personal and family resources to at least mitigate the problem.

MONITORING EXTERNAL PROVIDERS

Apart from individual case considerations, EAPs also must devote time and attention to maintaining their general resource network. The resource picture is constantly changing as new options present themselves and as existing facilities change their treatment philosophies, personnel, procedures, or general levels of effectiveness. This means EAP staff members must find the time to continually reevaluate and update their resource file in order to remain effective themselves. Currently, a number of EAPs already monitor referrals through required written or verbal reports from providers, but it still is common for counselors to rely on combinations of client feedback and occasional calls to the provider as a basis for evaluation. Although this information can be useful, it is likely that, as healthcare costs escalate and fewer employers or employees are able to pay these costs, more quantitative and verifiable information will have to be maintained about the effectiveness of treatment in relation to both individual clients and resources in general. EAPs will be expected to assume increased responsibility for monitoring the types and effectiveness of providers whose services are subsidized by health plans, as insurers are demanding more detailed information about EAP clients in treatment centers.[1] As the technological capability of many programs increases, various information systems need to be put in place to provide a basis for continuing evaluation of both the compliance rate and the effectiveness of referrals.

SELF-HELP GROUPS

Among the most commonly used resources in EAPs are self-help groups of one kind or another, a pattern that has existed since the original occupational alcoholism programs and their heavy reliance on AA as part of treatment when few other effective and accessible treatment resources were available. The self-help movement has mushroomed and there now exists a dizzying array of self-help and support groups that deal with all types of problems. In considering these groups as possible client resources, however, it is important to keep in mind that not all are alike. Some, such as Al-Anon or Narcotics Anonymous (NA), are strongly identified with the 12-Step philosophy of AA; others, including some codependency groups, are not. Still others have evolved distinct methodologies and operating styles of their own that owe nothing to the AA movement. What they all have in common is the fact that they are assemblages of nonprofessionals who have had a common experience and who believe they can help themselves and one another by sharing their personal stories.

AA and Al-Anon have been in operation the longest and have amassed a positive track record among both recovering people and the professionals who treat them, but this was not always the case. Even today, professionals in some settings see AA as a quasi-mystical movement, and the backlash that has emerged especially in relation to codependency groups (Kaminer, 1992; Katz & Liu, 1991) has not spared AA.[2] Although the nature of AA makes it difficult to mount major studies of its effectiveness, research does exist that indicates that AA can be very useful in helping certain alcoholics remain sober and that this effect may increase with the length of membership (National Institute on Alcohol Abuse and Alcoholism, 1990; Alcoholics Anonymous, 1989). It is not clear why AA is effective (a fact that is just as true of psychotherapy), but several possible reasons have been suggested.

These include AA's insistence on abstinence in contrast to some treatment modalities that accept controlled drinking as a treatment objective. AA is holistic in its approach and emphasizes social, emotional, and spiritual change as part of the recovery process. The 12-Step philosophy provides objective tasks that operationalize and reinforce change over time and foster a concept of self-responsibility for continued growth. Kurtz (1992) points to AA's effectiveness in helping alcoholics deal with issues of guilt and shame as a factor in its effectiveness with members.

Brown (1985) refers to the conversion experience that many members undergo once they acknowledge a Higher Power and surrender or turn over control of their drinking to that power. It is this surrendering of control that is so troublesome for a number of the critics of the movement (Katz & Liu, 1991), as it is viewed as a relinquishing of responsibility for all behavior and a cult-like reliance on the group to decide one's fate. However, this is not an accurate representation of the phenomenon as experienced by most members. Such a perspective suggests confusion between the concepts of control and responsibility, admittedly a difficult distinction to retain in most aspects of human behavior. Paradoxically, once a surrender occurs over the struggle to limit or stop the drinking, the addicted person no longer is enmeshed in either nonproductive control battles or attempts to deny his or her problems, both of which are struggles that leave little time or energy for growth. As the need to control the thoughts and behaviors of "the other" decline, the chemically dependent individual is better able to exert more control over other aspects of his or her life.

A similar phenomenon can occur in Al-Anon and some codependency groups when a person understands at some profound level that the effort to control the dysfunctional behaviors of others is counterproductive, and that it is only by retreating from that battlefield that more functional patterns of personal performance can be developed. Much of the strength of the 12-Step philosophy is its insistence that its members continue to assume greater degrees of responsibility for getting their lives in order, first acknowledging and in some way compensating for the damage to others that they may have caused and eventually assuming responsibility for helping other chemically dependent people to achieve sobriety.

Whatever the basis for the success of the 12-Step movement, it would be irresponsible for any professional in this field to ignore its potential for helping addicted persons to remain chemical free and to reconstruct their lives and relationships. For many patients the positive effects of both psychotherapy and AA can be enhanced when each part of the treatment partnership respects what the other has to offer. On the other hand, these groups are not a panacea or "magic bullet." Not everyone can make use of them, and for some clients other treatment options may be more effective. It is important to be sensitive to the timing of the referral. If clients are dealing with other overwhelming issues, they often are less receptive to a referral even though the practitioner understands that the group could be helpful in dealing with these very issues. It may be necessary, however, to wait until clients are emotionally ready to fully understand the basis for the recommendation—when, for example, they are able to find the locations, attend different groups, and get a sense of what the support groups can offer.

Because of the regard that so many EAP personnel have for 12-Step groups it is easy to make the assumption that all self-help groups are equally effective. This is as improbable as assuming that all therapists are equally effective. Counselors need to become as informed as possible about the different offerings in a given community—their objectives, membership profile, and procedures. In addition, it is helpful to obtain feedback about specific groups, feedback that typically comes from clients or other professionals. It also is extremely useful for practitioners to attend open meetings whenever possible as a means of obtaining more immediate and direct information about the experience.

NOTES

1. One EAP manager in a contracting firm complained that he had to assemble 87 separate bits of information regarding a single client for the insurer.

2. See Chapter 8 for additional discussion of these groups in relation to dysfunctional families and codependency.

Chapter 7

BEYOND ASSESSMENT AND REFERRAL

Although some EAPs define their services as limited to problem identification, assessment, and referral, most programs also provide help to selected clients on a continuing basis in either formal or informal arrangements. Formal provisions include those EAPs that specify a clear model of service that includes the option of short-term counseling, in 1 to as many as 10 or 12 sessions, for clients as an alternative to referral. Most settings also include provisions for follow-up and aftercare that can take the form of continuing treatment in some settings. In addition, ongoing treatment by the EAP counselor often is institutionalized in programs that have been in place for long periods of time because employees return periodically with new issues or new developments on old issues over a period of several years. They view the EAP as a dependable, handy resource in dealing with ongoing problems of living, and they participate in what amounts to a series of short-term treatment episodes. A few programs offer long-term treatment internally to selected employees, and in most internal EAPs certain sensitive cases may be handled in-house for confidentiality reasons regardless of the formal policy statement.

In addition to these fairly straightforward extended service arrangements, many counselors continue with clients informally because the case situation requires it, and they feel ethically bound to do so. It is not uncommon, for example, for some counselors to stretch out the number of available assessment interviews to provide continuing service to clients over time if it appears that a referral is unlikely or unnecessary. These arrangements often are more effective clinically than referrals to external providers, and they also can result in signifcant cost savings to the employer. To date, there has been relatively little exploration as to the professional implications of these extended service arrangements in EAPs. In this chapter I examine several forms of extended assistance to clients beyond the assessment stage and the clinical implications of these service arrangements. I discuss general techniques that can be of significant help to clients whether or not they are being seen for one session, several sessions, or over extended periods of time. Finally, I discuss both programmatic and clinical issues related to follow-up or aftercare.

The concept of extending EAP services beyond assessment and referral still is controversial. It is seen by some counselors and program managers as a departure from the real work of EAPs. The clinical methodology developed for earlier EAPs and OAPs was based on the assumption that their primary responsibility was the identification of either chronic, late-stage alcoholics or more seriously emotionally disturbed employees. For these clients, referrals to external providers was the most realistic course of action. Less severe problems in behavior were not seen as representing the same degree of risk to the people and systems involved, and their potential for affecting a company's bottom-line concerns was generally unrecognized. The changing nature of the EAP clientele now requires more diverse intervention options.

Many EAP counselors are skeptical about the value of short-term, in-house counseling because of their skepticism regarding short-term treatment in general. Most forms of interpersonal helping still are influenced by images of psychoanalytically based psychotherapy and a medical model in which the person with any kind of personal problem is viewed as "sick." The therapist is the doctor who can cure the problem through the application of esoteric techniques not otherwise available to the layperson. Some clients *are* sick, physically or mentally, and they do require specialized, intensive help, such as clients who are seriously chemically dependent. However, many other clients do not need such care.

EAP caseloads include a high proportion of people who are experiencing marginal adjustment problems and incipient conditions that can be helped through preventative, short-term intervention. This is equally true of most forms of psychotherapy. The contemporary EAP practitioner needs the skills and techniques required to assist both the less seriously disturbed client as well as the crisis-ridden and clearly dysfunctional employee. In addition, he or she needs to feel a conviction that it is important to the general welfare of the organization to treat this diversity of problems without making their degree of severity a type of means test to determine whether the client is worth the EAP counselor's time. A special benefit of workplace practice is the extent to which it allows clinicians the opportunity to intervene in situations early in the process of personal or interpersonal deterioration, before the erosion of resources and relationships and before irreparable damage occurs. Unfortunately, it is difficult to document the value of such help in dollar terms, but practice wisdom suggests its worth can be considerable.

Finally, most of the problem solving, healing, and repair that occur in treatment are accomplished by the client. Clinicians' value lies in their ability to foster and facilitate certain processes within the client's personal, interpersonal, and social reality that can bring about positive change if the client chooses or is capable of taking advantage of them. This perspective counters the notion that counselors must, either directly or through a referral, solve all of the client's presenting difficulties. Rather, the task is to provide an altered perspective on the choices clients have open to them. The counselor as catalyst rather than curer seems a more accurate representation of the reality of most treatment.

GENERAL TREATMENT INTERVENTIONS AND TECHNIQUES

EAP counselors engage in many of the same clinical behaviors as their coprofessionals in other service settings. A premise of this book, however, is that the special nature of the occupational environment and clientele foster certain forms of clinical practice that, if not unique to workplace settings, help to give this form of practice its special character and style. In a survey (Cunningham, 1990) practitioners were asked to describe what types of services they offered, what kinds of interventions or techniques were more or less helpful, and what they thought their clients found most helpful. Their responses provide the general framework for the following discussion.

Problem-Solving Strategies

The overall picture that emerged from the survey reflected a basic problem-solving strategy of clinical practice that is very compatible with the short-term nature of most EAP cases and the expectations of the employee clients. The model, however, is more than a common-sense, facts-oriented approach to problems; it is embedded in a profound understanding of human behavior, conscious and unconscious processes, and the confounding influences of interpersonal and intersystemic interactions. This form of problem solving requires a sensitive awareness on the part of the counselor of the client's capacity to participate in the process and an ability on the part of the counselor to adjust to the client's pace of movement. One counselor stated, "I may see all kinds of problems and issues, but the client may not be ready for them yet." Even more important is the need to facilitate the client's own problem-solving capabilities and not impose solutions generated by the counselor. Several problem-solving techniques are discussed below.

Problem Identification

Key elements in assisting clients are to help them arrive at a clear-cut identification of the nature of the difficulties causing them the most concern and to provide the kind of focused discussion that enables them to explore these issues in some depth.

A young woman manager trainee was referred to the EAP by her supervisor because of her irritability and argumentative interactions with coworkers and subordinates. In the initial interview she acknowledged that her behavior was due in part to loss of sleep, depression, and binge eating because her thirtieth birthday was approaching and her closest friend and roommate for 5 years was getting married. It became apparent that a major issue was her grief over the loss of both her friend and a familiar, comfortable lifestyle. In addition, she was confronting the possibility that she might never marry herself, which she felt was a clear indication that she was not making the grade as a woman. This self-perceived inadequacy was spilling over into her work role. She came to realize that her problem had less to do with uncooperative coworkers than with feelings about herself.

Reframing the Problem

Major services that counselors provide for workplace clients are the opportunities both to air their difficulties and to learn that their own views about these difficulties may be inaccurate and self-limiting. Clinicians offer what seem to clients to be novel or fresh perspectives that open up new avenues for action. In the example cited above, the counselor helped the client to reframe the problem as one of several major and stressful losses and changes in her life that were precipitating classic symptoms of a grief reaction. The counselor challenged the client's perception of herself as inadequate by pointing to her considerable accomplishments in several areas, including her work life. When the client commented that she had reached a major turning point, the counselor suggested this might represent an opportunity to start thinking more concretely about what she hoped this next phase of her life would be like.

Formation of Objectives

People can be very clear about the nature of the problems and still be stymied in their attempts to do anything about them because they are not certain what they would like to accomplish. They may need help in understanding what objectives are possible and realistic and something about the strategies and processes involved in achieving these objectives. It is helpful in any type of treatment to ask the client specifically what he or she would like to be different, and what changes the client would like to see in his or her life that would help resolve the problem. Clients often think that someone else or "the system" needs to change in order for them to feel better, and yet they believe they have little power to accomplish such changes. Part of helping them to formulate treatment objectives requires identifying what they do have the power to accomplish; this often means changes in the ways in which they think, feel, or interact with other people.

Again, in the example discussed above, the client gradually became aware of the fact that she was not all that upset about not being married. She was not sure marriage was something she truly wanted for herself, but she also did not want a life devoid of close relationships. She had become very dependent on her roommate for many of her social and affectional needs, and she resisted the idea of having to take the initiative in developing relationships with other men and women. Doing this, however, became one of her objectives, which was discussed for three interviews spread over a period of 2 months. She also determined that the time was ripe for her to position herself more advantageously for additional career advancement through further training. The need to "clean up her act" in her present position emerged as a primary goal, not just to satisfy her supervisor and subordinates but also because it had important implications for her own life.

Evolving and Evaluating Problem-Solving Options

Many clients are able to generate a series of different options during their interviews that they might not have been able to think of without the guided assessment and analysis of the supportive practitioner. Other clients may be under so much stress that they cannot do even this much problem-solving work on their own, and they must rely, instead, on the suggestions and options presented by the counselor. At times, just knowing there are several different ways to deal with their concerns is extremely therapeutic for those who have been immobilized by rigid or circular thinking. Helping clients to understand, for example, that it is not their responsibility to keep their spouse from drinking is profoundly liberating for any client, especially if the client has been bombarded with family and societal messages that the drinking is his or her fault. Instead, such clients can be helped to give up control of the other's behavior and concentrate on what they need to do to make their own lives more manageable. An employee experiencing marital difficulties might assume divorce is the only solution until he or she has the opportunity to reflect on specific elements of the relationship that are problematic and that can become options for change.

Workplace clients generally are not knowledgeable about social welfare resources, treatment centers, or self-help groups; often they may not even know about potential resources within their own company. At times, the counselor can help them find resources within their personal networks that have gone unrecognized.

> A single mother was referred for excessive absenteeism that seemed related to her need to find a child-care resource for her 9-year-old son, who was chronically ill with asthma. Most of her sitters were either unavailable or incapable of providing sick child care on the days when her son was unable to attend school. During a routine health screening, the client reminisced about the woman who cared for her "like a mother" when she was recuperating from surgery the year before. At the counselor's suggestion, she tracked the woman down and secured her help as a regular and competent caregiver for her child.

Certain clients may be unable to think much beyond their current needs and predicament. Even when problem-solving options are open to them, they cannot assess the longer-term consequences of pursuing such options. Others may be under such acute stress that their ability to judge the relative merits of different courses of action is affected. More typical, however, are those clients who simply need a sensitive and attentive listener who can support their own analysis of relative courses of action and introduce additional insights when appropriate. In contemplating inpatient care, for example, the client usually is better able to weigh the amount of disruption that will occur for other family members during the hospitalization. The counselor, however, usually is better able to talk about the relative advantages of inpatient and outpatient options, and how well different resources attend to the problems of other family members.

Rehearsal for Action

In a seminal article Perlman (1975) urged clinicians to help their clients bring about desired changes in their lives by providing them with opportunities to translate into action what they have learned through counseling through a *rehearsal for action*. It is not always enough to think more clearly or feel better about things; sometimes one must do something about the difficulty, not only to set change into motion but also to comprehend on a deeper level why the changes are important. Clients may recognize that they have to limit the demands others are placing on them, but it is not until they have the experience of putting this insight into action that they learn they can do so without being emotionally destroyed. The rehearsal for such action may occur within the counseling sessions through role playing or modeling by the practitioner. It can be presented in the form of homework or task assignments that clients can try and then process with the counselor. The client is helped to develop basic skills in carrying out the task, to anticipate their own and others' reactions as a way of defusing them, and to identify additional insights about how to proceed.

Validation and Normalization

The norm in most work settings is that the expression of strong emotion, either positive or negative, is somewhat aberrant. Many people grew up in homes in which their honest expression of feelings was repudiated or depreciated. Under these circumstances persons often simply do not know which of their affective responses are normal or abnormal. It is important to provide such individuals with the occasion to identify and express their emotions within the context of a supportive and nonjudgmental relationship where they will not be scolded for doing so and where they can be protected from their own self-punishing reactions.

It often is a novel experience for clients to learn that they do not have to be perfect, and in fact that nobody is. One very busy and accomplished professional woman with a husband and teenage children was absolutely astonished to hear that most women in her situation did not expect to have all the beds made before leaving for work in the morning. Later she credited this insight as one of the most helpful aspects of treatment because it led to an awareness of her own perfectionism and how out of touch she was with what constituted reasonable expectations.

A common theme running through clinical treatment in this field is the need of many clients for assurance that they are not going crazy, and that their intense feelings that have surfaced are consistent with the other aspects of their presenting problem. To hear a responsible professional assure them— of course, only when it is legitimate to do so—that they are not deranged or at risk for psychosis can be profoundly reassuring. Just this intervention alone can significantly reduce the person's stress and help reestablish confidence in his or her ability to manage current problems. Counselors provided the following comments illustrating these points when asked what types of interventions they thought clients found most helpful (Cunningham, 1988).

I see the relief in people's faces when I do some normalizing and they realize they're not crazy.

I do a lot of normalizing. Health-care professionals think they're supposed to have it all together. I let them know they don't have to be perfect [from a hospital-based EAP].

They think they're weird because they're struggling with all these feelings; they are such self-blamers. They respond to hearing that they are not always to blame.

Empowerment and Enhancing Self-Esteem

The EAP counselors in this study (Cunningham, 1990) were acutely aware of the pervasiveness of problems of low self-esteem among their clients and the extent to which so many felt unable to take any action in their own behalf. As a result, many make a special attempt to communicate to clients, when it is realistic to do so, that clients have control over their decisions and have the power to act in their own interests. Clients are encouraged to become self-solvers so they can deal more effectively not only with their presenting problems, but also with problems they may encounter in the future. Too much dependence on the counselor relationship is discouraged. The following comments from the respondents illustrate these concepts (Cunningham, 1988).

I empower clients through knowledge, support, role modeling. . . . I try to facilitate their ability to take care of themselves and reach for their own definition of success and contentment. [I help them] see themselves as human beings with a right to have problems.

I focus on their positives. They do enough self-beating and I tell them that I refuse to participate in that process.

People leave feeling more powerful and more in control with a broader perspective on what's bothering them.

Most are holding it together in spite of problems so I let them know they have more strength than they realize. They come in expecting me to solve their problems for them and they're surprised when I make them hear what they are already doing for themselves.

As these comments suggest, empowerment involves a variety of strategies directed at correcting client misperceptions or undervaluing of their own strengths, teaching them the skills necessary to become more self-actualizing, and identifying for them those occasions when they demonstrate their abilities to deal effectively with other systems or individuals.

Education

Counselors are for many clients the major source of learning about their predicaments and how to address them. Counselors educate clients about themselves; common human needs; problematic behaviors; the impact of other systems, especially work and family systems; and the resource network that they can access to improve their lives. Clients often lack the opportunity to engage in reality testing with others about their perceptions and experiences, and the counselor becomes a major source for doing so. In dealing with the death of someone close, for example, it becomes important for a client to hear that his or her depression, disorientation, and inability to remember the appearance of the deceased are fairly common responses to loss. Often during the assessment process a few sessions directed toward universalizing a client's feelings of confusion may be enough to stabilize him or her to the extent that the client's more characteristic coping strategies can be revitalized.

A middle-aged clerk/typist was referred to the EAP by her supervisor because of her bouts of crying at her desk. She confided to the counselor that she was growing more depressed over her daughter's "rejection" of her since her daughter's marriage a year ago. Exploration indicated that she saw her daughter and son-in-law regularly, but she was disappointed that they no longer returned "home" for Sunday dinner even though she extended an open invitation to them to do so. She interpreted their lack of interest in her as a critique of her mothering and disappointment with her as a person. In a short period of time she was able to acknowledge that none of her friends' adult children returned home so frequently and that perhaps her expectations were unrealistic. She accepted with relative ease the need for young couples to concentrate their efforts on establishing their own family. Her legitimate sense of loss was supported, and she was helped to find ways of dealing with it. This was easier for her when she became convinced that the separation was "normal" and not an indication that she had lost her child's love or respect.

Education also may take the form of informing clients about the corporate system, both how it functions and how it impacts on its employees. Understanding something about unarticulated norms of behavior can ease on-the-job interactions. Currently clients are reacting to the socioeconomic pressures businesses are experiencing and the tendency of many organizations to increase not only the actual work responsibilities of employees, but also the responsibility for failures to perform up to higher standards. Employees may need to understand what is realistic and unrealistic about such messages in order to function more responsibly in ways that enhance not only their lives but the well-being of the organization as well.

The Clinical Relationship

In the debate about the relative effectiveness of different models of psychotherapy, certain core features have emerged that cut across models. Chief among these is the nature of the helping relationship itself (Lambert et al., 1986).[1]

When respondents in my survey were asked what aspects of assistance the counselors thought were most helpful to clients in addition to those already mentioned, counselors described their efforts to create a positive treatment relationship by "being a good listener," offering support, allowing venting of emotions, empathy, individualizing their clients, and serving as a source of reality testing for clients (Cunningham, 1990). Both counselors and clients, but especially clients, saw the clinical relationship itself as a major source of help. The ten clients interviewed as a part of this study were a small and self-selected group, and their responses cannot be generalized. Their comments are interesting, however, because they communicated so much about the flavor of the relationship they experienced. All found the experience helpful, using phrases such as, "terrific,"

"They should give her the Counselor of the Year Award," or, "You have to ask if I thought she was good?" One recovering alcoholic said, "She saved my life; I was walking around dead, and now I'm part of the living again" (Cunningham, 1990, p. 42). In spite of their strongly positive comments they could discriminate between things they liked and did not like. For example, one client complained that her warm and caring counselor always finished her sentences for her, "as if she knew better than I did what I was thinking!" (p. 42). All found the clinical relationship with the counselor unique and overwhelming because of its difference from any other type of relationship they had experienced and *because of its reliability.* It was not simply that this was a nice person to whom they could talk, but that no matter how often they came they could count on the same level of concern, privacy, and professionalism. All but one experienced apprehension prior to their EAP interviews. They worried about being able to put their concerns into words, what they would find out about themselves, how it might affect their jobs, or whether the encounter would help. All commented on the skill of the counselor in dealing with these concerns in the first session.

Clients were better able to talk about the overall climate of the interaction rather than specific interventions they found helpful.

> She really cared. She let me know it was okay to be feeling like I did. When I was at my lowest she made me feel stronger than I knew I was.

> It was clear that she felt responsible for me as a whole person, not just my work performance. She wanted this to be a healing experience.

> I could talk to her like a priest; anonymity was sacred to her. She said she would try and [sic] help my wife and kids but that I was her main focus.

> She was very honest; everything was up front. She said, "You don't have to be lied to!" (Cunningham, 1992, p. 43)

In addition to commenting on the general warmth and acceptance provided by the counselors, clients talked about the helpfulness of the information they received, feeling that they had an ally in dealing with their problems, and not being pressured to follow any single course of action. An exception is the client who said that everyone else but the EAP counselor had failed to get him into a drug treatment program because, "She wouldn't accept my B.S.! Each time I came up with an excuse not to go, she just said 'Yes, yes, I know, *but. . .*' " (Cunningham, p. 43).

Generally clients left the first session feeling better about themselves and more hopeful about their presenting problems; some viewed the problem differently. Those who thought it was someone else's problem came to recognize that they were the ones who had to make changes: "I saw that the situation was not all my supervisor's fault; that I would have to work on myself if I wanted things to get better." New problems also emerged: "At first it was just about my drinking, but then I got cancer and she got me through that"; "After my husband died it was more about the grieving and how to get over it" (Cunningham, 1990, p. 44).

Other interventions the clients found helpful included the feedback counselors provided about why things were happening, how client behaviors impacted on others, and their own improvement. Also mentioned was the fact that counselors seemed to know the reasons for things and were able to anticipate events in the clients' lives. "She knows what she's talking about and can warn me about pitfalls as though she's been through it." "No one else seemed to know what I was going through the way she did." Although clients assumed their counselors had been through the same experiences, in fact, the counselors were operating from a theory base of knowledge and experience that allowed them to both understand their clients' problems and anticipate further events. A common thread running through all the clients' responses was an increase in self-understanding. "I was afraid if I really looked at myself I'd find no one at home; or if there was, it was demonic! Now, the more I find out, the more I like myself and the more open I become to other people." Even when their personal situations did not change dramatically, the encounter of these clients with their EAP counselors clearly was profound and beneficial.

An aspect of relationship building that may set EAP counselors apart from other clinicians is a seemingly more positive, optimistic view of client coping. In contrast, Beck and Jones (1973) and Maluccio (1979) note in their studies the practitioners' tendency to view clients as weaker, more pathological, and having more negative qualities and experiences than the clients' view of themselves. Maluccio notes, for example, that as clients continue in therapy they begin to make better use of their social networks and life experiences and see them in positive terms, whereas the social workers see the same networks and experiences as negative influences on their clients' lives. Few of the EAP counselors in our study expressed any pessimism about clients' abilities. This may be because the EAP client actually is higher functioning than agency clients—an opinion expressed by many respondents—or because the EAP counselors have fewer long-term clients and therefore do not experience the reverses and setbacks in treatment more observable in traditional settings. Maluccio suggests another reason. He comments that his sample of social workers did not have access to the life space of their clients and tended to place exaggerated importance on the worker/client relationship, unlike clients, who view the clinical relationship as just one of many systems with which they are involved. However, EAP counselors have a heightened sensitivity to the multiple life systems their clients inhabit; they are able to witness client progress in a major life role—their work—rather than in a treatment relationship alone, which by its very definition focuses on failures, deficits, and inadequacies. Whatever the reason, the extent to which EAP counselors communicate positive expectations about the outcome of assistance exerts a significant impact on the relationship itself and can be instrumental in helping more clients achieve positive outcomes (Beutler, Crago, & Arizmendi, 1986).

PLANNED SHORT-TERM TREATMENT

This term is used here to describe the conscious decision on the part of the client and the counselor to continue for several sessions beyond those needed for initial assessment of the presenting problems. At times such short-term help actually may be offered within the allotted quota for assessment interviews, but the focus has shifted toward problem resolution rather than problem identification. The exact nature of the presenting problems determines how the short-term treatment course is handled. Generally, however, it is important to be clear at the outset about the probable length of contact, to limit the focus to one or two clearly defined areas, and to identify with the client expected outcomes. Situations that might be addressed more effectively on a short-term, in-house basis generally are of two types: (a) when a clear-cut clinical decision has been made that the nature of the person/problem/situation is such that better help can be offered internally than through a referral and (b) when an appropriate referral cannot be made because of the unavailability of a resource, pressing client needs, or questionable client motivation.

The first category includes the use of short-term help for support or guidance when the client's problems are transitional in nature or do not represent severe pathology but there still is a need for limited direction to promote the employee's own problem-solving capabilities. For example, a municipal employee experiencing severe stress at home because of his wife's hospitalization was managing his family and work responsibilities adequately, but he could not handle the expectations of his coworkers that he continue to socialize with them after work. His anger at their good-natured teasing and lack of understanding resulted in uncharacteristic verbal battles between them over minor issues. In a few sessions, he was helped to understand the pervasive nature of the family stress, his guilt over not being always available to his wife and daughter, some displacement of anger onto his colleagues, and the transitory nature of the problem. By reframing the problem for him, the counselor reversed the employee's sense of losing control, validated his feelings, and restored a sense of competency along with the recognition that he was doing a very good job of managing things under difficult circumstances.

Some presenting problems involve work-related difficulties requiring interventions with managers or coworkers. EAP counselors usually are better informed about the personalities, the organizational culture, shifting political realities, and those aspects of the system most amenable to intervention than an external provider, and they can access them more readily within the context of in-house short-term treatment.

A woman in a clerical position petitioned for help from the EAP counselor because of serious conflict between her and her supervisor. In the initial interview it became clear that although there were a number of obvious communication problems between them, the client also was reacting to her supervisor in the same conflictual manner that characterized her relationship with her stepmother. In a few sessions the client learned to recognize the source of her reactions to both women, a process that was facilitated by the counselor's separate discussion with the supervisor conducted with the client's consent. The supervisor agreed to communicate her expectations of the client in writing so there would be no opportunity for confusion. The client agreed to moderate her aggressive style of raising questions about these expectations. Their relationship did not become harmonious, but the arguments stopped and the work flow improved.

There often are politically sensitive circumstances surrounding a referral in which the need for guaranteed confidentiality is so great that, it simply is not expedient to refer the client to an outside resource. A major executive experiencing an acute depression, an executive secretary confused about a deadend love affair with a coworker, or a key decision maker discovering he is HIV positive may be seen by the in-house EAP person as a means of offering greater protection to the client and the company.

At times the nature of the problem is so pressing or so severe that it would be professionally irresponsible not to engage the client in immediate, direct treatment.

> An elderly member of the union retiree program was found crying and disoriented in the parking lot by a union employee. She obviously had been assaulted and an immediate examination by the union's medical staff confirmed that she had been raped. A social worker from the membership assistance program (MAP) was called in immediately and stayed with her through-out the difficult process of reporting the event to the police. Mrs. A. absolutely refused to consider any type of referral for counseling. Her age and cultural background were such that the idea of discussing the event with strangers was almost as traumatic as the rape itself. The social worker made a series of follow-up home visits to monitor Mrs. A.'s physical and emotional health and to interpret the nature of the experience to family members. She also provided help in discussing Mrs. A.'s delayed reactions to trauma in at least a minimal way, because the social worker had become "like family." Later, Mrs. A. was given moral support to return to the activities of the retiree center. Eventually Mrs. A. assisted the MAP staff in developing an educational program for center members on issues of personal safety.

Even when referral options are available to clients, they are not always willing or able to take advantage of such options. Under such circumstances the counselor may choose either to extend the process of assessment in order to obtain a clearer picture of the issues or to engage the client in a period of short-term treatment, either as a test of motivation or to model what a period of externally provided treatment might be like. Sometimes clients may have to wait weeks or months before a community-based resource can begin treatment, especially in programs serving employees with limited benefit coverage. A short period of in-house counseling can resolve some immediate issues.

> A woman was referred to the EAP because of repeated wage assignments, and the counselor referred her, in turn, to a community debt counseling service with a long waiting list. In the interim the counselor helped free up the woman's salary, got her electricity turned on, and staved off a few of her creditors. In the process he noted that she had not claimed all the dependents to which she was entitled under IRS provisions. He helped her submit a revised IRS form and as a result she had more take-home pay to apply to her debts.

Grief Reactions

A typical use of short-term counseling involves nonpathological grief reactions in response to a loss. The loss can be real or symbolic: either an actual loss of someone or something through death, separation, or destruction or a less tangible injury such as a transition from one life stage to another. A fairly common grief reaction encountered by EAP staff is that associated with the chronic or terminal illness of clients themselves or of family members. The emotional and physiological pains of grief can feel like psychic decompensation and may even look like psychosis, when, in fact, they are a more or less normal response to an atypical event in a person's life. Physical illness, depression, and increased use of alcohol or tranquilizing drugs are associated with bereavement (Klerman & Clayton, 1984).

Most grief is time limited and does not require intense or long-term treatment, which might even do more harm than good if clients come to believe that their reactions were pathological. An employee in need of grief counseling often derives greater benefit from an immediate intervention by an EAP counselor, who can provide a consistent, reassuring relationship for a short period of time, interpretation of the universality of grief reactions, and assurance that the devastating effects the client is experiencing will pass. As is true of any form of timely and appropriate intervention, not only can it help an employee negotiate the difficult period of acute grief, but it has, in addition, the potential of preventing or defusing future difficulties associated with the loss.

Some grief experiences can precipitate more profound disturbances. They also may reflect past grieving situations to the extent that a client's physical and emotional distress in response to a current loss may trigger a whole series of past losses that still need to be processed in some way. Even normal reactions can create distressing situations at the workplace if clients cry, exhibit changes in behavior or dress, cannot maintain their work performance, or vacillate from one mood to another. A key diagnostic task for the counselor is to determine what type of grief the client is experiencing and whether it appears to be within the bounds of characteristic human reactions, or whether it suggests more severe pathology and the need for an external referral for more extended treatment. Assistance also may include helping clients reestablish usual patterns of relationships with coworkers as the grief work continues.

Loss and grief can precipitate or exacerbate addictive behavior (Greene & DiCuio, 1991). Persons in recovery typically deal with a range of losses while trying to restructure their lives, losses that they might be helped to cope with more effectively through anticipatory discussions about the dynamics of grieving. When unexpected losses develop for these clients, prompt intervention by an accessible EAP person can be instrumental in preventing relapse.

Budman and Gurman (1988) suggest that the therapeutic tasks involved in helping clients suffering from a major loss include helping clients specify and name the loss, universalizing the experience, educating them about the course of grief reactions, facilitating the grieving for the clients and others in their social systems who are affected by the loss, and bringing some closure to the experience. Sensitive EAP counselors have evolved varying models addressing these tasks by combining sequences of short-term supportive help with periodic "touching-base" interviews to help relieve some of the stresses such clients experience on the job. Sometimes an employee's need may be as simple as having a safe place to cry or to talk openly about a reality that cannot be shared with anyone else at the workplace.

Normal grief usually is time limited, but it is not possible to put an exact date on how long it will take a given client to work through his or her grief. Usually, the periods of deep mourning happen less frequently over time, with recurrences in relation to meaningful events in the person's life that are experienced differently because of the loss. Anniversary dates can precipitate new bouts of grieving almost as severe as the original distress. Some additional insights concerning grief are included in the following discussion of crisis intervention.

CRISIS INTERVENTION

Crisis intervention usually is short term in nature but it involves other therapeutic considerations not true of all short-term case situations. Many of the crises people experience are work related. In their list of life events that contribute to stress reactions, Holmes and Rahe (1967) identified job loss, retirement, changes in work tasks or responsibilities, spousal employment, and disagreement with superiors as contributing to life-stress reactions. Crises not directly related to employment nevertheless can result in symptomatic behavior that is played out on the job or in interaction with fellow employees (Parad, 1984). In addition, the workplace is at times the arena in which other unique crises occur, affecting everyone in the workplace: the accidental death of a coworker, plant closings, or armed robberies.

The special interventive techniques associated with critical incident debriefings are discussed in more detail in Chapter 9. Here I address the private crises that clients bring to the EAP counselor and the psychological changes most people experience when in a crisis state.

A major intervention in reducing the harmful effects of a crisis event is to reach the victim as soon as possible after the stressful incident has occurred. Otherwise the person may resort to more dysfunctional ways of coping with the trauma that reduce his or her ability to respond to any intervention later on. Because of the accessibility of the EAP and the work-related nature of many crises, the EAP counselor often is the first human service professional the client encounters to help deal with the overwhelming anxiety and sense of personal disequilibrium associated with private crises: the point, both temporally and emotionally, when clients are most vulnerable and most in need of immediate assistance. Even in those situations when a referral to an external provider is made, there are a number of significant interventions that the EAP counselor must consider at the point of the first contact with the client that may not be able to wait for a referral.

The counselor needs to determine whether a client is in a state of active crisis at the point of the initial interview. Not everyone exposed to a stressful event experiences crisis. It is the subjective psychological state of being in crisis that is of clinical concern to the counselor, not the event itself. A crisis state exists when clients feel that their usually reliable strategies for maintaining psychological equilibrium are, for the moment, inadequate to deal with the threat, loss, or challenge represented by the crisis event (Rapaport, 1970). When nothing seems to work, and when the problem cannot be resolved, postponed, or ignored in some way, people experience escalating tension and psychological disorganization. They will have feelings of inadequacy, high anxiety, and helplessness. They may regress to more primitive, childlike behaviors such as flight or rage. They may experience mild to gross distortions in bodily function, perception, and cognition (Parad & Parad, 1990). Characteristically a person in this state is extremely responsive to any promise of relief from such tension. It is this vulnerability to influence that gives crisis intervention its power to bring about change in a very short time.

The counselor needs to determine the severity of such clients' disequilibrium and their capacity to function, the unique meaning the crisis event may have for them, and how the current crisis relates to past patterns and personal themes of trauma, loss, mastery, and coping. All crises occur in a social context and it is important to understand how other people and circumstances in the clients' systems are affecting or affected by the clients' crisis state, in addition to how these people and circumstances may be exacerbating the crisis or how they can be mobilized as a source of support. Crisis intervention typically involves three different treatment objectives: relief of symptoms, prevention of further psychological regression and internal disorganization, and restoration of the person's precrisis level of adjustment (Golan, 1978). These objectives can be accomplished in several ways.

Reduction of Anxiety

Often it is enough to say "I'm here to help. Let's work together to see what needs to be done." Clients need reassurance that they are not losing their minds, that they were not responsible for the crisis (if this is true), that they could not have prevented it, or that it is not an indication of God's displeasure. In contrast to many other clinical situations, this may be a time when it is necessary to offer very direct advice to clients about what needs to be done, because disorganized and emotionally spent clients may not be able to do this for themselves. It may be necessary, too, to make arrangements for the mobilization of concrete resources: money, physical examination, anti-anxiety medication, housing. Any deficit that can be addressed immediately removes some of the pressure from clients and allows them the opportunity to reorganize and redirect their energies toward other aspects of their situation. Help in mobilizing a support system for the client, preferably from his or her own environment, enhances a client's sense of safety. If clients can do some of this work for themselves they should be supported in doing so as a means of restoring their sense of self-mastery. Simply providing factual information is a potent factor in reducing anxiety as the person is helped to attain a more realistic picture of what occurred and why.

Client Verbalization

Encouraging the client to talk about the crisis is not always possible, and sometimes the verbalization itself can be premature or increase anxiety if it requires reliving an event that the client is working hard to suppress. Budman and Gurman (1988), for example, suggest that in instances of bereavement, eliciting discussions too soon actually may interfere with the normal grief process. Generally, however, helping clients to talk about what happened soon after the trauma aids in the process of restoring equilibrium. It engages the cognitive functions of the personality and allows the person to put names to things that have been experienced only emotionally. This process makes the feelings more manageable, which in turn helps the client to feel more in control. It also allows clients to begin to achieve a temporal distancing from the crisis event. As they talk about it they can begin to discuss the crisis event in the past tense, which helps them to comprehend that it is over and they are not *in it* any longer.

Ventilation

This refers to the expression of the feelings associated with the crisis: anger, terror, anxiety, loss of control, panic, or pain and to the surrendering, neutralizing, and integration of these feelings emotionally. Under severe stress such feelings can be cemented off as a way of defending against the immobilizing anxiety they generate. The clinical effects of ventilation are similar to those of verbalization, and often the two processes occur simultaneously as crisis victims are supported in their attempts to encounter and conquer the threatening reality of the crisis event and the thoughts and feelings it stirs up.

Golan (1978) suggests that early in the initial encounter in crisis it is important for clinicians to make a *decision statement,* a clear-cut communication as to what the counselor thinks is occurring and what needs to be done about it:

> From everything you told me it doesn't sound like your job is in any jeopardy. It's probably most important for us to try to understand why your encounter with this customer provoked such an angry response on your part. It probably has a lot to do with all these other stresses in your life. We need to talk later on about what steps we may need to take with your supervisor and the other sales staff so you can get back to work.

Such communication provides a kind of anchoring thought or psychic "life preserver" for the client and assurance that he or she is being heard and understood. It helps a person in crisis understand that no matter how lost and ineffectual he or she may feel at that moment, the counselor can see above the crisis and can help the client make some choices and decisions that will get him or her through this difficult period.

Restoring Mastery

As soon as is reasonably possible, clients need to understand that the loss of their ability to control their reactions and the events in their lives is temporary. The clinician facilitates the process of psychological reorganization by identifying experiences in which the client is demonstrating greater ability to cope even in very small ways. The counselor also can generate tasks for clients to provide opportunities for demonstrating their increasing capacity for mastery, which in turn lessens the panic and frees up the psychic energy that had been directed toward simply holding themselves together. When the immediate effects of a crisis are identified and preliminary interventions have been made, it may be advisable to think in terms of the necessity for a referral, how best to time it, and what other interventions the EAP counselor may have to make to bring about the referral. Like all clinical decisions, this one should take into consideration the individual person-situation factors. What internal and external supports does the client have in dealing with crisis and any associated problems? How ready is he or she to make the transition? Current crises often stir up past, unresolved trauma that can complicate a simple resolution through crisis intervention, and clients may require a more intense period of therapy to help integrate such past traumas more successfully. Whether or not they are referred, clients may need to be prepared for the delayed effects of crisis, anniversary dates, and the availability of the counselor to help with such experiences if they occur. The crisis literature once was fairly universal in declaring that crisis states lasted 4 to 6 weeks; however, the reality is more complex and diverse, and if the counselor is operating under such assumptions, it can undermine the therapeutic efforts of those clients who need more time.

THE USE OF GROUPS IN EAPs

EAP counselors are involved in a range of activities that require a basic knowledge of group process and the skills needed to facilitate that process. Virtually all EAPs are responsible for in-house marketing of the EAP as discussed in Chapter 2, which requires group presentations with managers, line staff, and newly hired employees to keep them informed about the availability of the EAP, how supervisors and employees can make use of it, and any changes in policies, procedures, or the types of services being offered. However, the focus of this discussion is the group services geared specifically toward helping employees deal with problems in functioning encountered on the job or in their personal lives. The extent to which EAP staff engage in group work of one kind or another is determined partly by the extent to which they are professionally prepared to do so, the size and culture of the employing organization, and the degree of specialized task assignments that exist within their human resource departments. For example, in larger organizations some of the activities described below might be the responsibility of management development or training departments. In smaller companies or in those with less clearly defined areas of specialty, the EAP may be given primary or collaborative responsibility to perform these functions.

The subculture of the organization sometimes has its own ideas about what is or is not acceptable in group presentations, and these need to be understood. In certain settings any assembly of more than a handful of workers makes managers nervous if it looks too much like union organizing or a threat to hierarchical power structures. Interpretation to management about the nature of planned group meetings needs to be handled sensitively and with an awareness of the meanings people attach to such meetings. Certain topics may be more or less acceptable. For example, in some religious organizations, content concerning HIV infection, safe sex, and the use of condoms can be highly charged and controversial. At one time even discussions about alcoholism were extremely threatening in companies that had been denying the existence of the problem. These cautionary comments are not intended to discourage counselors from dealing with any subject that might make people feel uncomfortable. However, counselors must use their professional skills to evaluate the types of group offerings that are needed and possible, given a particular work group, and how the institutional climate might be influenced to become more accepting of the content. In addition, proposals to management about planned presentations need to be carefully prepared, and they should include consultation with key personnel about the implementation of the groups as well as professional documentation and support for the accuracy of the message.

Understanding Group Process

Although many practitioners have formal training in group process as part of their professional education or work experience, probably a greater number do not. Some facility in managing group process is a basic requirement for most EAP positions even if some of the specialized group functions are contracted out to those with the required training. EAP counselors often develop their own knowledge and experience by co-leading groups with skilled professionals, through consultation, and through other forms of self-instruction. For those who are new to this methodology, it can be very helpful to keep regular and detailed notes of group process over a period of time to develop sensitivity to the multiple facets of group inter-action. Such notes should include a statement as to the general goals of the group, the specific objectives for each meeting, a description of process and interaction, and an analysis of what occurred. It is important to complete these records as soon as possible after a meeting, as the memory of details can decay rapidly. An even better means of self-instruction is to arrange for videotaping of your own and other group meetings if this can be done in a way that does not constitute a threat to confidentiality or effective group process.

Each type of group requires a different assortment of skills; however, several basic considerations are necessary in all forms of group presentations. At the very least practitioners need to know what they are talking about, and they need to be skilled and attentive listeners. To perform as a change agent in any size of group means counselors must have knowledge and information about the central issues under consideration that are relevant and accurate and not a mere repetition of what already is known by the group members. It can be extremely costly for a company to send employees to such sessions during regular working hours. If the informal feedback about the content is that it was a waste of time, then it also was a waste of company funds. When there is a demonstrated need for certain areas of content to be covered and the EAP staff members are not experts in the field, arrangements need to be made either to contract for someone better informed to conduct the sessions or to allocate the time to educate EAP staff about the issue. Expertise in any field often is born out of a need to know or a need to inform others.

Whatever the size of the meeting, focused and sensitive listening is important to fully understand what the group members are communicating, what their overt and latent questions might be, and what specific ideas and points have to be made to accomplish group goals. This is especially difficult for practitioners trained in individual counseling, who are unaccustomed to the multiple levels of verbal and nonverbal interaction that are a part of group process. Cultural and gender factors also influence what happens in a group context, determining what gets discussed, who does the talking, and whether or not objectives will be achieved. Group presenters must have the essential skills for communicating the desired message, fielding questions, facilitating discussions, and analyzing group process to determine whether modifications in the pace, focus, or direction are indicated. Preparation for such meetings also requires a realistic and up-to-date understanding of the employing organization in general and the group being addressed in particular.

In addition to these skills, it is important for practitioners to cultivate a philosophy about group process that may be difficult initially. Although there are many different explanatory and practice theories concerning groups, a common theme for most is the importance of respecting the group's ability to produce its own answers and to facilitate the growth and healing of its members. This is true of all kinds of groups. The group leader may be more or less active in directing process, making interpretations, setting limits, or expanding the group's knowledge and understanding of certain issues, but part of the skill of leading groups is to know when to sit back and allow the process to move everyone forward. However, groups also can be powerful destructive forces because of inept leaders or dysfunctional members, who can negatively influence group communication and interaction in much the same way they do in their own families. I once witnessed a group presentation in which the total staff of several hundred workers was assembled ostensibly to discuss new Civil Service regulations. During the discussion a racial argument erupted between the presenter and an employee, which only the group planners knew was a role play. Their hidden agenda was to uncover some of the racial problems that existed in the workplace. The pandemonium that ensued almost resulted in physical violence among those attending and the inexperienced leaders were totally unprepared to deal with the consequences. Employees were deeply traumatized and any movement toward dealing with the racial problems was derailed.

Information/Education Groups

This type of group activity is very common in EAPs, and it is a model that can be especially effective in those settings that do not have abundant benefits to be used for external referrals or that lack adequate EAP staff to deal individually with all the employees who could benefit by the service. These groups typically take the form of workshops or seminars for 25 or more employees. The format is didactic and relatively little planned interaction occurs among group members. The attendees meet for about one to three sessions. Topics can include information on chemical dependency, work stress, holiday blues, single parenting, parent/child relationships, AIDS awareness, or any issue of personal, emotional, or family functioning deemed appropriate. In conducting these meetings counselors draw on their professional knowledge and experience as a basis for educating employees about these problems, their prevalence, key symptoms, and a person's options for obtaining help.

It is difficult to assess the impact of such meetings. Both formal evaluations and anecdotal information suggest that they can help employees in various ways. They can normalize certain types of experiences and their associated feeling states, potentially alleviating the concerns of some group participants that their feelings are somehow abnormal or pathological. Often the discussion may have been the employees' first exposure to information about such problems or the emotional reactions to them. For example, in a group presentation about the concerns and legal rights of divorced fathers, several of the men in attendance indicated that they had not realized that their profound grief and sense of total life dislocation were common. Our cultural inhibition against allowing men, especially men in authority positions, to talk about their feelings had kept each of them in emotional isolation both on and off the job.

Such groups also can be helpful in providing encouragement for some employees to contact the EAP for individual help or to seek help from other sources. Working people rarely are well informed about existing resources either within the company or in their communities. The opportunity to hear about alternative options without the often frustrating trial and error involved in obtaining such information on their own can reduce barriers to getting the help they need. It also is possible that some attendees can make use of the information covered in large group meetings to make important changes in their lives: to alter their perceptions about their personal problems, to make more informed choices about their behavior, or to contribute to a healthier work culture. In some settings, large group meetings provide a basis for the formation of continuing small treatment groups, self-help meetings, or brown-bag lunch groups in relation to specific problems.

As in other aspects of EAP practice, the success of such meetings or workshops is related to the degree to which they accurately address the concerns of a particular organization. A discussion of the psychological stresses of retirement is unlikely to capture the imaginations of the employees of fast-food chains, whose average age is 19. Relevant topics can be identified through a sensitive listening to individual clients and the patterns of concerns that emerge. A more direct approach is to conduct periodic employee surveys soliciting input about the types of discussions they would find useful. A similar survey that I conducted several years ago produced a large number of unanticipated requests for information on how to deal with sexual harassment. The company chose not to deal with the topic in group sessions, but the data provided the basis for upgrading the organization's policy statement and procedures for supporting individuals who needed help with this problem. In another EAP, survey results uncovered a strong interest in programming for single fathers, and the series of meetings that evolved were among the best attended of any that were scheduled. The EAP advisory council may be a source of information about other content areas of special interest to employees.

The logistics of how to advertise and when to schedule meetings are important to ensure that any given target group knows about meetings and is able to participate. This may mean scheduling such meetings several times so employees from all shifts can participate or making sure meetings take place in locations that are most accessible for the target group, such as at outlying plant sites rather than at central corporate office buildings.

Even when sessions are led by externally contracted professionals, it is important for EAP staff to be present at least for part of the time, particularly when initiating a program of group workshops. An exception would be when the nature of the topic or the circumstances are such that employee anonymity is important. Group meetings are opportunities for shared information among employees and EAP staff about these concerns and what the organization may be able to do about them. The types of questions asked by participants and the nature of shared discussion provide insight for EAP personnel about workers' response to the training sessions, how content may need to be modified, and topics of interest for future programming. It may be an employee's first opportunity to see EAP staff "up close" and to realize that a voluntary request for help from the EAP is not going to be impersonal or intimidating. Evaluations of the workshop discussions are an important part of the ongoing group program. They can be both oral and written, but they should be done as soon as possible after the session to ensure that there will be some feedback, as people are less likely to complete an evaluation once they leave the session. If time and budget permit, it may be helpful to do a follow-up evaluation of attendees to determine whether the information communicated in the sessions resulted in any alteration in their own situations. For example, did their attitudes or behavior change as a result, or did they seek help for problems they might be having in the area? Such information can be useful in assessing the impact of the EAP in areas other than individual counseling, and it provides a basis for further decision making about programming.

Problem-Solving Groups

Counselors may themselves identify work-related problems that need to be addressed or they may be invited to help a work unit or group of employees deal with specific problems related to their work. In a hospital setting, the patient care staff on an oncology unit started to encounter problems that seemed related to the unusually large number of young people being admitted to the unit who were terminal. In spite of all their professional preparation for dealing with terminal illness, staff members were caught off guard emotionally to see so many of their own age group succumbing to cancer. The EAP director was able to clarify the source of their collective depression and to offer immediate support and validation of their feelings. The group continued for several sessions and members were presented with options within and outside the hospital for continuing help as needed.

At times problem-solving groups can take the form of special-interest brown-bag meetings over lunch. The content can be similar to that offered in the large seminars discussed earlier, such as problems of single parenting, but brown-bag discussion groups are not just didactic presentations on a topic of common concern. Because of their smaller size, brown-bag meetings typically offer more opportunity for sharing reactions and personal experiences. Some of these groups have no formal leadership, whereas others may include professionals either as leaders or consultants who can provide insight and information about the shared concern. The focus of problem-solving discussion typically is directed toward developing realistic options for handling identified problems more effectively.

Small Treatment Groups

In contrast to the groups discussed above, treatment groups are established with the intent of using therapeutic group interaction to help troubled employees deal with common issues of personal functioning. Such groups can be as varied as those existing in any community treatment center and often cover the same topic areas as larger group meetings. Treatment groups, however, are professionally led; are of longer duration, even open ended; and deal with more personal problems in functioning. They allow for more group interaction among clients and the processing of the informational content in terms of their own lives. In addition, the professional group leader makes direct interpretations of and interventions into group interaction as a basis for facilitating changes in the attitudes, feelings, beliefs, and behavior of the participants. For example, in a group of managerial women the nonassertive behavior that characterized several of the participants was identified through their interaction within the group and became a basis for analyzing the extent to which such behavior interfered with their success on the job.

One counselor uses the large educational/informational meetings discussed earlier as the basis for spinning off a series of small treatment groups. She makes a point of scheduling several follow-up sessions after every large meeting for anyone interested in more information about the topic area. These usually produce a core of employees interested in an ongoing group experience. In another setting, a chemical dependency recovery group has been in operation for several years with gradual changes in membership over time. Members use this work-based group as part of their mix of individual counseling and 12-Step group participation without any apparent sense of conflict or confusion of roles.

This last example is somewhat atypical because of the long-term duration of the group. This EAP seems to have overcome a common barrier to establishing work-based groups that deal with highly personal problems: the perception by employees that confidentiality will not be maintained. Such concerns are realistic. As one counselor phrased it, "I'm trained to keep confidentiality; my clients aren't!" Although professional staff are very much aware of the damage that can occur when a client's confidentiality has been breached, this is a more difficult concept to communicate to group members, who can inadvertently or deliberately pass on information about membership in the groups and what was said. Discussion about these concerns and strategies to help group members protect one another's anonymity need to be aired fully at the outset of any group of this type and need to be repeated regularly.

Leading this type of group requires professional training, experience, or expert assistance about treatment groups in the form of consultation or the use of a co-leader who is prepared to teach group skills through demonstration and discussion. Not only must the leader understand the characteristics of group systems as discussed earlier; she or he also must be knowledgeable about internal psychological states, interactive processes, and how they manifest in group interaction, a process that is very different from their emergence in individual counseling. Leaders must be capable of remaining tuned in to both the content under discussion as well as the multiple levels of interaction among group members. Not only does the interaction provide important diagnostic information about the group as a whole and individual members, but it also provides important opportunities for the leaders to intervene in the process in ways that facilitate understanding of key behavioral issues for the members themselves. It is one type of experience to counsel employees in individual interviews about their tendencies to invite depreciating evaluations from others; it is quite another experience for such employees to hear themselves doing so in "here-and-now" group interaction.

Self-Help and Support Groups

In addition to professionally led groups, EAP staff often are instrumental in setting up the organizational conditions that make it possible for various self-help or support groups to operate within a system. Counselors may determine that there is a need for 12-Step, recovery, or other types of support or self-help groups to be held onsite, possibly because the nature of the work makes it difficult for employees to find such groups elsewhere, for example, on certain construction jobs or for shift workers. Preparing for such groups means a careful assessment of the organizational readiness to support this type of assistance on a continuing basis. Preparation involves not just the pragmatics of locating appropriate accommodations, but also dealing with the firm's attitudes about the issues the groups will be discussing, and their understanding about the confidential nature of the content even if EAP staff are not directly involved in the ongoing process. The nature of these groups is such that the counselor is not present during meetings except perhaps as a consultant from time to time or as an organizational facilitator. Similar problems exist, as with other types of groups, about possible violations of confidentiality and anonymity, and members need to be apprised of the importance of these issues when the groups are being formed if they do not identify the issues themselves.

FOLLOW-UP, AFTERCARE, AND CASE MONITORING

Most EAPs offer some type of follow-up or aftercare services to selected clients. A few programs may include all referred clients in aftercare; most reserve this for chemically dependent clients, the more severe psychiatric problems, or clients who are management referred. For the most part there is no clear consensus in the field as to the content of follow-up or aftercare services. At times it even is difficult to distinguish clearly between them, as there is a tendency to use the terms interchangeably. Typically these arrangements involve required reporting by the client to the counselor for a stipulated period of time, usually a year. Reporting may mean brief telephone contacts, but most programs ask that these clients come for in-person interviews on a weekly basis, at least initially. The frequency of visits diminishes over a period of 3 to 6 months with contact being on an as-needed basis for the last half of the year. A common focus for these interviews is to determine the extent to which a client is participating in his or her recovery plan, including attendance at therapy sessions or self-help group meetings, and the development of any behaviors or high-risk situations that would signal a relapse.

It can be difficult to define one's role with aftercare clients involved in treatment relationships with other professionals. Some counselors consider requirements to maintain follow-up contact with a referred client as intrusive and duplicating the work of the external provider, an unnecessary and costly misuse of the EAP's time. Others argue that it is unethical to interfere in a professional therapeutic relationship between a client and a provider, so EAP contacts are kept to a minimum. Still others believe that ethically they *must* maintain ongoing contact as part of their professional responsibility to the client and the organization. As one clinician commented, he does not want to know after the fact if a client is having difficulty, especially if it affects job performance: "If that manager calls me I want to be able to tell him that I know what's happening, and what needs to be done about it" (Cunningham, 1988). As suggested in Chapter 6, perhaps the most realistic role performance for EAP counselors in aftercare cases is for them to be recognized as part of a treatment team having a defined function in supporting the recovery process through procedures of interdisciplinary sharing of information and treatment tasks. Viewed in this way, the role of the EAP counselor is an important adjunct in the mutual tasks associated with preventing relapse or in dealing with it effectively when it occurs (Marlatt, 1985b). The EAP counselor can be a major asset in mediating work-stress problems, facilitating motivation, and providing accurate feedback about the results of clients' efforts to change their behavioral interactions with coworkers. If the EAP counselor is recognized as a member of the treatment team, it is not an issue of duplicating interventions but enhancing their impact.

Problems of denial do not end when the person enters or leaves treatment. The internal pressure to minimize, explain away, or forget the consequences of abusive behavior patterns reemerges throughout recovery. The EAP counselor is an important adjunct to other treatment personnel as an additional source for challenging these beliefs, exploring the facts with clients, and helping them recognize these attitudes for what they are: a feature of the illness of addiction and a threat to their recovery (Marlatt,

1985a). In addition, as recovery progresses other problems emerge. The client has to face all the ordinary problems of living encountered by most people, but now without the numbing effects of chemicals. Further, all the learning that has been delayed, all the past issues ignored, and all of the growing up that never occurred because of the addiction begin to surface during recovery and can be overwhelming. Most of these issues need to be dealt with within the primary treatment resource, but EAP counselors can alert clients and treatment teams to high-risk situations and they can provide emergency input and a holding environment until the primary therapist is available. A precondition of being able to perform effectively in this role is that the counselor understands that relapse is a ubiquitous aspect of chemical dependency and not an indication of treatment failure. Relapse is part of the recovery process for many afflicted men and women and not a demonstration of the inadequacy of the counselor, the treatment program, or the client (Marlatt & Gordon, 1985).

Finally, in Chapter 3, I presented a theoretical framework regarding addiction problems that addresses the diversity of factors that can play a role in generating and maintaining substance abuse and dependence. In Chapters 5 and 6, I emphasized the need for a comprehensive approach to clinical assessment that can help identify and individualize the mix of factors affecting a given client. This broadened conceptualization of the multiple factors involved in the assessment of chemical dependency is essential in order to be able to deal constructively with clients' recovery and problems of relapse (Donovan & Chaney, 1985). As either a monitor of resources, a case manager, or a treatment team member, the EAP counselor can ensure the quality of treatment and the odds of recovery for addicted clients by making sure the relevant factors identified during the assessment are attended to during follow-up. For example, if the assessment screening identified a family history of addiction or emotional disturbance among other family members, it is important to determine the current status of these family members and the client's degree of involvement with them. If the client's recovery is being undermined by a work group that considers on-the-job drinking normal "macho" behavior, some added support systems need to be constructed, such as contact with other recovering employees or onsite 12-Step groups (Fine, Akabas, & Bellinger, 1982). If the chemical dependency was complicated by emotional or mental illness, it is important to make sure that someone on the treatment team understands and can deal with the consequences of dual diagnosis. If a spouse or a child has been abused or subjected to violence because of the employee's behavior, their unique needs should be attended to so that more mutually healthy family interactions can be instituted.

NOTE

1. In her national study of the effects of counselor characteristics on treatment outcomes, Beck (1988) comments that the findings support "the critical importance to outcomes of the client's global perception of the counselor-client relationship" (p. 27). Orlinsky and Howard (1986) also stress the significance of the patient's global perception of the therapeutic bond to outcomes in their extensive review of outcome studies, and they explore some of the dimensions of this persistent finding in psychotherapy research. See also Patterson (1985); Sloane, Staples, Cristo, Yorkston, & Whipple (1975); Smith, Glass, & Miller (1980).

Chapter 8

UNDERSTANDING FAMILY ISSUES

A continuing trend in EAPs is the shifting ratio of cases to include proportionately more requests for help with problems other than addictions. EAPs are reporting that issues of marital and parent-child conflicts and emotional or interpersonal problems are equal to and sometimes surpass the numbers of referrals for alcohol and drug problems. Changes in both the culture and the makeup of the workforce (Galinsky, 1986; Kanter, 1977b), a more profound understanding of the family impact of chemical dependency (Brown, 1985; Steinglass, 1987), and an awareness of how a family treatment perspective can increase the effectiveness of short-term counseling in EAPs all are contributing toward a heightened interest in dealing directly with the concerns of family members of employees. Increasing numbers of clients—often self-diagnosed—are presenting with problems linked to having grown up in alcoholic or dysfunctional homes. Clients also request help for concerns not associated with problems of alcohol or drugs. Even though upon investigation many of these situations do, in fact, involve issues of substance abuse, others do not.

In this chapter I examine several sets of family issues that EAP counselors have been dealing with routinely for many years and others that have emerged more recently. These include general problems of family living that workers bring to EAPs (an accessible source of information and guidance), problems associated with the overlap between work and family life and the associated stresses this creates, and the special considerations involved in working with families of chemically addicted employees and with individuals who have been affected by family addiction either as children or as adults. Some of these issues were discussed in earlier chapters; the material here is introduced by way of providing more depth.

FAMILY ASSISTANCE

Family Issues and EAPs

Most EAP programs provide counseling services to dependents of employees. The definition of *dependent* varies depending on the employer, but generally this means family members living with the employee, adopted children, and, often, significant others in the home even if they are not living together in traditional or legal relationships. In spite of the flexibility of these eligibility provisions, most counseling in relation to family issues occurs with the employee; direct counseling with family members is not very common, and direct work with all family members or subunits of the family system is even less frequent although it is a feature of some EAPs. Saltzberg and Bryant (1988) describe a hospital-based EAP firmly rooted in family systems theory. Another EAP in a large urban police department provided a full range of both group and family treatment for their officers because of the staff's perception that community-based family service and mental health agencies held negative stereotypes of police.

Employees come to EAPs for information about marital tensions, about acting-out or disturbed children, and, increasingly, about ways to deal with the responsibilities of caring for their own aging parents as economic and societal supports become less reliable (Anastas, Gibeau, & Larson, 1990; Brice & Alegre, 1989; Gadon & Serwins, 1989; Winfield, 1988). Others recognize that they are dealing with current dilemmas and concerns that somehow are related to experiences in their own childhood. Even when family matters are not uppermost in the client's mind, it is not always possible to understand clients without an awareness of the intimate family systems with which they are involved. In addition, problems that originate in the family can become displaced or recreated with members of a work group to the extent that new difficulties arise in this apparently unrelated arena of a client's life (Friedman, 1985).

To recognize that problems in one sphere of life contribute to problems in another is not the same as attaching blame or responsibility to one or the other. It is, rather, an acknowledgment that human beings are holistic, not capsulated, entities, and that what happens in one part of their lives will have an effect on other areas. The application of systems theory constructs as outlined in Chapter 3 underscores the ripple effects from one system to another; it also can help organize the data in a way that provides insight to the client and direction as to how to intervene (Saltzberg & Bryant, 1988).

> Mrs. M. asked for help in locating a therapy resource for her teenage adopted daughter, who was having difficulties with her grades and peers in her new junior high school. The girl frequently seemed withdrawn and depressed. In addition to the new school, the child's natural mother, a family member, was back in the picture, asking for visitation privileges. The counselor was able to help Mrs. M. locate several resource possibilities in her community that were covered by her benefits. He also noted that Mrs. M. was experiencing problems of her own in several areas. Her preoccupation with her daughter was contributing to sleep disturbances, which in turn were affecting her work performance. She could not handle her work responsibilities because of worry, poor concentration, and fatigue. She was working overtime to keep up, a "solution" that also limited her contact with her daughter each day but that put greater stress on her husband of five years. He and the daughter had a reserved relationship that now was being tested as he assumed more responsibility for the girl's supervision. When Mrs. M. did go home at the end of a work day, it usually was to three-way arguments.

The counselor helped Mrs. M. reframe the problem as one belonging to the whole family. He suggested a resource that would offer family sessions along with individual interviews for the daughter, whom he believed still was dealing with the abuse she had experienced by both natural parents years before. He also talked to Mrs. M. about altering the family's vacation plans, an expensive trip to Disneyworld that they could not afford but that she hoped would magically lift her daughter's depression. As it turned out, no one was all that excited about the trip, and by substituting a simpler plan at a nearby resort, the family felt less pressured.

Work and Family Overlap

In addition to general family issues that come to the attention of EAPs, there are others that arise out of clients' dual sets of responsibilities to both their families and the organizations they work for. The workplace places many demands on employees, both men and women—demands that influence how they cope with the needs, goals, and objectives of family life and that undermine the ability of working individuals to adequately address both sets of responsibilities (Googins & Burden, 1987; Lambert, 1990; Rodgers & Rodgers, 1989). The overlap between work and family exists for virtually every employed person (Burden & Googins, 1986). Problems at home contribute to demoralized and unproductive laborers; pressures and tension on the job create difficulties for all family members. Although the competing pressures of work and family can be as severe for men as for women, it has been the dramatic increase of women entering the full-time workforce that has highlighted the need for the workplace to deal with the overlap in more systematic ways. More than 58% of all women age 20 or over now work outside the home, constituting 43% of the U.S. workforce ("Current Labor Statistics," 1993). Increasing numbers of these women are single parents; most still are relegated to the lower paying positions. It often is these women who are struggling unsuccessfully with multiple role demands and who find their way to EAPs.

Until the advent of the industrial revolution—only a little more than a century ago—most work was performed close to or as a part of the family group. In agricultural communities, small towns and villages, and family-run shops, the separation between the family and work was less distinct. Communication among family members was maintained throughout the day; children knew exactly what work their parents did and where they did it. Often, entire families participated in the process of earning the family's livelihood. The industrial revolution had the effect of not only separating work operations from the family, but also separating people from one another as family members, including mothers and children, worked in different settings. This reality reinforced a cultural ethic in the United States that places a value on an image of work and family as two very different and barely overlapping arenas in a person's life (Kanter, 1977b). People declare with pride, "I never take my work home with me!" or, "Yeah, my job is a bummer, but I make sure it doesn't affect my personal life."

Piotrowski (1978) sees such disclaimers as a type of denial workers resort to for various reasons: as more a wish or a hope than a statement of fact, because it preserves the illusion that they are more autonomous from the job than is actually the case, or, because their job is so energy draining, denying its impact is their only means of coping. For many men and women there is a perceived danger in letting their boss think they cannot handle multiple roles and stresses without complaint; to do so could be interpreted as personal inadequacy. Although our society generally is more willing to acknowledge the multiple ways in which personal, family, and work lives intersect, employees and companies still are a bit nervous about making the connection too overt. Corporate attitudes about the importance of accommodating family responsibilities will vary in response to the lack or surplus of workers. When it is in the employer's economic interests to retain valued employees, more provisions will be available to help workers balance work and family roles (Kammerman, 1984); when unemployment is high or new technology renders work functions obsolete, fewer supports will be offered.

The work conditions that most directly affect the family are those related to economic issues and the allocation of the worker's time and energy (Galinsky, 1986; Kanter, 1977b; Piotrowski, 1978). Many EAP clients can be classified as the working poor, those who work as regularly as possible but whose annual incomes still fall below the federal poverty line (currently $13,359 for a family of four). An even greater number of clients could be included in Wyers's (1988) secondary classification of economically insecure, those who may earn an income above the poverty level but who are at risk of slipping below it with any unanticipated crisis or economic downturn. He describes them as subsisting, surviving, struggling, and in constant dread that something will occur to bump them into poverty (Wyers, 1988, p. 18). In the 1990s, that unanticipated crisis often is the acute or long-term illness of a family member who no longer is fully covered by health-care benefits. The increasing number of clients who are economically insecure also are at risk for a host of other biopsychosocial problems including chemical abuse or relapse, marital and family problems, and stress-related illnesses.

The second area of tension between work and family is related to time, and the perception of many analysts that the typical workplace schedules its operations as though most workers were men with supportive spouses.

> Families where all adults work are still coping with rules and conditions of work designed . . . to the specifications of Ozzie and Harriet . . . [a] rigid adherence to a 40-hour work week, a concept of career path inconsistent with the life cycle of a person with serious family responsibilities, notions of equity formed in a different era, and performance-evaluation systems that confuse effort with results by equating hours of work with productivity. (Rodgers & Rodgers, 1989, p. 122)

Most family and personal activities have to be planned around work routines. When family members can eat, play, or pray together; fight; interact; or resolve problems still is largely determined by the structure of work. Family roles and functions can be dislocated by shift work, over-time hours, and rigid regular work schedules that allow no flexibility for family emergencies, children's school activities, or vacations when other family members are free. Expectations that employees will relocate to meet the needs of a company become major crises in dual-wage-earner families with school-age children.

Currently, a serious issue facing families is the need to find reliable and affordable options for dependent care for either children or parents. Problems are further complicated for workers who have several children of different ages, or adult or child dependents with chronic medical problems (Anastas et al., 1990). Most dependent-care arrangements are informal and most are very vulnerable to changes in the lives of the care providers. Increasingly, children are expected to assume responsibility for themselves and, at times, their younger siblings as well. There even is an identifiable "3:15 syndrome," when employed parents wait with increasing anxiety for the calls from their latchkey children to let them know the children arrived home from school safely.

Clinical Implications

When a client seeks help with family problems, the counselor needs to make preliminary decisions as to whether or not family members will be involved in counseling and the extent of any involvement. It is not uncommon for family members to be interviewed during the assessment phase, but it often is important to include them in follow-up interviews or referral planning as well. If, for example, the clinical assessment points to problems in communication or lack of awareness of one another's feelings or attitudes, much more can be accomplished in a short period of time in a joint interview during which such patterns and attitudes are acted out in ways that the counselor can observe and point out to the family members.

Several factors mitigate against including family members in EAP interviews. Organizational resistance to the concept is an issue with some employers, especially those who believe that work and family should be rigidly separated (Saltzberg & Bryant, 1988). If family service is not an established tradition in an EAP even though the service policy allows it, the clinical potential of involving family members can be overlooked. For counselors who have little experience or training in joint or family interviewing, the special tasks associated with conducting such sessions can be overwhelming. Also, it usually is easier to schedule meetings with employees than with family members, and the overall press of intake may discourage seeing anyone other than the employee. However, those who are experienced in multiple-client interviewing and the application of family systems concepts offer a strong argument for the effectiveness of such methods in helping to resolve problems that might never surface in single-client interviews (Saltzberg & Bryant, 1988). In the long run, working with larger units of the employees' families may produce more rapid and enduring changes in both work and family functioning that reduce costs to the employer in a variety of ways, including improved worker productivity.

Men and women who are experiencing difficulty in balancing family and work roles find their way to the EAP for all sorts of reasons, and the source of their problems may not be all that apparent to them or to the counselor at the outset. A basic requirement for the counselor, therefore, is to be sensitive to the significance of work/family overlap in general, and to incorporate this understanding into routine clinical screening practices. It is important that counselors not participate in the denial that minimizes the significance of these concerns and that their clients understand that discussions about job stress are allowed. Initial screening can include an assessment of the views of family members about presenting problems and those areas of traditional conflict between work and home.

Counselors usually cannot significantly alter the demands of work or family life. However, by using the techniques described in Chapter 6, counselors can help burdened employees problem solve more effectively, explore resource options that might help them in meeting multiple demands, and experience the support of a concerned, accessible, and interested person. Regardless of where the greatest pressure lies, to achieve immediate relief the best counseling strategy for a given client may be to focus problem-solving work on that part of the overlap over which he or she has some control. The counselor's knowledge of the organizational system may suggest avenues of assistance, such as arranging for temporary or permanent changes in work schedules that can help a family through an emergency situation.

Education and information about issues of family life also are helpful in reducing pressing family issues. Saltzberg and Bryant (1988) describe a full range of programmatic options developed in response to the needs of their particular employee group in a hospital setting. These options, which reflect a systems theory understanding of the work and family overlap, are applicable to most EAPs. They include providing information about relevant family issues in employee orientation and supervisory training sessions; brown-bag lunch groups; special training for select employees on issues of family violence; and support groups for single parents, caregivers of elderly relatives, family members of alcoholics, and those experiencing occupational stress.

EAP counselors also are in a position to make policy recommendations to the employer about family issues. They can bring certain types of issues to the attention of key administrators if these issues are negatively affecting the health of the total organization. The EAP program also can provide evidence of the economic and human costs of outdated or inefficient procedures that undermine the productivity of the workforce, especially if such problems can be addressed through strategies such as flex time, job sharing, or even granting supervisors more latitude in making decisions about released-time requests for family emergencies.

CHEMICAL DEPENDENCY AND THE FAMILY SYSTEM

The 12-Step self-help movement long has identified alcoholism as a family disease with profound effects on all family members, adults and children alike (AA, Al-Anon, Al-A-Teen). A major focus of these groups, however, is discussion of the strategies and mechanisms required to cope with and detach from the chemically dependent family member through one's own recovery process. Although groups vary in their preferred style and focus, the abuser and his or her addiction usually are the core of attention in ways similar to their centrality in the family system itself. In professional treatment centers the substance abuser and his or her recovery often are the major emphasis of treatment. Family involvement is directed primarily at helping to create a climate that will enhance the abuser's chances of recovery. Until recently such help involved sending different family members to their own therapy or self-help meetings, which frequently contributed more to the fragmentation than the cohesion of the family, with scant attention to the interactions of the family as a system. As Seilhamer (1991) points out, even the research and treatment literature tended to focus on the problems of the alcoholic *or* the spouse *or* the children, with concerns about the family as a system emerging just within the past 15 years.

EAP and addictions counselors are familiar with the effects of chemical dependency on families including family violence and incest; financial depletion; the threat of criminal involvement, especially through the illegal use of controlled substances; social isolation; recurrent losses; and the piercing pain associated with chronic states of fear, anxiety, shame, and guilt. The presence of chemical addiction creates major stresses for family members that at best ultimately interfere with their ability to live fully satisfying and actualized lives and at worst contribute to severe mental, emotional, and physical illness. However, many families of chemically dependent persons also display relatively stable, intact, and nonconflictual family styles without any of the more severe and debilitating consequences described above. Steinglass (1987) notes that members of alcoholic families evidence different levels of stress in response to the alcoholic's behavior that are related to what he termed a vulnerability factor, a pattern of susceptibility to the drinking that exists in some families and not in others. EAP counselors are likely to encounter these varying family styles among their clients, which in turn requires differential assessment and intervention.

For assessment purposes, therefore, two different types of judgments are indicated: whether or not substance abuse exists on the part of one or more family members and, second, whether or not the family is exhibiting clearly dysfunctional behavior. Steinglass (1987) defines a genuinely alcoholic family—as distinct from one that contains alcoholic members—as one in which the alcoholic behaviors have become major definers of the system's internal regulatory and developmental functions by the superimposition of an alcohol life history on the customary family life cycle:

> Emphasis is placed on short term stability to the detriment of all other issues. Thus challenges to this stability . . . are interpreted primarily as threats to the status quo; the possibilities for growth inherent in these challenges are ignored. . . . The family's current developmental phase is extended far beyond its natural life. The clinical impression is that the family is frozen in time. (Steinglass, 1987, p. 46)

A family systems perspective sensitizes observers to the extent to which the chemical addiction becomes, first of all, the core feature around which most of the behavior of family members becomes organized. Second, it illustrates how the addiction itself can come to promote certain family interactions and behaviors in ways that have a short-term benefit, such as fostering greater expressions of feelings or intimacy, but a long-term disadvantage in terms of family growth and health (Isaacson, 1991). Assessment screening needs to determine whether or not the addictive behavior itself creates chaotic, unpredictable, destructive experiences that can interfere with the normal tasks, roles, and responsibilities of family members and, if it does, how this occurs. To what extent are everyone's energies directed toward defending against or coping with the addictive behavior, further undermining the use of energy required to meet the usual and normal demands of maintaining a home, raising children, and structuring a lifestyle that is meaningful and gratifying? Even when the effects are not dramatic, afflicted family members may survive major debilitation only to lead what Steinglass (1987) refers to as "compromised lives" marked by marginal problems that they may not even be able to link to family alcoholism. "The 'ache' is there, but the attempt to localize the pain is unsuccessful" (p. 24).

Counselors need to examine the adaptive coping strategies family systems have used to withstand or mitigate the influence of chemical dependency. Have they managed to retain certain norms of interaction, openness of communication, tolerance for growth and change, and stability of values in spite of the drinking? Have they been more or less successful in refusing to allow the addictive behavior to take over the normal growth processes in the family? What other assaults may the family be facing that can contribute to its vulnerability, such as serious illness, job loss, or loss of extended family supports?

The intervention implications for EAP counselors are of two general types. Most practitioners agree that it is necessary to work with the families of chemically abusing employees from the outset to increase the odds of recovery for the abuser. An initial assessment that presents a clear picture of the extent of reconstructive work that the family system requires increases the probability of recovery for everyone. A referral to an appropriate provider who can address the family systems issues may be necessary. When EAP counselors are involved in discharge planning of a client from inpatient care, their understanding of the family system to which the client is returning can ease the transition home. The family will need help in anticipating the many changes in interaction that will occur, working through the emotional upset such changes produce, and learning new ways of communicating and interacting. Counselors make additional important interventions by alerting family members to their legitimate strengths and successful coping strategies. Even problems that erupt on the job may be better understood and handled in the light of the family system's struggles to become more functional.

Codependency

A professional conundrum has arisen for many practitioners who wish to provide responsible help to their clients involved in addictive relationships because of disagreements about what constitutes codependency:

whether it is a clear psychological disorder, a universal phenomenon, or even legitimately exists.

There are arguments to the effect that codependency constitutes a distinct mental/emotional illness with more or less discrete behavioral symptoms that should be included in standard classifications of mental and emotional illnesses (Cermak, 1986, 1989). Others have found these behaviors and personality traits to be so ubiquitous in our culture that they declare that we all are codependent to some degree (Whitfield, 1989). Feminist theoreticians and clinicians have questioned the extent to which codependency traits are indicative of further efforts to pathologize what our culture considers to be typical and even desirable female behaviors (Collins, 1993; O'Gorman, 1991) or are attempts to "blame the victim" (Frank & Golden, 1992), especially because most codependency studies have been in relation to women. There even has been a backlash developing against the codependency and ACA movements that sees them as either undermining personal responsibility for behavior, fostering "parent bashing" (Kaminer, 1992), or assuming cult-like control over their members as a way of sustaining the burgeoning addictions industry (Katz & Liu, 1991).

Most experienced practitioners will recognize elements of truth in each of these positions, which complicates decision making as to how best to assess and intervene with codependent clients. In reading the literature on codependency it appears that authors are operating under different assumptions about codependency, about the nature of human behavior and development, about what constitutes functional or dysfunctional behavior, and about the genesis of dysfunctional patterns of interaction. In this discussion I attempt an understanding of codependency issues that is straightforward and pragmatic but that neither minimizes the seriousness of the definitional debates nor needlessly pathologizes individuals who do not judge themselves and are not judged by others to be experiencing problems in functioning.

I propose several operating assumptions and assessment principles to be used to make more differential diagnostic decisions regarding codependency phenomena and to arrive at a more individualized treatment plan with employee clients. These are (a) that codependency is not a unitary condition or syndrome; (b) that the characteristics and symptoms associated with codependency occur for a variety of reasons, not all of which are associated with chemical abuse or dependence; (c) that the problems related to growing up in a drug- or alcohol-abusing family are qualitatively different from other types of codependency experiences; (d) that the presence of chemical dependence or abuse creates unique problems not associated with other types of compulsive behavior; and (e) that to have experienced chemical dependency in one's nuclear or birth family is not a sufficient basis for labeling that person dysfunctional.

An Assessment Framework

My first premise is that codependency is not a single or discrete condition. Much of the confusion about its nature and causes is due to the fact that different people are describing different sets of behavior that share some characteristics but that are not synonymous with one another. Most descriptions of codependency traits depict a wide range of behaviors (Beattie, 1987; Black, 1982; Pape, 1992; Woititz, 1983) representing a continuum from functional to dysfunctional. EAP practitioners are seeing clients from every point along this continuum. A number of these traits are common behaviors that most people resort to at one time or another and that may be appropriate to certain circumstances but that, if extended over long periods of time or carried to extremes, constitute dysfunction. Just as neurotic symptoms are more or less normal behaviors carried to extremes, codependency traits often are more or less normal ways of dealing with the exigencies of ordinary living. To be "overinvolved" with a sick child or dying relative in ways that require suspension of one's own needs is healthy if it means the well-being of the other is protected or the strength and integrity of the family system are ensured. However, when such behavior no longer is appropriate to the circumstances, when it signals clearly inflexible patterns of response that the person cannot control, and when it creates persistent problems in living for individuals or those close to them, then we can recognize the behavior as a more serious manifestation of emotional disability that may require special treatment.

A second premise governing my approach to assessment is that the characteristics and behaviors identified with codependency can occur for reasons other than dysfunctional or substance-abusing relationships. They often are associated with very different types of disorders just as apparent symptoms of substance abuse may be related to other factors. For example, extreme disorientation, depersonalization, hallucinations, and loss of contact with reality can be caused by actual psychotic processes, chemical intoxication or withdrawal, other physical conditions, or a major crisis event. In somewhat the same way, problems of intimacy, difficulties with affect management and expression, the need to control people and situations, and low self-esteem may be "caused" by developmental trauma or arrests, current relationship or situational realities, acute or long-term crises, or some combination of factors. I believe, for example, that otherwise healthy individuals exhibiting no prior pathology can evidence severely dysfunctional and seemingly codependent behavior in reaction to highly toxic environmental conditions such as noxious though temporary relationships or systems, including discriminatory or destructive job situations. Other individuals might have experienced early developmental deprivation and abuse and long-standing patterns of self-defeating actions and relationships that produce similar behavior. Although these two types of clients may look very much alike when they come into an EAP office, planning for the first will be different from trying to help the second. The fact that the behavioral manifestations are similar does not mean that the underlying condition is the same or that the clients will respond to or require the same interventions. If this is true, then efforts to find a single classification or disease entity that encompasses all such behavior will, in the long run, confound rather than clarify treatment options.

One of the implications of this second premise leads to a third: that although children and adult children of chemically dependent parents automatically are included in some definitions of codependency and may exhibit codependency behaviors, their social, emotional, and behavioral problems are qualitatively different from those of men and women who have learned codependency strategies in adult relationships. This observation in no way minimizes the seriousness and pain associated with spousal and other types of codependency relationships first encountered in adulthood. I am saying that differences exist between adult children and other codependents that are of great significance clinically. Problems are compounded for the individual who is both an adult child and someone compulsively involved in adult codependent relationships.

When children experience the abuse and inconsistencies of the chemically dependent family, they lack the emotional maturity, life experience, basic personality structure, and even language to process events meaningfully. They often lack external supports or alternative ways of thinking about themselves and their experiences that might lessen their trauma. There may be no compensatory nurturing either from other family members or from the nonabusing parent, who may be too caught up in the spouse's addictive behavior to attend to the child's needs. It is devastating for anyone to confront the fact that no amount of love, dedication, pleasing, or pleading can keep an addict from using his or her drug. It is much more profoundly damaging for the immature personality of the child, who lacks a basic sense of his or her own worth, to realize that the parent loves the next drink or the next fix more than the parent loves the child, no matter how careful, obedient, good, or lovable that child tries to be. The profound narcissistic injury associated with such abuse is difficult to comprehend, much less to manage. Because the hurt is so intense and the repertoire of coping behavior so limited for children, they are far more likely to bury or capsulate these memories in their unconscious, and their own healing and recovery may involve many more layers of uncovering and a different set of procedures than is true of other codependents.

The extent and seriousness of the problems encountered by children in addicted families are affected by the child's age when the abusive behavior began; other types of abuse that may have occurred; other strengths or deficits in the family system; other cultural or environmental forces; and the presence or absence of additional physical, mental, or emotional problems. For these reasons I discuss the clinical implications of the child (COA) or adult child of the alcoholic/addicted (ACOA) family in a separate section below.

A fourth operating assumption in my assessment of codependency is that, although other types of abusive and destructive relationships can precipitate behaviors that fit descriptions of codependency, those relationships with individuals who are abusing or chemically dependent on alcohol and drugs are clinically distinct. The biomedical factors that either predispose or are consequences of chemical abuse introduce a whole separate set of intervention considerations that does not apply to similar patterns of behavior not related to chemical abuse and that may be better understood through the application of different diagnostic criteria. Further, the social, legal, and economic consequences associated with the illicit use of controlled substances introduce yet another set of factors that complicates both diagnosis and treatment. Although a knowledge of dysfunctional family processes may provide insights into other types of obsessive or compulsive behaviors, more accurate and informed insights are found in the emerging bodies of research related to these other disorders and in alternative, personality-based diagnostic criteria that have more explanatory power. Trying to make all types of personal or family difficulties fit into a fairly loose, nondiscriminating, all-purpose definition of codependency contributes to failures in diagnoses and inadequate treatment plans.

Finally, I also believe that someone having grown up in or having been a part of a substance-abusing family is not an adequate basis for labeling that person codependent. There is a fatalistic quality to much of the literature on the subject of codependency that suggests that to have had

these experiences means the damage has been done and is irreparable unless the person agrees to treatment directed toward this condition. Such a
deterministic view does not do justice to either the variability or the resiliency of human beings, and their ability to extract compensatory gratifica-
tions from one part of their experiences to deal with the deficiencies of
another (Ackerman, 1987). Research already cited indicates that a high
degree of variability exists in how different families respond to alcoholism (Steinglass, 1987), and others speak to the thrust toward health that
characterizes so much of human functioning (Anthony & Cohler, 1987;
Garmezy & Rutter, 1983). The behaviors and characteristics that are supposed to identify ACOAs fail to describe all or even most adult children
who grew up in families with a history of alcoholism, nor do they
accurately differentiate between ACOAs and adult children from homes
in which there is no history of alcoholism (National Institute on Alcohol
Abuse and Alcoholism, 1990). The thrust of the research also indicates
that children from alcoholic homes score within the normal range for all
types of performance measures as adults (Windle & Searles, 1990). There
currently is no basis for being able to predict that an alcoholic family
history or other forms of drug abuse will produce a certain kind of adult.

Children of Alcoholics

Although definitions of codependency and the assumptions upon which
they are based are open to disagreement and debate, we are far more
clear about the traumatic effects on children of growing up in substance-
abusing homes (Cork, 1969; Freeman, 1992a; National Institute on Alcohol
Abuse and Alcoholism, 1990; Seilhamer, 1991). Children in such settings
are at risk physically, emotionally, educationally (Pilat & Jones, 1985),
and economically. Children born to addicted parents are more likely to
experience (a) prenatal damage leading to usually nonreversible effects
of retardation, (b) emotional instability, and (c) higher morbidity rates for
a range of medical problems (Freeman, 1992a). Fetal alcohol syndrome
(FAS) has a longer history of investigation than is true of other drugs, and
the data are more detailed although still incomplete (National Institute on
Alcohol Abuse and Alcoholism, 1990). For example, not all women who
drink heavily have FAS infants or children with fetal alcoholism effects
(FAE), and there is no clear indication as to what contributes to this
differential result. The cocaine epidemic has spawned a growing number of
addicted infants whose long-term prognosis is yet unknown but who evidence a range of behavioral, cognitive, and biomedical disorders. Children

born into addicted environments are at risk for HIV infection (Freeman, 1992a; Leukefeld & Battjes, 1992), physical and sexual abuse (Pilat & Boomhower-Kresser, 1992), and other medical conditions related to neglect or poverty, and some are at greater risk to develop alcoholism than the population at large.

Adult children raised in addictive homes have other needs and problems that require specific and comprehensive treatment beyond that involved in either learning to cope with the addict or contributing toward his or her recovery (Brown, 1985). They often have additional issues of missed developmental experiences, impaired or underdeveloped capacities in forming relationships, uncorrected self-perceptions, and childlike needs that persist throughout adulthood. Many also carry with them into adulthood repressed memories of physical or sexual abuse, abandonment, or other severe trauma that never have been addressed in any way. But, as is true with chemical dependence and codependency, there is great variability in how individuals respond to an addictive environment, their actual degree of disturbance, their treatment needs, and their responses to different forms of intervention. Unfortunately, there is no magic-bullet theory or all-purpose methodology that will answer all of a counselor's questions about survivors of dysfunctional family environments. It is clear, however, that blanket diagnoses of children from addicted homes and cookie-cutter approaches to treatment intervention are no longer tenable in working with adult children. EAP clients who evidence characteristics of an ACOA need to be assessed thoroughly along several dimensions before any treatment is initiated. The key diagnostic fact is not that the person is a product of an addicted home, but rather how his or her current problematic functioning may or may not be related to family-of-origin issues and/or other current and past life experiences.

Clinical Implications

As is true of clinical assessment in general, basic tasks associated with codependency issues are to discover which aspects of clients' lives are causing them pain; to assess the cognitive, affective, behavioral, and situational factors related to these problems; and to set a course of action that offers clients hope for improvement. Applying the assumptions described above to the task of diagnostic assessment involves making several types of distinctions. First, is the behavior a product of systems involving chemically addicted or abusing members, or is it in response to other types of relationships? It is important to spend some time understanding the conditions that have contributed to the behavior rather than assuming, for example, that everyone with low self-esteem comes from an alcoholic home. It may be, instead, that the self-esteem problem is more directly related to years of sexual harassment from supervisors and coworkers that the client is afraid to discuss with anyone. Referral options and intervention strategies will differ, depending on the picture that emerges during the assessment.

Next it is important to determine the extent to which clients' behaviors represent a genuinely dysfunctional response to their current reality or a more or less realistic attempt to protect themselves from threatening circumstances. The more severe manifestations of dysfunction include a high degree of preoccupation with either controlling or defending against, possibly through denial, another's addictive behavior; an inflexibility and rigidity in their own behavioral responses to any new event or relationship; a pervasive inability to fully attend to other responsibilities and areas of performance; an erosion of a sense of their own identity; and, for some, an eventual lack of control over their own feelings or behavior including a failure to deal adequately with emotions of shame, anger, anxiety, and depression.

Clients evidence different degrees and types of reactions, but it is the persistence of self-defeating, ineffective, and destructive behaviors that interfere with most aspects of living that helps in defining dysfunctional behavior, especially if the addictive behavior has stopped. Studies of wives of recovering alcoholics indicated that they exhibited fewer problems in psychological functioning than those whose husbands were actively drinking (Moos, Finney, & Gamble, 1982). In another study, wives experienced a marked decrease in symptoms of anxiety and depression the longer their husbands maintained sobriety (Paolino & McCrady, 1977). This points to the resiliency of human functioning referred to earlier and why it is important to assess behavior in the light of current as well as past realities.

Although the lists of codependent characteristics are too broad and general to provide a precise diagnosis of codependency, anecdotal reports from practitioners clearly suggest that clients are helped through reading about and discussing codependency traits, and that the help often is dramatic, powerful, and life changing. The use of the characteristics can be a valuable tool in helping clients arrive at a general understanding of their own functioning as long as such lists are used carefully and with a sound understanding of their limitations, especially the understanding that having some of the behaviors is not the same thing as being mentally ill. Beattie (1987) groups the characteristics into several categories including inappropriate caretaking, low self-worth, repression of feelings, obsessive attachments, controlling situations and events, denial, dependency, problems of communication, and personal boundary issues, among others. Assisting clients to, perhaps, locate themselves within these more general areas of functioning opens the door to recollections, narratives of family interaction, the experiencing of emotions long denied, and new ways of thinking about themselves and their problems. This approach often circumvents ingrained patterns of denial and provides clients with a way of organizing aspects of their experience that they were partially aware of but that they could not fit together in any meaningful way. This can be a major help to people whether their problems are marginal or profound, long-standing or recent.

Finally, the clinical assessment needs to clarify the extent to which a client's behavior is a product of interactions with addicted members from the client's family of origin, more recent associations, or both. If the clinical assessment reveals that the destructive relationships are current or of fairly recent onset, treatment can be toward helping clients detach emotionally from the compulsive involvement and refocus their attention on their own needs and those of other family members. Interventions also may be directed toward moving the addicted member into treatment if the EAP counselor has access to him or her. Al-Anon can be especially helpful in the process of detachment from the addictive behavior, not necessarily from the addicted person. As clients learn to separate from compulsive involvement in the addictive behavior, they are better able to attend to personal and family issues, which in turn helps reduce their vulnerability to further damaging interactions with either the addict or other destructive encounters. Longer-term individual psychotherapy, family treatment, therapy groups, or couples counseling each can be helpful to clients, separately or in combination, but it is important that the EAP counselor be familiar with the providers of such services, their theoretical base regarding codependency, and their track record in providing realistic assistance.

If we do not have the right answers yet regarding COAs and ACOAs, an amazing array of research conducted by many different disciplines over the past decade makes it possible for us to ask more of the right questions. Windle and Searles (1990) and an interdisciplinary panel of experts reviewed approximately 1,000 studies conducted during this period. Their analysis points to major trends and themes in the emerging knowledge base about children of alcoholics that are relevant to assessment and treatment. For example, of major significance for the clinician is the extent to which a vulnerability to alcohol addiction is inherited. Research now can help confirm that alcoholism can be inherited and that many, but apparently not all, ACOAs are at greater risk to become alcoholics (Chan, 1990; National Institute on Alcohol Abuse and Alcoholism, 1990). Furthermore, certain additional risk factors have been isolated that may contribute to a person's vulnerability (Searles, 1990). As already mentioned, lists of characteristics of COAs are so inclusive and even contradictory (for example, super-responsible to irresponsible) that most people could find some basis for seeing themselves represented regardless of their family history. To date, the research studies reviewed by Windle and Searles (1990) have not been able to support any single set of personality characteristics that is found in most COAs although combinations of factors, such as hyperactivity and conduct disorders, may be more common in COAs. More attention is being directed toward identifying those factors that seem to protect at-risk children from succumbing to the more severe effects of parental substance abuse, knowledge that ultimately may point both researchers and clinicians toward those familial, social, and environmental factors that can be modified to increase a child's resilience and long-term emotional health.

Although the research cited above does not support that either general personality characteristics or family roles can be specifically linked to adult children from alcoholic homes, this does not mean that the work initiated by Beattie (1987), Black (1982), Wegscheider (1981), or Woititz (1983) is irrelevant in working with these clients or that it is akin to astrological predictions. These and other authors did, in fact, alert our society to what still is for many a group of forgotten and underserved children and adults. Although the bandwagon phenomenon has helped to undermine the importance of this message, the point still needs to be made in general and with clients that terrible things can happen to children when their parents drink or use drugs, and that the scars of such trauma are not all physical; they can lie buried and denied long into adulthood, influencing in negative ways the lives of other families and unborn children.

Clients can use the information provided by the COA and ACOA literature to discover, often for the first time, that the residual difficulties they are encountering are not typical of most adults, that the roots of their current difficulty may lie in their childhood, and that there are ways of reversing the effects of such childhood events at any point in life. Such discussions can penetrate denial both about the seriousness of the addictive behavior and often about other losses, trauma, or abuse, although this often may occur much later.

Mrs. C. came for help in deciding whether or not to divorce her alcohol-abusing husband. Although she recognized that such abuse was a multi-generational reality in her husband's family, she had not thought of herself as having been reared in an alcoholic home. During the assessment, however, she recalled that both parents drank daily before, during, and after dinner. Although she never saw them drunk, she remembered that the children were sent to spend the night with their nearby grandparents on a regular basis; she now realized it was because the parents were drunk. Her emerging awareness about her own troubled childhood allowed her to concentrate on her own issues through treatment and Al-Anon and to set limits as to what she was prepared to tolerate from her husband, who subsequently entered treatment. It was more than a year later before she began to remember incidents of sexual abuse that she and a sister experienced from their father and an uncle, which she finally recognized were contributing to the continuing sexual problems with her husband.

The hidden nature of so many of the traumas experienced by ACOAs complicates the clinical process. Denial in many such situations serves an adaptive purpose for some people, in that it allows them to continue to perform the necessary tasks of ordinary living without having to manage as well the overwhelming anxiety and personal decompensation such recollections can produce. Decisions as to what material to discuss in EAP counseling sessions, referrals to ACOA or other self-help groups, or other alternative interventions need to be based on a conviction that the client is in a position to process the material and to deal with the consequences that any treatment can precipitate. The supportive help of a sensitive psychotherapy relationship combined with a reliable ACOA group that has a clear sense of its boundaries and the 12-Step philosophy often are the best combination for very traumatized or vulnerable clients.

It can be important to draw on the conclusions available from the research to counsel adults from addicted families about their own drinking or substance-use patterns. The equivocal nature of the data is such that even though we cannot say that all such offspring are at greater risk, it makes sense for anyone with such a history to be cautious about his or her use of potentially addictive substances of any kind. Also important is the guidance offered to parents about child-rearing strategies that can be implemented to reduce the risk of addiction for their offspring who have been exposed to substance abuse in the home. It is important, for example, to maintain regular family rituals, to minimize other sources of stress on family members, and to recognize how easily children and their needs can be lost in the struggle to control the addictive behavior. For both adult clients and their children it also is important to communicate the message that growing up in such a home is not a condemnation either to eventual addiction or to emotional disturbance. Affixing such labels indiscriminately can lead to self-fulfilling prophesies. It is essential that clients recognize that there are choices and options available to help them lead gratifying and sober lives.

Chapter 9

ORGANIZATIONAL ASSISTANCE

A unique feature of employee assistance practice is the dual responsibility that its professionals have toward both the companies they work for, either as paid employees or contractors, and the individual workers in those organizations who require assistance. The special responsibilities toward the organization go beyond those that social workers, for example, have toward their agencies and organizations because the occupational setting also is a client of the EAP toward which EAP staff have distinct professional service obligations. At times this dual responsibility creates ethical dilemmas for practitioners, but to a great extent EAPs operate within a conflict-free sphere in which both the organization and its employees benefit by EAP services (Kurzman, 1983). In this chapter I discuss specific procedures designed to provide help to different systems and subsystems of the organization, interventions that I term organizational assistance.[1]

The very existence of a well-functioning EAP is a major source of assistance to the organization as a whole, not just to the individual clients who receive direct services. Through the EAP's routine educational and preventative activities the entire work community benefits. The direct service to individuals, families, and large and small groups as described in earlier chapters has positive institutional repercussions, many of which could not even be tracked or documented. Other types of EAP activities have a significant organizational impact as well. For example, practitioners indicate that much of their work in behalf of individual clients requires interventions with supervisors, coworkers, or department heads. In addition, often they must call upon their clinical skills to mediate interpersonal difficulties, to resolve problems of communication, or to assist in the identification of enabling behaviors on the part of coworkers or managers. When large-scale crises befall an organization, EAPs typically are involved in critical incident debriefings directed toward restoring the organization and its members to precrisis levels of functioning. Practitioners also are increasingly involved in other facets of organizational life often not tied to specific case situations.

They are asked to provide consultative services on occupational welfare issues, to lend their expertise to intraorganizational disputes, and to use their problem-solving skills to provide insight into certain management issues. Involvement in such issues is by no means a universal experience for EAPs, but the trend is especially apparent in mid-sized or downsizing organizations that lack a broad range of specialized human resource functions, or in settings in which the EAP staff over time has generated a high degree of credibility as having special knowledge about people and systems that can benefit an employer in a variety of ways.

Some EAP counselors see such activities as an unfortunate departure from the "real" work of EAPs. Also, a number of factors discourage EAP involvement in other areas of organizational life. These include, first, traditional organizational resistance to apparent system changing by anyone, but especially by those not generally thought of by corporate managers as being system changers. In the competitive world of EAP marketing it is not always prudent to negotiate the concept of organizational intervention. Contracts can be lost if the idea is inadequately represented. Finally, the early focus of EAPs clearly was the substance-abusing employee. Except for the EAP's responsibility to educate the work environment about the seriousness of substance abuse, the concept of intervening in the workplace in other ways was not well developed or endorsed. Part of the philosophy of alcoholism treatment was that the abuser must learn to accept responsibility for his or her own recovery. Anyone providing an "easy out" by blaming the drug or alcohol abuse on work stress or an antagonistic boss was viewed as enabling the drug abuse.

Although organizational assistance may not be right for every program or every counselor, it is a reality of practice that exists and that needs more attention. I became aware of its prevalence during a practice survey (Cunningham, 1988) that originally did not anticipate the amount of time and effort practitioners were devoting to this aspect of their work. The details the respondents provided about the organizational service beyond that involved in routine program administration prompted me to include additional inquiries directed at capturing this aspect of their work that seemed to generate so much interest and gratification. It appears that organizations develop their own paradigms as to what role the EAP plays based on their own needs and their acquired experience with EAP professionals. As described by Ozawa (1980), it is the credibility and expertise of the program professionals that move them into additional practice roles within a company. Although there are similarities between organizational assistance and organizational development (OD), my impression is that EAP personnel have different objectives in mind, use different sets of skills, and approach the tasks in ways unlike those of OD professionals. Practice situations illustrating the application of organizational assistance are discussed below. They include the use of organizational interventions to reach greater numbers of troubled employees, direct intervention with others in the client's work life who are involved in the presenting problem or significant in its resolution, help with specific work groups that are experiencing special problems, participation in critical incident debriefings at times of organizational crisis, work with the organizational culture to support the recovery and health of employees, and, finally, interventions directed toward other health and welfare issues not directly related to troubled workers.

MAXIMIZING THE EAP's IMPACT

A very gifted counselor in terms of organizational assistance was forced to direct more of her energies toward the company as a target of change because she could influence greater numbers of people by doing so. As the only EAP counselor in a large firm of almost 10,000 employees on three different shifts at several different sites, she had the choice of remaining in her office all day seeing individual employees or becoming a visible presence with managers, decision makers, and department heads in order to educate, inform, and evolve a network of internal resources who could help with issues of concern to both workers and management. Although individual requests for services remained her top priority, much of her time was directed toward (a) scheduling large education/information groups led by a cadre of in-house professionals concerning community-based resources to help with personal problems; (b) mediating in certain types of work unit problems; and (c) sensitizing the workforce through articles, posters, brochures, and video presentations about the interactional and environmental circumstances that can foster personal and family problems. This style of EAP practice carries some risk as it is difficult to amass the service statistics some firms require as a condition of their continuing support. In this organization, however, the EAP director significantly influenced how the total organization viewed personal problems, substance abuse, counseling, and the work environment. The organizational commitment to the EAP shifted from one of ambivalence to viewing it as a mark of status and an indication of the company's concern for its workers. For similar reasons, but in a very different type of setting, another counselor is intimately involved in all types of organizational activities, including recruitment, staff development, and the planning of recreational events for employees. In other firms such involvement would be thought of as inappropriate; however, this is a small, family-oriented company of fewer than 1,200 employees. One of its valued traditions is that "if a job needs doing, everyone pitches in to get it done." Job descriptions and functional specialties give way to this pragmatic and apparently effective way of doing business in this setting. If the EAP director had ignored this expectation, it might have meant the end of the program. The director has been vocal and unambiguous about what she can and cannot do, based on the need to respect the privacy of individuals who come to her for help. In doing so she has increased everyone's understanding of the work of the program. In addition, as in the first example, her visibility in the organization has garnered tremendous support for the EAP to the extent that it is virtually untouchable at times of budget review. The EAP has a continuing flow of individual clients, and it has been a major resource for employees in this small suburban town with declining community-based service alternatives.

ORGANIZATIONAL ASSISTANCE AS AN EXTENSION OF CLIENT SERVICE

A more typical form of organizational assistance occurs in behalf of individual assistance to employees in reference to their own personal difficulties. This occurs in several ways: as a form of advocacy in relation to specific client needs, as interventions designed to modify the attitudes or behaviors of significant others at the workplace that contribute to an employee's dysfunction, or through informal mediation when interpersonal problems between a client and coworkers are the issue. Frequently, for example, managers or coworkers collaborate in a client's denial about the seriousness of a drug problem. Often, personal problems get played out in work groups with each member contributing part of his or her own disturbance to a troubled work environment. A systems orientation illustrates the many ways in which a problem in one area of life has repercussions in every other area, and a systems-oriented treatment style often points to the need to intervene in the workplace as well as with individual employees and their families. This may be as basic as arranging for a period of in-patient treatment in such a way as to ensure that the information is handled appropriately by managers and human resource departments and that medical coverage will be available. In other situations, however, it may mean contacting managers or coworkers in an effort to work out personal problems between a client and such persons.

A client came to the EAP because he "hated his supervisor." The disagreements between the client and the supervisor were severe and their relationship had deteriorated to the point that it was affecting the work of the entire unit. A single joint interview was arranged in which specific communication problems between the two men were addressed. They were helped to evolve a set of working agreements about how to exchange the information necessary to get the work done without resorting to verbal abuse of one another. Meanwhile, the client continued to receive help with personal issues relating to chronic depression and deteriorating relationships with other significant people in his life.

Yet another type of intervention in behalf of troubled employees occurs when a supervisor or manager calls for help with an employee who may never appear at the EAP. In many organizations supervisors are promoted into their positions because they understand the details of production, not because of their people-handling skills. Nevertheless, they are expected to deal with all types of personal and interpersonal problems, and the failure of just one worker in an operation becomes a failure for the manager as well. Some organizations provide management development training to help with these issues, but even when such training is available managers may be reluctant to take advantage of it because to do so could be interpreted as admitting their personal inadequacy for the managerial role. Under such circumstances the EAP becomes a confidential source of information and guidance for those who are overwhelmed or simply perplexed by employee behavior they do not understand. In offering assistance the counselor makes use of his or her assessment skills to determine the relevant facts of the situation and what actions might help bring about improvement. In addition, it is important to alert managers to the fact that their own feelings and attitudes often are involved and that acknowledging these feelings and attitudes is not an indication that they are at fault.

A manager called the EAP because of serious problems he was having with two employees. One, a supervisor, was convinced that one of her new subordinates was sabotaging her efforts to complete a major project and she blamed the new worker for her own failures in performance. The second woman, the subordinate, was upset at the supervisor's attempts to control her every move and at the supervisor's inconsistent and contradictory work directives. Each had come to the manager complaining of the other's behavior, and the new worker was threatening to quit in spite of a promising first year with the company. As the manager discussed the situation with the EAP counselor it became clear that the supervisor was having other problems that signaled a more pervasive disturbance. Her appearance was deteriorating, she was quite withdrawn, her suspiciousness extended to other workers as well as to family, and she was complaining of physical symptoms suggestive of either physical or emotional illness. The manager was given guidance as to how to get help for her through either the EAP or the medical unit. He decided to assign the other employee a new project that would remove her gracefully from the supervisor's responsibility. He also was helped to deal with his own feelings toward the supervisor. She had been one of his own mentors who had trained him for his present role. It was disturbing for him to see her in this new light as someone he needed to protect. Neither employee ever came to the EAP. The manager later informed the counselor that the supervisor had been suffering from a serious medical condition that might have gone unnoticed for a longer period of time if the EAP had not been prepared to help.

ORGANIZATIONAL ASSISTANCE
TO WORK UNITS

Counselors may learn about work-related problems affecting a particular work group, or managers may invite the EAP in to deal with certain conflict situations that influence the overall performance of the unit. In one company it became apparent that the turnover in the female sales force was higher than that for males, a fact that was costing the company thousands of dollars annually in lost training costs. The EAP contractor was asked for ideas as to why this was happening. On the basis of preliminary research about the circumstances of the problem and individual and group discussions with saleswomen, the EAP counselor determined that a major factor contributing to the problem was divergent communication styles between the male supervisors and the female staff. The increase in the numbers of saleswomen was a recent development in the life cycle of this company, and the supervisors assumed they could conduct their training as they did with men. The women, on the other hand, brought with them their own assumptions about the work, how expectations should be communicated, and how production objectives would be prioritized—attitudes that their male supervisors had not encountered before. In this instance the decision was made to provide a series of group meetings to help the supervisors deal with the issues and with their own frustrations at being well intentioned but misunderstood, as well as to offer some basic content about how men and women communicate differently. The training for new saleswomen was modified to incorporate a number of the insights gleaned from all of the discussions.

In another program, a similar problem was recognized by the in-house EAP counselor, who identified several women managers who felt they were being stymied in their professional advancement because of a "glass ceiling" that allowed them to get so far and no further. A time-limited and confidential series of group meetings led by the counselor dealt with both the emotional battering these women were experiencing as well as various strategies they could generate and use to counteract the unreceptive organizational environment.

In a hospital setting, a large number of employees from a particular unit were coming to the EAP individually because of what turned out to be escalating pressures for overtime work. With the consent of these employees, the EAP counselor contacted the unit manager, who was similarly overwhelmed by expectations for performance that neither she nor her staff could realistically fulfill. With the manager's support, the counselor initiated a series of unit meetings in which the problems were redefined as residing within the organization, not the individual workers. Simply acknowledging this fact helped to relieve some of the stress all unit members were experiencing and the conflictual relationship that had been developing between the manager and her staff. They were able to redirect their energies toward using existing mechanisms within the human resource department to make a case for additional staff and reduced overtime.

Features of this type of assistance include the work-related focus of the discussion and a relatively small target group. This does not mean the personal and emotional implications of the work problems are ignored; frequently, discussions about these issues are a major part of dealing with the problem effectively. Although the target group may represent only a small slice of the total organizational profile, the consequences of the problem and its reduction can be far reaching, having profound effects on others not directly involved.

ORGANIZATIONAL TRAUMA—
CRITICAL INCIDENT DEBRIEFING

At one time or another most EAP counselors will encounter special problems that occur at the workplace that generally are acknowledged to be traumatic or of crisis proportions to a significant percentage of the workforce. Common examples are company mergers, downsizing, or the death—perhaps onsite—of a coworker. Less common examples include incidents of physical or psychological violence (Engel, 1987) perpetrated by either other coworkers or the public, such as attacks on transit workers (Gallo & Reisner, 1992). EAPs are typically among the first units of a company asked to deal with such events. In some settings EAP staff may have primary responsibility for coordinating all of the activities required to minimize the effects of the trauma while supporting the organization's need to carry out its normal work responsibilities.

A therapeutic response to such crises usually requires various combinations of individual counseling, organizational consultation, and group sessions ranging from small discussion groups to organization-wide informational meetings. In addition, it is likely to require the involvement of a number of different groups and offices within the organization to address the problem. Professional EAP counselors typically draw from a knowledge base rooted in crisis theory (see Chapter 7) and post-traumatic stress disorders (PTSD) as a basis for intervening in these emergency situations. Crisis theory provides both (a) a powerful explanatory theory base for helping counselors and clients understand the confusing internal and behavioral manifestations of a crisis state and (b) a predictable and time-tested set of interventions that are effective in diminishing the consequences of a crisis. An understanding of PTSD allows the counselor to interpret to others the potential long-term effects of a crisis reaction, knowledge that can help to diminish the force of such reactions or help to determine when other types of treatment and supportive help are indicated (Figley, 1985; McFarlane, 1990).

Trauma Response Plan

Ideally, the place to start dealing with crisis situations is before they occur. Increasingly employers are recognizing the advantages of having an existing written plan in place that spells out general guidelines, areas of responsibility, and operating principles to be followed in the event of an organizational crisis. Although such plans cannot anticipate all of the emergencies that might occur, they can diminish a portion of the disorganization, immobilization, and anxiety that can turn a serious problem into a major disaster (Walsh & Ruez, 1987). Certain work sites are prone to certain types of problems. Law enforcement personnel are potential victims of violence each time they go out on the streets (Brennan, Kyster, Vinton, & Citta, 1987). Cashiers, bank clerks, and others who handle money are at risk for burglary, assault, and both physical and psychological injuries. Jobs that involve high risk for physical injury, such as construction or the handling of hazardous substances, are also work settings that have a greater potential for trauma and that need to prepare an organizational response in the event that one occurs. However, any workplace can experience the death of an employee on the job, the suicide of a manager, or the maiming of a line worker in an industrial accident, and these, too, can benefit by a well-thought-out plan of organizational response. The tasks associated with instituting such a policy, however, can be difficult and time-consuming.

Walsh and Ruez (1987) suggest that a trauma response plan needs to take into consideration two key elements: certain principles of operation that will serve as a basis for making choices and decisions and a set of guidelines that spells out what needs to be done, in what order, and who is responsible for doing each task (see Table 9.1). An example of a statement of principle would be that in the event of a trauma the safety, security, and psychological well-being of victims and their families will be the prime concerns. In a patient care setting the principle might be restated to place the well-being of patients as the priority concern. Guidelines should include statements as to who should be in charge when a trauma occurs, such as the senior onsite person; who will have responsibility for coordinating security, medical care, and communication internally and externally; and what follow-up interventions will be required of managers or auxiliary staff (Walsh & Ruez, 1987). Companies have different internal resources that can be called upon to participate in a trauma response. Hospitals, for example, often have both medical and psychiatric personnel and usually chaplains or religious consultants who can be called upon to see victims of trauma as soon as possible. Most firms have security staff or communications officers who can play a major role in minimizing the spread of panic.

In working with an institution in the development of the plan, a place to start is often a review of its history to determine the types of situations that might have occurred in the past and how they were handled. People's reminiscences of their own reactions and concerns demonstrate the value

Table 9.1

Examples of Principles and Guidelines That Can Be Followed When Dealing
With Worksite Trauma

Principles and Guidelines

Examples of Principles

In a trauma situation, the safety, security, and psychological well-being of the victim and those surrounding the victim, as well as their families, will be the prime concern.

Securing the dangerous area or the perpetrator, as applicable, to avert further trauma will be of first-order importance.

Communication about the event to employees in the worksite and to their families, when indicated, will be accomplished swiftly and through company officials rather than usual media processes.

A major effort will be made to provide employees with as much factual information as possible about the event and to respond in an organized, systematic, and swift way to the proliferation of nonfactual rumors about the traumatic event and its ramifications.

Traumatic events generally create physical, psychological, and social symptoms of distress for victims, and intervention should address all these facets. Immediate relatives of victims are also victims and should have access, through the auspices of the organization, to the same array of intervention services.

Examples of Guidelines

The senior person on-site at a trauma scene will have responsibility for initiating a response to the event.

Communication of specific trauma facts to the senior official in the work division will be a first order of business, and that person will coordinate the various personnel activities and services that may be needed (e.g., medical, industrial relations, substitute workers, communications, and family contacts).

As early as possible, formal authoritative information will be given to all worksite employees about what has happened and what responses are being planned. A fact sheet is highly desirable, and verbal communication in addition is better still.

Communication with the media should be the designated duty of one person, and all external communications should be made through that individual.

Responsibility for contact with immediate relatives of victims should be designated by the senior division official and, if the relatives are needed on site, transportation should be made available for them.

With appropriate consultation, the on-site medical unit (or personnel unit if no medical unit is present) will be responsible for triage for those affected by the trauma. Prominent physical and psychological concerns take first priority, followed by services to those who are clearly affected but uninjured. When indicated, relatives of employees will be contacted so that their capacity for support may be activated. When public information about the trauma is abundant, employees should be encouraged to contact their relatives in order to provide accurate information about their well-being.

In the days and weeks immediately following the trauma, brief factual updates should be provided to employees, along with reminders regarding how to gain access to medical and/or psychological services if needed.

Within 4 to 6 weeks after the trauma, managerial personnel should review the event and the responses made to it; evaluate these components with an eye toward the prevention of similar events, when possible; and critique corporate responses to the event. Such evaluations should be narratively summarized and employees should be informed about the conclusions.

The use of an external consultant for dealing with the psychological and medical aspects of a trauma is highly recommended. Such a person, simply because of being removed from the direct corporate impact of the event, can offer knowledge and perspective about appropriate alternatives and can serve as a buffer to the often harsh reactions experienced by employees. When an internal consultant is used, he or she should play the lead role and the external consultant should be used as a more general resource. Prior specifications of both an internal and an external consultant and the roles to be taken by each will expedite the intervention activities.

SOURCE: Walsh & Ruez (1987). *EAP Digest,* July/August 1987. Reprinted with permission of *EAP Digest.*

of being better prepared to deal with emergencies of any type. As with most institutional interventions, it is important to involve as many levels of the organization as possible in the task of identifying key elements of the trauma plan. Not only does this ensure that the plan will be sensitive to the unique requirements of a particular workforce; the shared problem solving involved in its development also helps to educate people about its existence.

Earlier I referred to the cultural attitudes that still perpetuate an image of the worker as someone who should be able to handle all the stresses of the job without allowing them to negatively influence his or her personal life. Engel (1987) suggests that individual and institutional denial of the effects of violence and trauma on employees and their families is widespread as well. Employers, employees, and coworkers minimize, ignore, and even ridicule the after-effects of a crisis event. This is especially true among workers who believe that such traumas are a normal and expected part of their job experience because of the nature of their work or among those in caretaking positions, such as medical personnel, who think that because they are responsible for the well-being of others they should not be experiencing job-related behavioral symptoms themselves. Managers often feel that they should have the knowledge and skills necessary to handle any situation, even those for which they have had no preparation. Such unrealistic attitudes can inhibit the development of a trauma response plan.

Education of significant individuals and groups within a company is, therefore, a major component of developing a trauma response policy statement. If the organization remains indifferent to the need for such a statement, it is important that the EAP devise one for its own personnel so they have a basis on which to act quickly in an emergency situation.

It is important that any plan and the organizational education associated with its development include reference to the psychological as well as the physical effects of trauma and how closely the two are linked in crisis reactions. It is relatively easy for the average layperson to understand that physical wounds require attention and an opportunity to heal; it is more difficult for most to acknowledge either the extensive psychological damage caused by crises or the time and attention required to heal such wounds. Often managers and coworkers assume that employee reactions to unseen emotional wounds are a form of malingering, and their intolerance and lack of understanding can complicate recovery. Communicating the message to everyone in an organization that the emotional effects of crises are as devastating as physical damage can lessen the impact of crisis and the confounding effects of having to deal with unfamiliar and unanticipated emotional reactions, both one's own and those of others.

Gallo and Reisner (1992) developed an effective and poignant way of communicating these concepts in a public transit organization through the use of training sessions developed and now taught by employees who are survivors of personal and organizational crises. Both face-to-face training sessions and videos are used. The videos include interviews with bus drivers and other employees who have been victims of physical attacks or "jumpers," who are people who attempt suicide by throwing themselves in front of a bus or a train, which apparently is a fairly common event. In the video these employees share their intense feelings of guilt and terror at returning to the job, as well as their experiences in recovering from the trauma, communicating a powerful and authentic statement to coworkers about how to handle such events should they occur.

Whenever possible, some rehearsal of the trauma plan is important to provide training to key personnel in how to behave should a crisis occur. Included in such training is the recognition that an actual crisis probably will not unfold in exactly the same way as the rehearsal, but the experience of moving through the stages of a trauma response can significantly reduce both confusion and panic in an actual occurrence.

Dealing With the Crisis

In the event of an actual trauma EAP counselors need to be systems orientated in their assessment of the crisis; they need to think of how the total organization and its subunits have been influenced. A priority concern is to determine as quickly and accurately as possible what happened, where, and who has been most immediately affected. Later, the definition as to who are the victims of the crisis may be broadened to include others whose exposure to the full dimensions of the trauma were unrecognized, delayed, or blunted. It may be necessary to see the site of the event to make these assessments, but this is not always possible, particularly if there is any continuing danger. Generally, in most situations a manager or department head will assume responsibility for both immediate decisions and delegation of responsibilities, such as deciding what parts of the organization need to be mobilized, who determines which employees are at greatest risk, who will notify family members, or how Worker's Compensation claims are to be dealt with.

The major responsibilities of EAP counselors are to make quick determinations as to the emotional state of employees most directly exposed to the trauma, to initiate immediate crisis intervention, and to prepare for critical incident debriefings (Mitchell, 1983). As stated earlier, crisis theory informs us of the importance of immediate intervention to prevent greater emotional decompensation and to forestall any premature efforts on the part of victims to minimize, disassociate from, or otherwise deny their feelings (Golan, 1978; Parad & Parad, 1990). Because of the recognized importance of immediate intervention, attendance at the debriefings should be mandatory for those directly involved. Too many costs are associated either with failure to identify seriously traumatized employees or with communicating an ambivalent message as to the importance of getting help. If large numbers of employees are affected it may be necessary to collaborate with other human resource personnel, consultants, or contracted professionals to reach as many potential victims as possible within the shortest time after the event.

Crisis debriefings can be conducted in large group meetings, smaller group discussions, or individual counseling sessions. Large group meetings should include no more than 25 people as larger groups may be difficult to manage. Fundamental objectives of the interventions include help in diminishing the debilitating effects of fear, anxiety, and psychological dislocation generated by the trauma; helping employees to reestablish their normal functioning as soon as possible; and, finally, a preventative thrust directed toward reducing the probability of related problems erupting at a later time up to and including full-blown post-traumatic stress disorders (McFarlane, 1990). The interventive technology is similar to that discussed in Chapter 6. Although it is important to know the actual events associated with the trauma, the perceptions and special meanings people place on these events are equally important (McFarlane, 1990). Debriefing sessions include encouragment of discussion among members about what occurred. Constructing a chronology of events and the use of group process restores these events to full consciousness and reduces the probability of the events becoming repressed or forgotten. It is helpful to acknowledge with the group that not everyone will react to a traumatic event in the same way, and that different reactions should not be a source of concern.

Whatever form the intervention takes, a priority consideration is to communicate accurate information to employees about what has occurred. Cognitive confusion and distortions are inevitable aspects of crisis. As described by Walsh and Ruez (1987), the rumors surrounding any crisis begin immediately, and if left unchecked they serve to fuel the terror of the victims. Accurate information, even distressing information, is likely to have a calming effect because people then know the reality they are faced with. Not knowing, only imagining, the full dimensions of a crisis frustrates people's problem-solving ability and their sense that they have control over either themselves or what is happening to them. The need for accurate information continues, and part of the development of the trauma plan should include attention to who is responsible for ensuring that accurate information is consistently available, possibly including periodic fact sheets with updated information (Walsh & Ruez, 1987).

Following the immediate effects of trauma, it is important to identify and reach out to others who may have special issues associated with the crisis that could be overlooked. One EAP contractor, in addition to running a series of groups for laid off employees, conducted special groups for the managers who had to decide who would be terminated while simultaneously dealing with their guilt about doing so and their fears that they might be next on somebody else's list. In another situation (Walsh & Ruez, 1987), an attacker could not find his own supervisor and so killed another instead. Support to the actual victim's family was immediate, but the counselor soon realized that the intended victim and his family also would need assistance. Other special target groups included the employees who had worked side by side with the perpetrator without recognizing his potential for violence and those employees responsible for cleaning up the murder site afterward. Many employees develop unrealistic guilt about what they did or did not do to precipitate the crisis; this is especially true of immediate coworkers or those in authority or decision-making roles. Such feelings and other delayed reactions can continue to erupt over long periods of time.

This points to the need to include, as part of the total response to trauma, follow-up assessments of its continuing impact, both institutionally and in terms of individual employees. A major crisis can truly poison the life of an organization, eroding the effectiveness and drive of people at every level. The need to educate about both the event itself and the longer-term effects of crisis continues, with special attention directed toward helping managers recognize delayed reactions among their unit members. There is likely to be a thrust from some quarters of the company to "put it behind us" and get back to business as usual. This can be healthy and part of the recovery process, but often it is premature and represents an effort to stifle still unresolved emotions and continuing problems. The EAP counselor needs to be able to make this distinction and to discourage, when necessary, any efforts to pretend that nothing really serious occurred. In most situations a permissive rather than an overly restrictive policy regarding the timing of the official closure of trauma services will be of greater benefit to the organization.

It may be helpful to involve all levels of a company in a post mortem when the immediate problems have been dealt with to analyze all that has occurred, why it happened, the short- and long-term consequences, and what needs to be done to reduce the risk of the same thing happening again. Employees find it gratifying just to be listened to and to be assured that the company is making an effort to protect them from future trauma. When there have been severe injuries or loss of life, memorial services and ritual closures can honor the victims and facilitate the healing of the survivors. As in the case of private, individual crisis, organizations may experience problems on anniversary dates or when conditions are similar to those that preceded the crisis. Education and information again become potent tools in helping people and systems anticipate, understand, and assimilate the associated feeling states. Anniversary memorials and rituals can be helpful here as well.

An often overlooked element in considering how to handle an organizational trauma is the significance of the consequences of the crisis to EAP counselors and other helpers. The EAP staff are just as vulnerable to the personal trauma induced by a worksite crisis as are any other employees (Webb, 1990). Ruez describes her own close-to-overwhelming personal reactions upon rushing to the site of an onsite homicide and seeing the bloody room where the assault occurred (Walsh & Ruez, 1987). Having a trauma response plan can keep counselors functioning in spite of their own crisis reactions, but at some point attention must be directed toward allowing the helpers to acknowledge that they are also in crisis and need to process the feelings and events in a personal context. This can be done with each other, with other professionals, or through a support group formed for this purpose (Epperson-SeBour, 1990; Webb, 1990). The key interventions, as with clients, are to talk about what has occurred; to acknowledge the grief, fear, guilt, and inadequacy that helpers typically feel; and to allow time at the worksite and in private to process continuing reactions as they occur.

INFLUENCING
THE ORGANIZATIONAL CULTURE

At times the EAP can intervene in the organization to bring about changes in attitudes that are undermining the welfare of both the company and those employees trying to achieve recovery from addictions or emotional illness. Certain firmly held stereotypes about what constitutes preferred behavior can have seriously erosive effects on employees, frustrating their attempts to function more productively on the job or to make better use of the services available to them. Counselors experience difficulty in supporting recovering clients in organizations where alcohol abuse is the norm and drugs are bought and sold openly on the job. Assistance directed toward helping chemically dependent employees in such settings is undermined by the organizational subculture that places a positive value on regular and heavy drinking and other forms of substance abuse (Fine et al., 1982). As one person put it, in her organization there was no stigma attached to drug use, only to being in recovery.

In some settings characterized by such attitudes, EAPs have mounted full-scale efforts directed at all levels of the organization to change beliefs and to create a climate that, at the very least, will not dilute the efforts of the EAP staff. A typical strategy includes informational and educational efforts directed toward employees and their families about substance abuse in terms of costs, illness, accidents, family disorganization, and productivity. Information can be dispensed in meetings (often poorly attended), bulletins, posters, fliers, paycheck inserts, and even direct mailings to the homes of employees. The same techniques can be applied to problems of discrimination or harassment and to the issues involved in working with terminally ill coworkers.

In an effort to provide help to recovering clients, EAPs also have directed efforts toward establishing alternative subcultures as an onsite refuge for individuals who are experiencing difficulty coping with the toxic effects of their work situation. For example, in one setting, if consent could be obtained, recovering clients were put in touch with one another to establish an informal buddy system so they would have an immediate on-the-job resource besides the EAP for those times when organizational pressures became too great. One organization, after mounting a campaign of several years' duration directed at altering attitudes about drinking and drug use, established an onsite recovery group after earlier efforts to do so had failed. Although the overall organizational culture has remained somewhat "soft" on drug use, the situation has improved enough that participation in the recovery group is assuming a status of its own.

THE EAP AND ORGANIZATIONAL POLICY

This form of organizational assistance involves the use of the expertise of the EAP staff to help develop various policy positions especially relevant to the health and welfare of employees. EAP staff, for example, have been directly involved in translating the directives of the Drug-Free Workplace Act (DFWA) to specific workplaces. Other examples include the development of the trauma response plan discussed earlier, the formation of an organizational response to HIV-infected employees, enhancing the multicultural adaptation of a workforce, and the decision to establish a family leave policy. Depending on the size, makeup, and style of the workplace, initiatives for such policies may occur in the EAP or another part of the firm. In most settings the EAP typically is involved in some aspect of the decision making or the implementation of the policy.

Involvement in such activities assumes that EAP personnel bring to the process specialized knowledge and expertise. Their direct work with troubled employees provides a unique perspective on the many forms of social, psychological, and medical concerns the workforce is experiencing and something of the costs to the employer that these issues involve. Counselors also need to be sensitive to the larger organizational needs and stresses that shape what an employer can and cannot do, or to which particular subcultural factors need to be taken into consideration in planning or initiating policy decisions. Finally, it is most important that EAP staff be well informed about the issues under consideration. This usually requires research or investigation into topics of concern and an analysis of how the information is relevant to each particular workplace.

Currently many firms are experiencing their first encounters with HIV-infected employees and discovering in the process that neither individuals nor companies are well prepared for the complex reactions the knowledge of infection generates in the victim, coworkers, managers, and staff. Although many other types of problems lend themselves to policy planning at the organizational level, the issue of the HIV-infected employee provides a case example of the activities EAP counselors might encounter in assisting an organization in its efforts to cope responsibly with this growing concern.

Knowledge about the existence and extent of HIV-infected employees can become available in different ways, such as through claims for medical benefits, from managers and supervisors, as a result of self-referrals to the EAP, and sometimes through general rumors. Whatever the source, to develop a responsible policy regarding this issue it is necessary to obtain accurate information from reliable sources within the organization, particularly from human resources. Furthermore, the development and implementation of the policy almost certainly will require a collaborative effort from these departments.

As is true of the trauma response plan discussed earlier, it is desirable to have in operation a plan for dealing with HIV-infected employees before the need arises, but in reality most organizations choose not to deal with the problem until the first case becomes a reality. The nature of the illness is such that individuals and systems participate in the denial that it can touch so close to home. Persistent myths about who does or does not get the disease lull people into the belief that the problem will remain the concern of someone else or that the numbers in any company will be so small that they can be handled on an ad hoc basis. Paul Hewitt, Midwest regional director of Archeus, Inc., a national EAP contractor, suggests that it may be more effective to develop a policy that pertains to all types of serious chronic and/or terminal illness rather than just to AIDS or HIV infections.[2] Doing so helps to mitigate some of the denial associated with AIDS and HIV, and helps to make the point that other illnesses carry psychosocial problems and stigma similar to those associated with AIDS. The larger numbers of employees experiencing other serious medical conditions argues for the desirability of adopting a broader policy.

Employers are faced with rising insurance costs, and terminally ill employees or dependents can bankrupt smaller firms or organizations. The important issue of medical costs will certainly be the central feature in any organizational response. The ultimate decision about the extent of coverage depends on multiple factors, including the options offered by different insurance providers, the size and makeup of the workforce, and a changing governmental role in health-care policy. However, a clear-sighted policy can include, for example, consideration of how affected employees can be assured that all of the services that a person is eligible for under their insurance are actually being received whatever the nature of the coverage. Such a policy also could note other types of services employees and their families might need that are available through means other than medical insurance, such as respite care, self-help or other groups, volunteer organizations, or government assistance.

EAP staff can play a major role in becoming as informed as possible about the problem. This is often more difficult than it sounds, as counselors must come to terms with their own ignorance, stereotypes, and fears (Gilman, 1991). Education of the total workforce is, of course, a major aspect of dealing with the issue of AIDS and HIV infection, but even before this is possible it is necessary to make sure that those persons involved in creating corporate policy are themselves well briefed. In addition to general knowledge about the nature of the illness and people's reactions to it, they also need to understand issues such as the organizational implications of any antidiscriminatory state or local statutes relevant to their situation. Once management and the policy framers have an understanding of the full scope of the issues, the next level of education should be directed toward the overall workforce. Information about the extent of AIDS and HIV infection within the general population, who is and who is not at risk, basic factors related to prevention, and the availability of services to detect or treat the problem are relevant areas of education.

In addition to the medical progression of the illness and legal and cost factors to the company, it is also important to be aware of the emotional and psychological impacts of the condition on employee victims and those close to them. The EAP often is involved in interventions with both these individuals and their families, and with those in the work environment who need information, reassurance, the opportunity to ventilate, and often the opportunity to be of realistic help. Dealing with the threat of terminal illness in a colleague or family member, or confronting the fears of such a threat to oneself, provokes a type of emotional reaction that must be handled as a crisis, requiring the crisis intervention techniques discussed above. Managers certainly are not immune to these concerns and may require EAP staff support. Having a well-developed policy in place can help them respond more effectively to reduce their own anxiety and organizational stress.

In summary, EAP counselors can assume a number of roles in influencing the development of organizational policy in reference to serious illness or other health and welfare concerns: as an informational resource about the issues in terms of both general knowledge about the topic and its specific significance to this organization; as educators of management and employees about its impact on the work environment; in the development of both internal and external resources that will help deal with the problem; in the coordination of these resources; as counselors to affected employees, their families, and coworkers; and as case managers to ensure that the victims and their families are in touch with the mix of services they need and that these services are providing the full range of help needed.

NOTES

1. I am indebted to Joanne Tolbert, former director of the Personal Consultation Service of Loyola University, Chicago, for this descriptive term and for her conceptualization about how to provide such assistance to organizations.
2. Personal conversation.

Chapter 10

PERSONAL AND
PROFESSIONAL ISSUES

Occupational practice has great appeal to professionals who work in traditional social service or welfare settings, often with seriously impaired
clients who have limited economic, emotional, or social resources. Although there are advantages and compensations for work of this type, the
rewards, in terms of income, recognition, and autonomous functioning are
often less than those assumed to be operating in private firms and corporations. The number of professionals interested in making a career shift from
traditional practice to the occupational setting always has outpaced the
expansion of employment opportunities in the occupational field. In addition, there is a growing cadre of professionals whose graduate education
includes specialized training for employee assistance practice, practitioners
who expect to spend their professional careers in work-based counseling
programs.

However, not everyone entering the field or making a career shift from
another form of practice finds the workplace a compatible professional
environment. Just as not all counselors can work effectively in child welfare
or criminal justice, others will find corporations confusing in terms of their
expectations or EAP contracting firms too demanding of their employees'
time and personal commitment. In this chapter I discuss a number of the
organizational, professional, and value issues associated with occupational practice, and I suggest several personal and professional considerations
that should enter into decisions either to commit to or to leave employee
assistance. These comments should not discourage interested professionals

from considering employee assistance as a career choice. They are intended to introduce a note of reality into the career planning process and to help practitioners formulate the types of questions to ask prospective EAP employers.

ORGANIZATIONAL ISSUES

Throughout this book I have emphasized the need to understand that the workplace is a unique practice arena compared to traditional settings. I have stressed how important it is for EAP counselors and would-be counselors to learn how to evaluate both the factors that apply to occupational systems in general and the specific characteristics that define a particular setting. It is equally important that the professional take the time to assess the implication of these factors for one's own personal working style, clinical philosophy, and career objectives.

Long-Term Career Options

Respondents in my survey (Cunningham, 1990) commented on an inherent problem in occupational practice: the lack of any clear, recognizable career path in workplace settings. To some extent this is a problem for human service professionals in general, a problem made worse by declines in overall economic growth. Entry into the EAP field is still difficult. In spite of expanding opportunities, there continues to be a great deal of competition for openings that occur, and position applicants are expected to have stronger credentials in terms of both clinical and EAP experience. After investing so much time and effort in locating that first job in the field, new practitioners often are not prepared for some of the limitations that exist in terms of long-term career advancement.

Career advancement in employee assistance usually occurs in one of several ways: moving up the administrative ladder within a firm into non-EAP positions, being promoted within EAP contracting firms as they expand, assuming a program director position, or moving to the directorship of a larger EAP. Some practitioners leave their EAPs to move into organizational development, benefits management, and other human resource employment. Usually such moves occur only after the person has obtained additional training or education, but this is not always the case. Other EAP personnel achieve professional advancement through new administrative roles in larger companies or nationally known EAPs. Competition for such positions is fierce, and most practitioners are faced with the alternative of remaining with the same organization for a number of years or negotiating lateral transfers to other positions that may offer more personal or monetary attractions. This situation may be changing as EAPs are merged with other types of health-care and benefits operations; the picture is currently too fluid to make any hard and fast predictions.

Although most of the respondents in the survey (Cunningham, 1990, 1992) were very satisfied with their decision to enter the EAP field, some expressed ambivalence about remaining in it, usually because of increasing limitations on clinical work and direct client contact. When asked what they would like to be doing 5 years into the future, only one third were fairly certain about remaining in the EAP field. Most of these expected to be practicing in some other context, to be further up the administrative ladder, or to be more involved in clinical work. Others either were quite definite that they would be in another form of practice or were uncertain that they wanted to remain in an EAP. As an alternative to, or in combination with, EAP work, counselors expected to be doing more direct practice, teaching, and either managerial or clinical consultation.

Adversarial Nature of the Workplace

Social workers and other mental health practitioners are conditioned by training to assume a neutral, mediating stance among various elements of a system as they work with troubled individuals and families. It is sometimes difficult to translate this into a workplace setting where adversarial and competitive relationships are frequently the norm. These attitudes are not viewed as negative but rather as facilitative of the goals of the organization and its members. It is sometimes necessary for EAP staff to recognize that there is a perceived benefit to retaining a degree of tension and conflict—a competitive edge—within organizations that are themselves competing with other firms for customers, contracts, and expanding market shares. Whether such beliefs actually are supportive of a company's goals or the general economic well-being of a community can be debated. What needs to be understood by EAP staff, however, are the overt and latent convictions on the part of managers and hourly employees alike that competition is desirable. This belief drives much of the decision making and process in most profit-making organizations. It also is present in varying degrees in not-for-profit settings that must compete for their share of philanthropic or tax dollars.

The continuing life of an EAP may depend on the director's ability to understand and work with this reality. For example, program directors may have to adopt a similar competitive stance at the point of budget reviews or contract renewals to justify the allocation of a company's resources to the EAP instead of to some other division within the organization. Even more important is the recognition that the internal marketing of the program never really stops, and that all exchanges with management need to communicate information and conviction about how the EAP is contributing to the organization's goals. Understanding the adversarial aspects of work settings is also important in understanding clients: how these attitudes may be contributing to personal problems, how they may be frustrating attempts to resolve difficulties, and why it is so crucial that worker confidentiality be maintained if knowledge of a personal problem can be used to undermine the perception of the employee's value to a company. In addition, if an employee group is acculturated to a climate in which every exchange is tinged with self-serving, adversarial, or competitive attitudes, it is often difficult to explain to clients that the EAP is different. (One practitioner I know has a large map of Switzerland on her office door as a way of communicating this message.) Counselors need to adopt a flexible stance that allows them to recognize when adversarial positions are functional for the organization, the employees, or the program, and when they are not.

Discrimination

EAPs are not unlike other parts of the U.S. workforce in terms of latent and sometimes overt examples of discrimination. Teare's study (1987) documented a wage inequity of almost $10,000 annually between men and women in the field. Successive studies conducted by the Association of Labor and Management Consultants on Alcoholism, recently changed to the Employee Assistant Professionals Association (ALMACA/EAPA), have reported smaller but persistent wage ratios in spite of the fact that many women have more advanced degrees than their male counterparts. Women and minorities are less likely to be in administrative or leadership positions within their companies and in the field generally. Ageist bias may be more an issue for younger persons interested in the EAP field than for older professionals. EAP personnel are expected to be able to function with a high degree of autonomy and to have both counseling and managerial experience. Also, the mature professional is seen as communicating a more reassuring image as someone to confide in about personal problems. In view of these expectations it is often difficult for younger persons to be taken seriously as potential EAP counselors.

Clientele

Practitioners find both advantages and disadvantages in the type of client and the clinical work required of EAP staff. For the most part counselors are captivated by the higher-functioning clients, who differ normatively from the more severely disabled and disadvantaged clients in traditional settings. EAP clients often demonstrate an ability to apply the insights gained in their EAP interviews rapidly and constructively, to the extent that these gains may be viewed suspiciously by traditional clinicians. The short-term nature of most client cases is viewed as a disadvantage by some counselors, although experiences and attitudes vary depending on the nature of the program. In settings that rely primarily on external providers for ongoing contact, the EAP counselor rarely has the opportunity to witness eventual outcomes. In in-house programs or those that provide ongoing treatment, the situation may provide more of an opportunity to see the continuing effects of intervention, not just within counseling sessions, but also in the person's work life. As one practitioner noted, it was particularly gratifying to be able to see former clients doing well in their job-related relationships long after they had been helped to resolve pressing problems through the EAP.

One of the strongest motivations for people remaining in the field is the fact that they have the opportunity to see clients in a very short time after their problem has become manifest. Although this sometimes contributes to the sense of burnout, it also is viewed as a positive by many clinicians. It facilitates accurate diagnosis. The client's high level of motivation to relieve the stress helps in the referral process, and the personal and concrete resources that employed clients possess become assets in carrying through any treatment plan. Occupational practice also provides the opportunity to intervene quickly before problems grow so severe that the probability of resolution is decreased. Primary prevention becomes a realistic objective in EAP practice, not just an ideal, because of the related activities associated with the program's educational functions. Informing a workplace about early symptoms of drug or alcohol abuse, potential problems of fetal alcoholism syndrome, ways to handle holiday depression, or the development of better parenting skills allows employees to deal with incipient problems on their own before such problems ever reach the stage of actual dysfunction.

Most traditional counseling practice is carried out in settings that are not part of the normal life space of the clients. For the most part clients come to the attention of agencies or welfare services when they can no longer function in their usual life roles. Such clients generally are seen in hospitals, mental health centers, or residential treatment centers at points in their lives when they are most vulnerable and marginal in their abilities to function. In occupational practice, however, counselors deal with clients in their normal life space. This fosters an attitude toward help-giving based more on a health rather than a pathology or "failure" model. EAP clients are apt to feel less stigmatized by services received at the workplace (Kurzman, 1983), and employee clients increasingly tend to see such services as a benefit or an entitlement. The thrust of the research concerning optimum conditions for service delivery suggests that such positive attitudes in and of themselves contribute to treatment effectiveness (Garfield, 1986).

The workplace confers a degree of power and credibility on the clinician very different from traditional settings, influencing how the counselor interacts with the client, the organization, and the community. Although negatives can be associated with the EAP's identification with management, as in issues of perceived threats to confidentiality, counselors also are seen as having both special insight into the workings of the organization and the power to intervene in ways not available to most employees. This is especially true of in-house programs, in which the counselor and the client are coworkers. The practitioner usually does have more understanding than clients as to the organizational realities that may be influencing their problems and has the ability to influence organizational process in ways not available to clients. This enhances the counselor's credibility as a problem solver and fosters in clients the belief in the counselor as a powerful ally.

Counselors' powers of expertise are as important in communicating with managers as with workers. This specialized knowledge about issues of human growth and development, interpersonal interactions, and effective means of intervention is expertise not generally shared within the organization. As one counselor described it: "A lot say that it's the first time they've talked about these things to anyone . . . ; many respond to the fact that I go beyond the obvious and can see things about their behavior they've never been aware of. It's like a light going on for them." In addition, the exceptional skills most counselors possess in being able to sort through the maze of external resources can assume almost epic proportions to the average layperson. For clinicians coming from traditional settings in which this expertise is routine, it is easy to underestimate the value placed on it in the field of occupational practice.

The Occupational Welfare System

Practice at the workplace provides counselors with a whole set of resources, part of what Titmus (1966) referred to as the occupational social welfare system. Such clients have access to a range of benefits through their company or union. Although these benefits are under increasing attack, the fact that EAP clients have incomes, savings, and personal and work-related support networks means that problem-solving options exist that frequently are not available to the unemployed or underclass clients encountered in many other fields of practice.

The workplace provides opportunities for linkages with some very powerful constituencies. As a society, we have a tendency to blame the victim for failures in functioning, and the massive failures considered typical of social welfare systems in general lend support to a cultural belief that people who require welfare are expendable. So, too, are those who are identified with welfare receivers as service providers. It is often difficult to secure resources for these residual clients no matter how genuine their need. This is less of a problem in the workplace because the well-being of a workforce is recognized as being important to the overall organization.

The location of EAPs in profit-making corporate structures confers a form of power on practitioners that facilitates their ability to access quality external providers quickly, a reality made possible because of the greater availability of funds, but also because of the status our culture assigns to business as compared to social welfare. As one pioneer in the field characterized his experiences, "When I worked for the . . . family service agency and tried to get a resource for a client, we could wait months. Now when I call and say, 'I'm with [a multinational corporation],' my requests get immediate attention."

Issues of status and prestige may seen trivial considerations to many; however, their absence can undermine a professional's energy, sense of worth, and commitment when continued over time. EAP work may provide a welcome combination of employment that is altruistic and capable of making a difference in the lives of troubled people, while at the same time providing a degree of power and societal validation of one's own professionalism.

Professional Autonomy

A major appeal of this work for many EAP professionals is the greater degree of professional autonomy they experience when compared to traditional practice other than private practice. The counselor is often the EAP manager, with continuing responsibility for shaping the ongoing life of the program. Associated with this fact is the opportunity EAPs provide for the development and exercise of a combination of skills—administrative, clinical, consultative, and educational—a combination that is rarely developed in other types of professional work.

Worker Burnout

These same circumstances also can contribute to worker burnout. Work stress is a realistic problem in many EAPs. Counselors are faced daily with the expectation that they will respond immediately and responsibly to an unfiltered variety of personal and organizational problems and crises. They must do so with a minimum of supervisory, consultant, or peer support. The labor-intensive nature of most programs does not allow much leeway for periods of high intake, staff illnesses, or other unpredictable alterations in the normal work flow. As with other types of professional burnout one of the remedies is to assume a balanced lifestyle that allows for practitioners' needs to be met as positively as possible. Even more important is the documentation of the need for internal supports such as consultation, stand-by personnel, adequate clerical staff, and expansion so the work of the EAP can be optimized.

PERSONAL ISSUES

Knowledge and Skill Gaps

Anyone entering occupational practice must be prepared to address any limitations in their knowledge and skills, limitations that can handicap their effectiveness as EAP counselors. Social workers or other mental health professionals may lack knowledge of economic theory, organizational structure, labor-management relations, substance abuse, and adult functioning and work role issues, among others. On the other hand, persons with a business or human resource background or those who have worked exclusively in substance-abuse treatment centers may lack a knowledge of various forms of emotional disorders or an understanding of different patterns of family functioning. They may lack the skills necessary to work with the medical and social welfare resource network to ensure that a client will be able to make the best use of the opportunities for help that are available.

Professional education specifically directed toward employee assistance counseling has been increasingly effective in preparing people more fully for work in this field, but no single educational design can anticipate all the unique variations of EAP practice or the changes that might occur in the field in the future. What is essential is the type of education that provides its initiates with the attitudes and skills necessary to maintain a process of continuing self-development and education to accommodate the inevitable changes and growth that will occur. This is part of the definition of a professional: someone who is capable of redefining his or her competence in the light of new issues and new challenges.

Personal Issues Regarding Addiction and Codependency

Even though the pattern of referrals in employee assistance has been shifting from an exclusive focus on chemical dependency to a broader range of problems, alcoholism and other forms of drug dependence remain major issues. Most people in our culture are exposed to addictions and addicted people in a variety of encounters. A significant proportion are likely to have experienced problems of alcoholism or other forms of substance abuse in their own families. To work effectively with chemically dependent and other troubled people it is important to come to terms with how these encounters have affected one's own life in the past and how they may be influencing behavior currently. It is too easily assumed that cognitive knowledge and academic training about such conditions somehow obviate the need to be concerned about the projection of one's own feelings onto client situations.

This is simply not true. It is my personal belief that one of the reasons psychodynamic explanations of addictions carried such force in the mental health community was because they fed into the denial systems of professionals concerning their own use or abuse of chemicals. If it could be argued that only certain types of inadequate personalities were capable of addiction, then seemingly stable, well-structured, functional individuals such as psychologists, psychiatrists, psychoanalysts, social workers, and academics were obviously immune. The extent to which such professionals could define addictions as belonging to classes or types of people very unlike themselves meant they could exempt their own behavior as a source of concern. Professionals must come to terms with their own behavior and that of their colleagues as a basic condition of presuming to extend help to others (Bissell & Haberman, 1984; Fausel, 1988; Reamer, 1992). It is important that people entering the EAP field engage in a period of self-analysis and review to assess their readiness to deal with problems and people that parallel their own experiences and concerns. Otherwise, too great a risk exists of being seduced into codependent and countertherapeutic exchanges with clients who are exquisitely adept at recognizing such vulnerabilities and exploiting them. A good place to begin this self-review is through self-help groups such as AA, Al-Anon, ACOA, and others. Personal therapy and informed consultation also are helpful in identifying potentially destructive countertransference behavior on the part of EAP practitioners.

VALUE ISSUES:
PROFESSIONAL IDENTITY AND CO-OPTATION

Professional identity is formed or challenged not just by the immediate circumstances in which practitioners find themselves; it is influenced as well by the larger body of professionals with whom they are associated. The first social workers to enter occupational practice in the 1970s had a particularly difficult time, as they were viewed with suspicion both by their EAP colleagues, who had different training backgrounds, and by other social workers, who often took a dim view of EAP practice in general, seeing it either as an abandonment of the traditional social-work clientele —the poor, the disadvantaged, the underdogs—or as a threat to the concept of clinical social work because of the short-term nature of client contact. One EAP director described the change in attitude she experienced when she moved from a traditional treatment position within a community mental health agency to its EAP contracting division. Although her credentials as a knowledgeable and gifted clinician were impeccable, her former colleagues reacted toward her in her new role as if she suddenly were less professionally reliable or clinically competent.

It takes very secure practitioners to withstand such dystonic images of their activities, persons who know the depths of their own professionalism and the value of the work they do regardless of the distortions that might occur. It may be helpful to keep in mind that EAP clients most often are the working poor and marginally independent men and women who are either ineligible for or unable to access other helping services. The EAP may be their sole source of getting timely professional help to deal with major problems in their lives, problems that are no less significant simply because the clients are employed. It is difficult to develop an ethical rationale for withholding professional services from any group of potential clients who wish to make use of them, particularly when these clients are largely responsible for funding many of the programs in which social workers operate through their tax dollars or charitable giving.

A particularly insidious aspect of negative attitudes toward occupational practice was an underlying assumption that people who chose the field were somehow less professional, less ethical, and more easily coopted than those who entered other types of practice. Bakalinsky (1980) raised the issue that the values of the social work profession were inherently incompatible with those of the profit-making sector, which was interpreted as impersonal and as seeing people as resources in the process of production, representing a means to an end and being essentially disposable. This was in contrast to a social welfare perspective that placed the individual at the center of a society's interest. In addition, there was concern that the confidentiality and general welfare of EAP clients would be placed in jeopardy by bosses and managers who would want to access records or influence the counseling process in ways that supported the company's interests rather than those of the client. From the perspective of more than a decade of changes in both professional counseling and U.S. business, Bakalinsky's concerns sound, on the one hand, naive and uninformed and, on the other hand, understated.

To a great extent the reality has been that EAPs are left mostly undisturbed by corporate managers in carrying out their day-to-day counseling responsibilities. There are, unquestionably, those settings and occasions in which varying types of interference do occur, but this is not the norm. It is clear to most firms that the confidentiality of the EAP is the most significant guarantee that it will be used by those employees who need it, and to compromise the program by undermining its credibility with staff is not in anyone's best interest. In addition, local and federal statutes concerning client rights to privacy and confidentiality have supported the EAP's insistence on confidentiality in the handling of employee interviews and records, and to do otherwise may expose the company to litigation. It should be noted that EAP staff must be actively involved in communicating these messages to an organization through a clear-cut policy statement, employee and managerial training, and interpretation to managers in individual case situations.

Nevertheless, there is a legitimate basis for concern that a number of fundamental professional and ethical positions are under attack in occupational practice, and this concern needs to be taken seriously by individuals and organizations in the EAP field. In both for-profit and not-for-profit organizations, bottom-line concerns that drive so much of the organization's formal and informal decision making can be a constraint on clinical work. This is also very true of EAP contracting firms, which must structure their organizations and services in ways that will ensure their own economic survival. The influences and pressures implied in such arrangements are far more complex than the kinds of concerns voiced more than a decade ago (Bakalinsky, 1980). It is not so much a question of the EAP counselor being at risk of becoming a tool of management by revealing the contents of client records or by using counseling sessions to steer clients in the direction of corporate goals and agendas. Rather, it is a question of having services curtailed or compromised by budgetary cutbacks, benefit restrictions, and escalating accountability forms and procedures that compete with the time needed to provide adequate service to employees.

Even more serious are those circumstances in which the counselor discovers that he or she is actually in competition with his or her own clients for the system's resources. This situation is not unique to occupational practice; it exists in social welfare agencies and private practice as well. The clinician needs to be aware of the extent to which such realities can influence assessment, intervention, and the choices and options made available to clients. Awareness contributes toward a more objective process of balancing the multiple needs of the client, the organization, and oneself when resources are limited or shrinking.

The availability of generous benefit packages helped finance the growth of the EAP field, private psychotherapy practice, and costly inpatient treatment for a wide variety of problems, as well as the attitude that this model constituted the best service to a company and its employees. It is my opinion that the unquestioned application of this model to all types of clients coming to EAPs has achieved the opposite effect, overtreating many conditions and creating a two-tier type of EAP service driven more by the availability of benefits than by client need and contributing unnecessarily to the rising cost of health benefits for client companies (De Rosa & Hickle, 1986). The complex network of providers that are dependent upon EAP referrals has introduced other ethical problems in the form of fee splitting, cronyism, and some of the abuses noted in Chapter 6. Although such problems can occur in any sector, contracting firms may be under particular pressure to provide quality service to companies and clients while at the same time remaining competitive in relation to other firms and to the escalating costs of doing business. Many EAP counselors are feeling the pressure of having to make clinical decisions based more on economic issues than on client need. It becomes more difficult for them to recite the rhetoric of policy statements about the nature of the EAP service in the light of shortcuts, disqualifications, and less than satisfactory decisions required of them on a day-to-day basis. In summary, if cooptation has occurred in this field it is likely that it is less in relation to interference by corporate bosses than as a result of the need for EAPs to identify with the values and methods of U.S. business in order to be taken seriously in an increasingly competitive arena or to flourish or simply survive economically.

The EAP field came partly of age—achieving its adolescence, so to speak —in the 1980s, a period of U.S. history characterized by the inflated evaluation of business and profit making, and by a view of growth and expansion that repudiated as "un-American" controls or sanctions on any money-making endeavor. Greed, growth, and expansion were values in their own right, and few, other than the most ingenuous, truly believed that the larger society would benefit from the "trickle-down" effects of such fervid self-promotion. It was a difficult era for EAP personnel to argue in favor of the prominence of individual rights or the expenditure of funds for humanitarian reasons alone. It was difficult, too, to find ways of meshing their own values as counselors with those of the corporate world in the light of existing stereotypes about "shrinks," social workers, and naive "do-gooders."

The time is at hand for EAP practitioners to decide whether it is more important to be identified as professionals capable of providing services not otherwise available at the workplace or as entrepreneurs able to buy, sell, or barter certain commodities like the "big boys" do. The decision in favor of professional standards is not counter to our best interests. For example, rather than dissipating our energies and powers by undermining the reputations of competitors in order to expand our own contract base, we accomplish more to ensure the continuation of the EAP field by re-affirming the value and the uniqueness of the service itself. To be professional implies, among other factors, an explicit code of ethics that provides a basis for the self-policing of behavior that guarantees that neither clients nor companies will be exploited in the interests of personal gain. There has been a growing disenchantment within and outside of the business world with the self-deception and dubious values of the 1980s to the extent that it is no longer hopelessly unfashionable to talk about ethics.

Appendix

MODEL ASSESSMENT TOOL

The following is a model client intake form. Instructions to the EAP counselor appear in parentheses. The initial client-problem question differs in respect to a voluntary referral or a supervisory referral. All other questions apply to all types of consultations.

Despite the length of the assessment tool, it is usually administered in one or two sessions. Administering the tool over a longer period of time, however, is left to the discretion of the EAP counselor.

In regard to interpreting the data gathered from this Model Assessment Tool: The following code (scoring) indicates the possible degree of seriousness and action to be taken to address the problem.

- A positive response to a one-star (*) question reflects a problem in an early stage.
- A positive response to a two-star (**) question reflects a critical problem; if a client has more than two positives in this category, immediate action is required.
- A positive response to a three-star (***) question reflects an emergency and need for immediate action.

A full drug use history would be done by the referral source, especially in outpatient and inpatient programs.

SOURCE: U.S. Department of Health and Human Services, Public Health Service, Alcohol, Drug Abuse, and Mental Health Administration. (1989). DHHS Publication No. (ADM) 89-158.

General Information

NAME _____

CURRENT ADDRESS _____

_____

_____

1. DATE OF BIRTH   ___ / ___ / ___

2. RACE (check one)

_____ White (Not of Hispanic Origin)

_____ Black (Not of Hispanic Origin)

_____ American Indian

_____ Alaskan Native

_____ Asian or Pacific Islander

_____ Hispanic—Mexican

_____ Hispanic—Puerto Rican

_____ Hispanic—Cuban

_____ Other Hispanic

3. RELIGIOUS PREFERENCE (check one)

_____ Protestant

_____ Catholic

_____ Jewish

_____ Islamic

_____ Other

_____ None

I.D. NUMBER _____

DATE OF INTERVIEW   ___ / ___ / ___

TIME BEGUN   ___:___

TIME ENDED   ___:___

CLASS:
_____ Intake
_____ Follow-up
_____ *Enter session number if appropriate

GENDER:
_____ Female
_____ Male

Employment/Support Status

1. Education Completed (GED = 12 years)

   _____ years   _____ months

2. Do you have a valid driver's license?

   _____ yes   _____ no

3. Do you have an automobile available for your use?
   (answer NO if no valid driver's license)

   _____ no   _____ yes

4. Company Position: (specify in detail)

   _____

5. Does someone contribute to your support in any way?

   _____ yes   _____ no

6. How many people depend on you for the majority of their food, shelter, etc.?

   _____

7. Salary Range:

    _____ Under 25,000

    _____ 25-40,000

    _____ 40-65,000

    _____ 65-100,000

    _____ 100-200,000

    _____ 200,000+

8. How long have you been working for the company?

_____

9. What was your first position?

_____

10. How long were you in that position?

_____

11. How many different positions have you held in the company?

_____

_____

12. Have you ever been disciplined?

_____

13. How many different employers have you worked for full-time since entering the work force?

_____

_____

**14. If voluntary referral, "What is it that brings you to the EAP office today?"

_____

_____

**15. If supervisory referral, "What is your understanding as to the circumstance that brought you to the EAP office today?"

_____

_____

_____

Now, we would like to ask you a few questions about your lifestyle.

Family Social Relationships

1. Marital Status:

_____ Married   _____ How many times?

_____ Remarried

_____ Widowed

_____ Separated

_____ Divorced

_____ Never Married

_____ Cohabitated

2. How long have you been in this marital status?

_____ years

_____ months

3. Are you satisfied with this situation?

_____ yes _____ no _____ indifferent

4. Usual living arrangements (past 3 years)

_____ With partner and children

_____ With sexual partner alone

_____ With children alone

_____ With parents

_____ With friends

_____ Alone

_____ Controlled environment

_____ No stable arrangements

5. How long have you lived in these arrangements?

_____ years   _____ months

6. Are you satisfied with these living arrangements?

_____ yes   _____ no   _____ indifferent

7. With whom do you spend most of your free time?

_____ Family

_____ Friends

_____ Alone

8. Are you satisfied with spending your free time this way?

_____ yes   _____ no   _____ indifferent

9. How many *close* friends (seen at least monthly) do you have?

_____

10. How many days in the past 30 have you had serious conflicts:

A. With your family?   _____

B. With other people? (excluding family)   _____

11. Have you had significant periods in which you have experienced serious problems with: (circle yes or no in both columns)

		Past 30 days		*In your life*	
A.	Mother	yes	no	yes	no
B.	Father	yes	no	yes	no
C.	Brothers/Sisters	yes	no	yes	no
D.	Sexual partner/Spouse	yes	no	yes	no
E.	Children	yes	no	yes	no
F.	Other significant family member	yes	no	yes	no
G.	Close friends	yes	no	yes	no
H.	Neighbors	yes	no	yes	no
I.	Coworkers	yes	no	yes	no

**Do any of the above have an alcohol problem? _____

Specify which group(s) by letters: _____

**Do any of the above have a drug problem? _____

Specify which group(s) by letters: _____

Health History

1. Explain your diet (i.e., supplements? When do you eat?)

_____

_____

2. How do you sleep? _____

_____

3. Are you troubled by frightening dreams?

Yes _____

No _____

If so, please explain: _____

_____

4. Are you under a doctor's care for any illness?

Yes _____

No _____

If so, please explain: _____

_____

5. Do you take any medication?

Yes _____

No _____

If so, please explain: _____

_____

6. How many times in your life have you been hospitalized for medical problems?

_____

(Include ODs, DTs, exclude detox.)

7. How long ago was your last hospitalization for a physical problem?

_____ (years)

_____ (months)

8. Do you have any chronic medical problems that continue to interfere with your life?

_____ Yes

_____ No

9. How many days have you experienced medical problems in the past 30?

_____

10. Do you use caffeine-containing products? How old were you when you started? How much do you use?

_____

_____

11. With regard to use of tobacco products:

a. Have you ever used tobacco products?

Yes _____
No _____

b. Approximate age at which you began to use tobacco products?

_____

c. How much do you use now? _____

_____

d. Regular (daily) use started at age _____

e. Describe briefly the pattern of tobacco use: _____

_____

_____

f. Do you perceive tobacco use as a problem in your life today?

_____

_____

g. What, if any, have been the consequences of tobacco use in your life?

_____

_____

*12. Do you sometimes need medication to sleep well; e.g., Sleep-eze, Pheno-barbital, Seconal, Doriden, or anything similar to these?

Yes _____

No _____

(If the answer to question 12 is No, move on to next question.)

If so, please explain: _____

_____

_____

If yes, how many times have you taken these?

a. Within the past month _____

b. Within the past 6 months _____

c. Over 6 months _____

**d. How has the use of this drug presented problems at work?

_____

_____

*e. Do you ever mix any of these with alcohol?

    Yes _____

    No _____

    If yes, please explain: _____

    _____

    _____

f. Person refuses to answer any of the above questions.

    _____

13. Do you sometimes need medications to stay calm, like tranquilizers or "downers," such as Valium, Compoz, Quaaludes, Librium, or anything similar to these?

    Yes _____

    No _____

    If No, move on to question 14.
    If yes, how often have you taken any of these?

    a. Within the past month? _____

    b. Within the past 6 months? _____

    c. More than 6 months? _____

    d. How has the use of this drug presented problems at work? _____

    _____

  **e. Do you ever take any of these before or during work hours?

    Yes _____

    No _____

If yes, please explain: _____

_____

f. Do you ever mix any of these with alcohol or with other drugs?

Yes _____

No _____

If yes, please explain: _____

_____

g. Person refuses to answer any of the above questions.

_____

14. Which substance is the major problem?

Drug   _____

Alcohol   _____

Drug and alcohol (dual addiction)   _____

Polydrug   _____

Other substance   _____

No problem   _____

15. How long was your last period of voluntary abstinence from this major substance?

_____

16. How many months ago did this abstinence end?

_____

**17. How many times have you?

Had alcohol DTs _____

Overdosed on drugs _____

**18. How many times in your life have you been treated for:

Alcohol abuse _____

Drug abuse _____

**19. How many of these were detox only?

Alcohol _____

Drug _____

**20. How many days in the past 30 have you experienced:

Alcohol problems _____

Drug problems _____

*21. Do you use or have you ever used marijuana or hashish?

Yes _____

No _____

If No, move on to question 22.
If Yes, how often?

a. Within the past month _____

b. Within the past 6 months _____

c. More than 6 months _____

d. How has using marijuana or hashish presented problems for you at work?

_____

e. Do you ever get high before or during working hours?

Yes _____

No _____

If yes, please explain: _____

_____

_____

*22. Do you use or have you ever used heroin or any other narcotics (morphine, codeine, dilaudid, etc.)?

Yes _____

No _____

If no, move on to question 23.
If yes, how often:

a. Within the past month? _____

b. Within the past 6 months? _____

c. More than 6 months? _____

d. How has the use of these drugs presented any problems for you at work?

_____

_____

**e. Do you ever use any of these before work or during working hours?

Yes _____

No _____

If yes, please explain: _____

_____

f. Do you ever mix any of these with alcohol or with other drugs?

Yes _____

No _____

If yes, please explain: _____

_____

_____

**g. Have you ever lost large amounts of money as a direct result of the use of narcotics?

Yes _____

No _____

If yes, please explain: _____

_____

_____

h. Person refuses to answer any of the above questions.

_____

*23. Do you use or have you ever used any street (nonprescribed) drugs not already mentioned, such as?

a. Hallucinogens (PCP, LSD, mescaline, peyote, psilocybin, etc.)

b. Inhalants (glue, paint, gasoline, etc.)

c. Amphetamines, speed

d. Crack, cocaine

e. Other drugs not mentioned

Yes _____   No _____

If no, move on to question 24.
If yes, how often:

a. Within the past month? _____

b. Within the past 6 months? _____

c. More than 6 months? _____

d. How has the use of any of these drugs presented problems for you at work?

_____

_____

_____

***e. Do you ever use any of these before work or during work hours?

Yes _____

No _____

If yes, please explain: _____

_____

_____

f. Do you ever mix any of these drugs with alcohol or with other drugs?

Yes _____

No _____

If yes, please explain: _____

_____

_____

g. What do you get out of the drug?

_____

_____

h. Person refuses to answer any of the above questions.

_____

Let's talk about your work . . .

Work History

24. Are you satisfied with your present work situation?

Yes _____

No _____

a. If not, why not? _____

_____

_____

b. If so, why? _____

_____

_____

c. How does the problem for which you come to the EAP affect your work?

_____

_____

e. Have you ever discussed this problem with your supervisor?

Yes _____

No _____

**25. Have you missed work, had an accident, or become ill because of drugs?

Yes _____

No _____

If yes, please explain: _____

_____

_____

**26. Do you believe your work performance is affected by your drug use?

Yes _____

No _____

If yes, please explain: _____

_____

_____

**27. Has your drug use ever resulted in poor performance at work in terms of a suspension, adverse action or performance evaluation, or any similar actions taken against you?

Yes _____

No _____

If yes, please explain: _____

_____

_____

**28. Have you ever been fired from a job because of drug use?

Yes _____

No _____

If yes, please explain: _____

_____

_____

*29. Have you ever failed to get a job or promotion because of drug use?

Yes _____

No _____

If yes, please explain: _____

_____

_____

**30. Are you often irritable at work and finding yourself arguing with coworkers?

Yes _____

No _____

If yes, please explain: _____

_____

_____

**31. Are you using more drugs than you did in the past? (could include both prescribed and street drugs)

If yes, please explain: _____

_____

_____

**32. Have you ever had a drug habit?

Yes _____

No _____

If yes, please explain: _____

_____

_____

**33. If so, have you ever tried to stop?

Yes _____

No _____

**34. Have you ever sought help to stop?

Yes _____

No _____

If yes, please explain: _____

_____

_____

**35. How are you supporting your drug habit/use? _____

_____

_____

**36. How many times in your life have you been charged with the following:

Disorderly conduct, vagrancy, public intoxication   _____

Driving while intoxicated   _____

Major driving violations (reckless driving, speeding, no license, etc.) _____

***37. Do you ever drive while under the influence of alcohol or drugs?

      Yes _____

      No _____

**38. Have you ever perpetrated the preceding without conviction or detection from others?

      Yes _____

      No _____

      If yes, please explain: _____

_____

_____

**39. Have you ever physically harmed anyone else? _____

***40. Are you harming anyone at the present time? _____

_____

**41. Have you ever been physically harmed? _____

_____

***42. Are you being physically harmed at the present time? _____

_____

43. What are:

    a. The three best things that ever happened to you in your life? _____

_____

_____

_____

b. The three worst things that ever happened to you in your life? _____

_____

_____

_____

44. Is there any other information you think is important in your evaluation?

_____

_____

_____

_____

INTERVIEW CHECKLIST

1. Obviously depressed/withdrawn

   Yes _____

   No _____

2. Obviously hostile

   Yes _____

   No _____

3. Obviously anxious/nervous

   Yes _____

   No _____

4. Having trouble with reality testing, thought disorders, paranoid thinking

   Yes _____

   No _____

5. Having trouble comprehending, concentrating, remembering

   Yes _____

   No _____

6. Having suicidal thoughts

   Yes _____

   No _____

DRUG USE QUESTIONNAIRE (DAST-20)

The following questions concern information about your potential involvement with drugs not including alcoholic beverages during the past 12 months. Carefully read each statement and decide if your answer is "Yes" or "No." Then, circle the appropriate response beside the question.

In the statements "drug abuse" refers to (1) the use of prescribed or over-the-counter drugs in excess of the directions and (2) any nonmedical use of drugs. The various classes of drugs may include: cannabis (e.g., marijuana, hashish), solvents, tranquilizers (e.g., Valium), barbiturates, cocaine, stimulants (e.g., speed), hallucinogens (e.g., LSD), or narcotics (e.g., heroin). Remember that the questions *do not* include alcoholic beverages.

Please answer every question. If you have difficulty with a statement, then choose the response that is mostly right.

Circle Your Response

1. Have you used drugs other than those required
   for medical reasons?   Yes   No

2. Have you abused prescription drugs?   Yes   No

3. Do you abuse more than one drug at a time?   Yes   No

4. Can you get through the week without using drugs?   Yes   No

5. Are you always able to stop using drugs when you want to?   Yes   No

6. Have you had "blackouts" or "flashbacks" as a result
   of drug use?   Yes   No

7. Do you ever feel bad or guilty about your drug use?   Yes   No

8. Does your spouse (or parents) ever complain about your
   involvement with drugs?   Yes   No

9. Has drug abuse ever created problems between you
   and your spouse (or parents)?   Yes   No

10. Have you ever lost friends because of your use of drugs?   Yes   No

11. Have you ever neglected your family because of your
    use of drugs?   Yes   No

Circle Your Response

12. Have you ever been in trouble at work because of
drug abuse?   Yes   No

13. Have you ever lost a job because of drug abuse?   Yes   No

14. Have you gotten into fights when under the
influence of drugs?   Yes   No

15. Have you ever engaged in illegal activities in order to
obtain drugs?   Yes   No

16. Have you ever been arrested for possession of illegal drugs?   Yes   No

17. Have you ever experienced withdrawal symptoms as
a result of heavy drug intake?   Yes   No

18. Have you had medical problems as a result of your drug use
(e.g., memory loss, hepatitis, convulsions, bleeding, etc.)?   Yes   No

19. Have you ever gone to anyone for help for a drug problem?   Yes   No

20. Have you ever been involved in a treatment program
specifically related to drug use?   Yes   No

SOURCES: H. A. Skinner. (1982). The Drug Abuse Screening Test. *Addictive Behaviors, 7,* 363-371; H. A. Skinner & A. E. Goldberg. (1986). Evidence for a drug dependence syndrome among narcotic users. *British Journal of Addiction, 81,* 479-484. © 1982 by the Addiction Research Foundation, 33 Russell St., Toronto, Ontario, Canada, M5S 2S1. Permission from the Addiction Research Foundation is required for use of this Drug Abuse Screening Test (DAST-20).

REFERENCES

Ackerman, R. J. (1987). A new perspective on adult children of alcoholics. *EAP Digest, 7*(1), 25-29.

Akabas, S. (1977). Labor and social policy and human services. *Encyclopedia of Social Work,* 17th ed. (pp. 738-744). Washington, DC: National Association of Social Workers.

Akabas, S. H., & Kurzman, P. A. (1982). *Work, workers and work organizations: A view from social work.* Englewood Cliffs, NJ: Prentice Hall.

Alcoholics Anonymous. (1989). *Analysis of the 1986 survey of the membership of A.A.* New York: Alcoholics Anonymous, General Service Office.

American Psychiatric Association. (1987). *Diagnostic and statistical manual of mental disorders* (3rd ed., rev.). Washington, DC: Author.

Anastas, J. W., Gibeau, J. L., & Larson, P. J. (1990). Working families and eldercare: A national perspective in an aging America. *Social Work, 35,* 405-411.

Anderson, D. (1991, August 18). A haven for whistle blowers. *Parade Magazine,* p. 16.

Angarola, R. T. (1991). Drug testing in the workplace: Legal issues and corporate responses. In R. H. Coombs & L. J. West (Eds.), *Drug testing: Issues and options* (pp. 155-189). New York: Oxford University Press.

Anthony, E. J., & Cohler, B. J. (Eds.). (1987). *The invulnerable child.* New York: Guilford.

Antoniades, R. (1984). Social work in a trade union setting: A network of volunteers and professionals in self-help groups. *Social Work Papers: Industrial Social Work* (University of Southern California, School of Social Work), *18,* 47-56.

Ausubel, D. P. (1980). An interactional approach to narcotic addiction. In D. J. Letteri, M. Sayers, & H. W. Pearson (Eds.), *Theories on drug abuse: Selected theoretical perspectives* (pp. 4-7). Rockville, MD: National Institute on Drug Abuse.

Axel, H. (1991). Drug testing in private industry. In R. H. Coombs & L. J. West (Eds.), *Drug testing: Issues and options* (pp. 140-154). New York: Oxford University Press.

Backer, T. E., & O'Hara, K. B. (1991). Drug abuse service in the workplace. *EAP Digest, 11*(5), 23-27, 62-65.

Bakalinsky, R. (1980). People vs. profits: Social work in industry. *Social Work, 25,* 471-475.

Bateson, G., Jackson, D., Haley, J., & Weakland, J. (1956). Toward a theory of schizophrenia. *Behavioral Science, 1,* 251-264.

Beattie, M. (1987). *Codependent no more: How to stop controlling others and start caring for yourself.* New York: Harper/Hazelden.

Beck, D. F. (1988). *Counselor characteristics: How they affect outcomes.* New York: Family Service Association of America.

Beck, D. F., & Jones, M. A. (1973). *Progress on family problems.* New York: Family Service Association of America.

Behavioral benefits. (1991, February). *Employee Benefit Plan Review, 26-27.*

Bell, P., & Evans, J. (1981). *Counseling the black alcoholic client: Alcohol use and abuse in black America.* Center City, MN: Hazelden.

Bergin, A. E. (1971). The evaluation of therapeutic outcomes. In A. E. Bergin & S. L. Garfield (Eds.), *Handbook of psychotherapy and behavior change* (pp. 217-270). New York: John Wiley.

Bergin, A. E., & Lambert, M. J. (1978). The evaluation of therapeutic outcomes. In S. L. Garfield & A. E. Bergin (Eds.), *Handbook of psychotherapy and behavior change: An empirical analysis* (2nd ed., pp. 139-189). New York: John Wiley.

Beschner, G. M., & Thompson, P. (1981). *Women and drug abuse treatment: Needs and services.* Rockville, MD: National Institute on Drug Abuse.

Beutler, L. E., Crago, M., & Arizmendi, T. G. (1986). Therapist variable in psychotherapy process and outcome. In S. L. Garfield & A. E. Bergin (Eds.), *Handbook of psychotherapy and behavior change* (3rd ed., pp. 257-310). New York: John Wiley.

Billings, A. G., & Moos, R. H. (1983). Psychosocial processes of recovery among alcoholics and their families: Implications for clinicians and program evaluators. *Addictive Behaviors, 8,* 205-218.

Bissell, L., & Haberman, P. W. (1984). *Alcoholism in the professions.* New York: Oxford University Press.

Black, C. (1982). *It will never happen to me.* Denver, CO: M.A.G. Printing.

Blackmon, P. (1985). Networking community services for elderly clients with alcohol problems. In E. Freeman (Ed.), *Social work practice with clients who have alcohol problems* (pp. 189-201). Springfield, IL: Thomas.

Blankfield, A. (1986). Psychiatric symptoms in alcohol dependence: Diagnostic and treatment implications. *Journal of Substance Abuse Treatment, 3,* 275-278.

Blum, E. M. (1966). Psychoanalytic views of alcoholism. *Quarterly Journal of Studies on Alcoholism, 27,* 259-299.

Blum, T. C., Martin, J., & Roman, P. M. (1992). A research note on EAP prevalence, components, and utilization. *Journal of Employee Assistance Research, 1,* 209-229.

Brennan, K. N., Kyster, T. L., Vinton, M. E., & Citta, J. (1987). A police department EAP: Innovative design reaches a closed system. *EAP Digest, 7*(5), 46-51.

Brice, G. C., & Alegre, M. R. (1989). Eldercare as an EAP concern. *EAP Digest, 9,* 31-33.

Brisbane, F. L., & Womble, M. (Eds.). (1985). *Treatment of black alcoholics.* New York: Haworth.

Brown, S. (1985). *Treating the alcoholic: A developmental model of recovery.* Somerset, ND: John Wiley.

Brown, S. A., & Schuckit, M. A. (1988). Changes in depression among abstinent alcoholics. *Journal of Studies of Alcohol, 49,* 412-417.

Brown, V., Ridgely, M., Pepper, B., Levine, I., & Ryglewicz, H. (1989). The dual crisis: Mental illness and substance abuse. *American Psychologist, 44,* 565-569.

Buckstein, O., Brent, D., & Kaminer, V. (1989). Comorbidity of substance abuse and other psychiatric disorders in adolescents. *American Journal of Psychiatry, 16,* 1131-1141.

Budman, S. H., & Gurman, A. S. (1988). *Theory and practice of brief therapy.* New York: Guilford.

Burden, D., & Googins, B. (1986). *Boston University balancing job and homelife study.* Boston: Boston University, School of Social Work.

Burrows, B. A. (1992). Research on the etiology and maintenance of eating disorders. In E. M. Freeman (Ed.), *The addiction process: Effective social work approaches* (pp. 149-160). New York: Longman.

Cacciola, J., Griffith, J., & McLellan, A. J. (Eds.). (1985). *Addiction severity index instruction manual* (4th ed.). Rockville, MD: National Institute on Drug Abuse.

Carter, I. D. (1977, Winter). Social work in industry: A history and a viewpoint. *Social Thought, 3,* 7-17.

Cermak, T. L. (1986). *Diagnosing and treating co-dependence.* Minneapolis, MN: Johnson Institute.

Cermak, T. L. (1989). *A primer on adult children of alcoholics* (2nd ed.). Deerfield Beach, FL: Health Communications.

Chan, A. W. K. (1990). Biochemical markers for alcoholism. In M. Windle & S. Searles (Eds.), *Children of alcoholics: Critical perspectives.* New York: Guilford.

Christner, A. M. (Ed.). (1991). *Reference guide to addiction counseling.* Providence, RI: Manisses Communications Group.

Clark, L. (1993, February). *Interface of EAP and organizational development.* Presentation at the regional meeting of the Employee Assistance Society of North America, Chicago, IL.

Cloninger, C. R. (1987). Neurogenetic adaptive mechanisms in alcoholism. *Science, 236,* 410-416.

Collins, B. G. (1993). Reconstruing codependence using self in relation theory: A feminist perspective. *Social Work, 38,* 470-476.

Coombs, R. H., & West, L. J. (1991). *Drug testing: Issues and options.* New York: Oxford University Press.

Cork, R. J. (1969). *The forgotten children: A study of children with alcoholic parents.* Toronto: Alcoholism and Drug Addiction Research Foundation of Ontario.

Cornett, C. (1992). Toward a more comprehensive personality: Integrating a spiritual perspective in social work practice. *Social Work, 37,* 101-102.

Corrigan, E. M. (1980). *Alcoholic women in treatment.* New York: Oxford University Press.

Cox, W. M. (1985). Personality correlates of substance abuse. In M. Galizio & S. A. Maisto (Eds.), *Determinants of substance abuse treatment: Biological, psychological and environmental factors* (pp. 209-246). New York: Plenum.

Cunningham, G. (1988). Study of clinical practices in EAPs. Unpublished raw data.

Cunningham, G. (1990). *Clinical practice in EAPs.* Unpublished research.

Cunningham, G. (1992). The EAP counselor: Attitudes, knowledge and beliefs. *Employee Assistance Quarterly, 8,* 13-25.

Current labor statistics. (1993, May). *Monthly Labor Review, 116*(5), 71-123.

De Rosa, J., & Hickle, R. (1986, March/April). Is direct service disappearing? *EAP Digest, 6*(2), 57-59.

DeSoto, C. B., O'Donnell, W. E., Allred, L. J., & Lopes, C. E. (1985). Symptomatology in alcoholics at various stages of abstinence. *Alcoholism, 9,* 505-512.

Donovan, D. M. (1988). Assessment of addictive behaviors: Implications of an emerging biopsychosocial model. In D. M. Donovan & G. A. Marlatt (Eds.), *Assessment of addictive behaviors* (pp. 3-48). New York: Guilford.

Donovan, D. M., & Chaney, E. F. (1985). Alcoholic relapse prevention and intervention: Models and methods. In G. A. Marlatt & J. R. Gordon (Eds.), *Relapse prevention* (pp. 351-416). New York: Guilford.

Dorus, W., Kennedy, J., Gibbons, R. D., & Ravi, S. D. (1987). Symptoms and diagnosis of depression in alcoholics. *Alcoholism (NY), 11,* 150-154.

Drake, R. R., Osher, F. C., & Wallach, M. A. (1989). Alcohol use and abuse in schizophrenics: A proscriptive community study. *Journal of Nervous and Mental Disease, 177,* 408-414.

Edwards, D. W. (1975). The evaluation of troubled employees and occupational alcoholism programs. In R. L. Willimand & G. H. Moffatt (Eds.), *Occupational alcoholism programs* (pp. 40-135). Springfield, IL: Charles C. Thomas.

Eldred, C. A., & Washington, M. N. (1975). Female heroin addicts in a city treatment program: The forgotten minority. *Psychiatry, 38,* 75-85.

Engel, F. (1987). Violence, crime and trauma at work: An overlooked problem. *EAP Digest, 7*(5), 29-33.

Epperson-SeBour, M. (1990). Psychosocial crisis services in the Maryland Emergency Medical Services system. In H. J. Parad & L. G. Parad (Eds.), *Crisis intervention book 2: A practitioners sourcebook for brief therapy* (pp. 209-226). Milwaukee, WI: Family Service America.

Erickson, P. G., & Murray, G. F. (1989). Sex differences in cocaine use and experiences: A double standard revived? *American Journal of Drug and Alcoholism Abuse, 15,* 135-152.

Fausel, D. F. (1988). Helping the helper heal: Co-dependency in helping professionals. *Journal of Independent Social Work, 3,* 35-45.

Feldman, S. (1991). Today's EAPs make the grade. *Personnel, 68*(3), 8-13.

Fewell, C. H. (1985). Psychodynamic treatment of women alcoholics. In E. Freeman (Ed.), *Social work practice with clients who have alcohol problems* (pp. 172-188). Springfield, IL: Charles C. Thomas.

Fienstein, B., & Brown, E. G. (1982). *The new partnership: Human services, business and industry.* Cambridge, MA: Schenkman.

Figley, C. R. (1985). *Trauma and its wake: The study of post-traumatic stress disorder.* New York: Brunner/Mazel.

Fine, M., Akabas, S. H., & Bellinger, S. (1982). Cultures of drinking: A workplace perspective. *Social Work, 27,* 435-550.

Fizek, L. S., & Zare, N. (1988). Factors affecting referrals from employee assistance programs to community agencies. *Employee Assistance Quarterly, 4,* 2, 31-43.

Foote, A., & Erfurt, J. C. (1978). *Cost-effectiveness of occupational employee assistance programs.* Ann Arbor: University of Michigan-Wayne State University, Institute of Labor and Industrial Relations.

Ford, D. H., & Urban, H. B. (1963). *Systems of psychotherapy: A comparative study.* New York: John Wiley.

Frank, F., & Streeter, C. (1985). Identifying roles for social workers in industrial settings. *Social Work Papers: School of Social Work, USC, 19,* 1-22.

Frank, J. D. (1974). *Persuasion and healing* (rev. ed.). Baltimore, MD: Johns Hopkins University Press.

Frank, P. B., & Golden, G. K. (1992). Blaming by naming: Battered women and the epidemic of codependence. *Social Work, 37,* 5-6.

Freeman, E. M. (1990). Assessment of substance abuse problems: Implications for clinical supervision. *The Clinical Supervisor, 8,* 91-108.

Freeman, E. M. (1992a). Addicted mothers-addicted infants and children: Social work strategies for building support networks. In E. M. Freeman (Ed.), *The addiction process: Effective social work approaches* (pp. 108-122). New York: Longman.

Freeman, E. M. (1992b). *The addiction process: Effective social work approaches.* New York: Longman.

Freeman, E. M., & Landesman, T. (1992). Differential diagnosis and the least restrictive treatment. In E. M. Freeman (Ed.), *The addiction process: Effective social work approaches* (pp. 27-42). New York: Longman.

Friedman, E. H. (1985). *Generation to generation: Family process in church and synagogue.* New York: Guilford.

Gadon, B., & Serwins, S. (1989). Eldercare: Its impact in the workplace. *EAP Digest, 9,* 33-38.

Galanter, M., Castaneda, R., & Ferman, J. (1988). Substance abuse among general psychiatric patients: Place of prevention. *American Journal of Drug and Alcohol Abuse, 14,* 211-235.

Galinsky, E. (1986). Work and family: Getting it together. *EAP Digest, 6*(6), 27-32.

Gallo, C., & Reisner, E. (1992, July). *Violence and PTSD in the workplace: Using video as a learning medium and therapeutic tool for social workers.* Paper presented at the National Association of Social Workers Meeting of the Profession and the 12th International Symposium of the International Federation of Social Workers, Washington, DC.

Garfield, S. L. (1986). Research on client variables in psychotherapy. In S. L. Garfield & A. E. Bergin (Eds.), *Handbook of psychotherapy and behavior change* (pp. 213-256). New York: John Wiley.

Garfield, S. L., & Bergin, A. E. (1986). Introduction and historical overview. In S. L. Garfield & A. E. Bergin (Eds.), *Handbook of psychotherapy and behavior change* (pp. 3-22). New York: John Wiley.

Garmezy, N., & Rutter, M. (1983). *Stress, coping, and development in children.* New York: McGraw-Hill.

Germain, C. B., & Gitterman, A. (1980). *The life model of social work practice.* New York: Columbia University Press.

Gilligan, C. (1982). *In a different voice: Psychological theory and women's development.* Cambridge, MA: Harvard University Press.

Gilman, A. G., Goodman, L. S., Rall, T. W., & Murad, F. (Eds.). (1985). *The pharmacological base of therapeutics.* New York: Macmillan.

Gilman, R. (1991). Social workers' experiences and attitudes towards AIDS. *Families in Society, 72,* 593-601.

Golan, N. (1978). *Treatment in crisis situations.* New York: Free Press.

Gold, M. S., Washton, A. M., & Dackis, C. A. (1985). Cocaine abuse: Neurochemistry, phenomenology, and treatment. In N. J. Kozel & E. H. Adams (Eds.), *Cocaine use in America: Epidemiologic and clinical perspectives* (pp. 130-150) (NIDA Research Monograph No. 61, DHHS Publication No. ADM 85-1414). Washington, DC: Government Printing Office.

Goldstein, E. G. (1980). Knowledge base of clinical social work. In P. I. Ewalt (Ed.), *Toward a definition of clinical social work* (pp. 42-53). Washington, DC: National Association of Social Workers.

Googins, B. (1987). *Occupational social work.* Englewood Cliffs, NJ: Prentice Hall.

Googins, B., & Burden, D. (1987). Vulnerability of working parents: Balancing work and home roles. *Social Work, 32,* 295-300.

Greene, S., & DiCuio, R. (1991). An EAP guide to bereavement. *EAP Digest, 11*(5), 29-32, 69-72.

Grissom, G. R., Baldadian, K. C., & Swisher, J. D. (1988). The case for needs assessment: A study in three disparate work settings. *Employee Assistance Quarterly, 4*(3), 11-25.

Gunther, J. F., Jolly, E. J., & Wedel, K. R. (1985). Alcoholism and the Indian people: Problem and promise. In E. M. Freeman (Ed.), *Social work practice with people who have alcohol problems* (pp. 214-228). Springfield, IL: Charles C. Thomas.

Gupta, S. D. (1990). Extent and pattern of drug abuse and dependence. In H. Ghodse & D. Maxwell (Eds.), *Substance abuse and dependence: An introduction for the caring professions* (pp. 22-34). Houndsmills, UK: Macmillan.

Haley, J. (1976). *Problem solving therapy: New strategies for effective family therapy.* San Francisco: Jossey-Bass.

Hartman, A. (1978). The diagrammatic assessment of family relationships. *Social Casework, 59,* 465-476.

Hartog, J., & Tusel, D. (1987). Valium use and abuse by methadone maintenance clients. *International Journal of Addictions, 22,* 1147-1154.

Helzer, J., & Pryzbeck, T. (1988). The co-occurrence of alcoholism with other psychiatric disorders in the general population and its impact on treatment. *Journal of Studies on Alcohol, 43,* 219-224.

Hepworth, D. H., & Larsen, J. A. (1990). *Direct social work practice* (3rd ed.). Belmont, CA: Wadsworth.

Hepworth, D. H., & Larsen, J. A. (1993). *Direct social work practice: Theory and skills* (4th ed.). Belmont, CA: Wadsworth.

Holmes, T. H., & Rahe, R. H. (1967). Life changes and illness susceptibility. *Journal of Psychosomatic Research, 11,* 213-218.

Inciardi, J. A., Lockwood, D., & Pottieger, A. E. (1993). *Women and crack-cocaine.* New York: Macmillan.

Isaacson, E. B. (1991). Chemical addiction: Individual and family systems. *Employee Assistance Quarterly, 6,* 7-27.

Jaffe, J. H., Cascella, N. G., Kumor, K. M., & Sherer, M. A. (1989). Cocaine-induced cocaine craving. *Psychopharmacology, 97,* 59-64.

Jayaratne, S. (1982). Characteristics and theoretical orientation of social workers: A national survey. *Journal of Social Service Research, 4*(2), 17-30.

Jerrell, J. M., & Rightmeyer, J. F. (1982). Evaluating employee assistance programs: A review of methods, outcomes, and future directions. *Evaluation and Program Planning, 5,* 225-267.

Johns, A. (1990). What is dependence? In H. Ghodse & D. Maxwell (Eds.), *Substance abuse and dependence: An introduction for the caring professions* (pp. 5-29). London: Macmillan.

Kaminer, W. (1992). *I'm dysfunctional, you're dysfunctional: The recovery movement and other self-help fashions.* Reading, MA: Addison-Wesley.

Kammerman, S. B. (1984). *Meeting family needs: The corporate response. Highlights of the literature.* New York: Pergamon.

Kanter, R. M. (1977a). *Men and women of the corporation.* New York: Basic Books.

Kanter, R. M. (1977b). *Work and family in the United States: A critical review and agenda for research and policy.* New York: Russel Sage Foundation.

Kantor, D., & Lehr, W. (1975). *Inside the family: Toward a theory of family process.* San Francisco: Jossey-Bass.

Katz, S. J., & Liu, A. E. (1991). *The codependency conspiracy: How to break the recovery habit and take charge of your life.* New York: Warner.

Kaul, B., & Davidow, B. (1981). Drug abuse patterns of patients on methadone treatment in New York City. *American Journal of Alcohol and Drug Abuse, 8,* 17-25.

Klerman, G. L., & Clayton, P. (1984). Epidemiologic perspectives on the health consequences of bereavement. In M. Osterweis, F. Solomon, & M. Green (Eds.), *Bereavement: Reactions, consequences, and care* (pp. 15-44). Washington, DC: Academy.

Kohn, M. (1980). Job complexity and adult personality. In N. J. Smelser & E. Erikson (Eds.), *Themes of work and love in adulthood* (pp. 193-210). Cambridge, MA: Harvard University Press.

Koss, M. B., & Butcher, J. N. (1986). Research on brief psychotherapy. In S. A. Garfield & A. E. Bergin (Eds.), *Handbook of psychotherapy and behavior change* (pp. 627-670). New York: John Wiley.

Kurtz, L. F. (1992). Research on alcohol abuse and recovery: From natural helping to formal treatment to mutual aid. In E. Freeman (Ed.), *The addiction process: Effective social work approaches* (pp. 13-26). New York: Longman.

Kurtz, N. R., Googins, B., & Howard, C. (1984). Measuring the success of occupational alcoholism programs. *Journal of Studies on Alcohol, 45*(1), 33-45.

Kurzman, P. (1983). Ethical issues in industrial social work practice. *Social Casework, 64*(2), 105-111.

Kurzman, P. (1987). Industrial social work (occupational social work). *Encyclopedia of social work* (18th ed., Vol. 1, pp. 899-910). Washington, DC: National Association of Social Workers.

Laing, R. (1965). Mystification, confusion and conflict. In I. Boszormenyi-Nazy & J. Framo (Eds.), *Intensive family therapy: Theoretical and practical aspects* (pp. 343-363). New York: Harper & Row.

Lambert, M. J., Shapiro, D. A., & Bergin, A. E. (1986). The effectiveness of psychotherapy. In S. L. Garfield & A. E. Bergin (Eds.), *Handbook of psychotherapy and behavior change* (3rd ed., pp. 157-212). New York: John Wiley.

Lambert, S. G. (1990). Process linking work and family: A critical review and research agenda. *Human Relations, 43,* 239-257.

Lazarus, A. (1967). In support of technical eclecticism. *Psychological Reports, 21.*

Leavitt, R. L. (1983). *Employee assistance and counseling programs: Findings from recent research on employer-sponsored human services.* New York: Community Council of Greater New York.

Lesieur, H., & Custer, R. (1984). Pathological gambling: Roots, phases, and treatment. *Annals of the American Academy of Political and Social Sciences, 474,* 146-156.

Leukefeld, C. J., & Battjes, R. J. (1992). Intravenous drug use and AIDS. In E. M. Freeman (Ed.), *The addiction process: Effective social work approaches* (pp. 123-135). New York: Longman.

Levinson, D. S. (1980). Toward a conception of the adult life course. In N. J. Smelser & E. H. Erikson (Eds.), *Themes of work and love in adulthood* (pp. 265-290). Cambridge, MA: Harvard University Press.

Levy, S. J., & Doyle, K. M. (1974). Attitudes toward women in a drug abuse treatment program. *Journal of Drug Issues, 4,* 428-434.

Lewis, J., Beavers, W., Gossett, J., & Phillips, V. (1976). *No single thread: Psychological health in family systems.* New York: Brunner/Mazel.

Lo, B. (1990). Ethical issues in drug testing. In R. H. Coombs & L. J. West (Eds.), *Drug testing: Issues and options* (pp. 190-201). New York: Oxford University Press.

Lowenstein, S. F. (1983). A feminist perspective. In A. Rosenblatt & D. Waldfogel (Eds.), *Handbook of clinical social work* (pp. 518-548). San Francisco: Jossey-Bass.

Lundberg, M. (1974). *The incomplete adult: Social class constraints on personality development.* Westport, CT: Greenwood.

Madanes, C., & Haley, J. (1977). Dimensions of family therapy. *Journal of Nervous and Mental Disease, 165,* 88-98.

Madden, S. (1990). Effects of drug dependence. In H. Ghodse & D. Maxwell (Eds.), *Substance abuse and dependence: An introduction for the caring professions* (pp. 30-53). Houndsmills, UK: Macmillan.

Maiden, P. R., Kimble, S. L., & Sudtelgte, S. L. (1993). A consortium EAP for rural employers: The Princeton option. *EAP Digest, 13*(3), 36-41, 47-48.

Maluccio, A. N. (1979). *Learning from clients: Interpersonal helping as viewed by clients and social workers.* New York: Free Press.

Marketers complain of sex offers. (1992, March 1). *The Dallas Morning News,* p. 45A.

Marlatt, G. A. (1985a). Cognitive assessment and intervention procedures for relapse prevention. In G. A. Marlatt & J. R. Gordon (Eds.), *Relapse prevention* (pp. 201-279). New York: Guilford.

Marlatt, G. A. (1985b). Relapse prevention: Theoretical rationale and overview of the model. In G. A. Marlatt & J. R. Gordon (Eds.), *Relapse prevention* (pp. 3-70). New York: Guilford.

Marlatt, G. A., & Baer, J. S. (1988). Addictive behaviors: Etiology and treatment. *Annual Review of Psychology, 39,* 223-252.

Marlatt, G. A., & Gordon, J. R. (Eds.). (1985). *Relapse prevention.* New York: Guilford.

Masi, D. (1982). *Human services in industry.* Lexington, MA: Lexington.

Masi, D. (1985). *Designing employee assistance programs.* New York: American Management Association.

McClellan, A. T., Luborsky, L., Woody, G. E., & O'Brien, C. P. (1980). An improved diagnostic evaluation instrument for substance abuse patients: The addiction severity index. *Journal of Nervous and Mental Disorders, 168,* 26-33.

McClellan, K. (1987). A profile of an EAP center and its caseload, 1980-1986. *Employee Assistance Quarterly, 2*(4), 31-44.

McFarlane, A. C. (1990). Post traumatic stress syndrome revisited. In H. J. Parad & L. G. Parad (Eds.), *Crisis intervention book 2: A practitioners sourcebook for brief therapy* (pp. 69-92). Milwaukee, WI: Family Service America.

McGilly, F. (1985). American historical antecedents to industrial social work. *Social Work Papers, 19,* 1-13.

Meltzoff, J., & Kornreich, M. (1970). *Research in psychotherapy.* New York: Atherton.

Meyer, C. H. (Ed.). (1983). *Clinical social work in the ecosystems perspective.* New York: Columbia University Press.

Miller, M. (1991). Addictions and the disease concept. In A. M. Christner (Ed.), *Reference guide to addictions counseling* (sect. 1, unpag.). Providence, RI: Manisses Communication Group.

Miller, T. W., Jones, D., & Miller, J. M. (1992). Stress in the workplace. *EAP Digest, 12*(4), 26-29.

Minuchin, S. (1974). *Families and family therapy.* Cambridge, MA: Harvard University Press.

Mitchell, J. T. (1983). When disaster strikes: The critical incident stress debriefing process. *Journal of Emergency Medical Services, 8,* 36-39.

Molloy, D., & Burmeister, L. (1990). Social workers in union based programs. In S. H. A. Straussner (Ed.), *Occupational social work today* (pp. 37-51). New York: Haworth.

Moncher, M. S., Schinke, S. P., & Holden, G. W. (1992). Tobacco addiction: Correlates, prevention, and treatment. In E. M. Freeman (Ed.), *The addiction process: Effective social work approaches* (pp. 222-236). New York: Longman.

Moos, R. H., Finney, J. W., & Gamble, W. (1982). The process of recovery from alcoholism, II: Comparing spouses of alcoholic patients and matched community controls. *Journal of Studies on Alcohol, 43*(9), 888-909.

Mortimer, J. T., & Borman, K. T. (Eds.). (1988). *Work experience and psychological development.* Boulder, CO: Westview.

Moss, H. B., Blackstone, T. C., Martin, C. S., & Tartar, R. E. (1992). Heightened motor activity level in male offspring of substance abusing fathers. *Biological Psychiatry, 32,* 1135-1147.

Nathan, P. E. (1987). The addictive personality: How valid? How useful? *Journal of Consulting and Clinical Psychology, 55*(3), 332-340.

National Association of Social Workers. (1980). NASW code of ethics. *NASW News, 25,* 24-25.

National Institute on Alcohol Abuse and Alcoholism. (1990). *Seventh special report to Congress on alcohol and health* (Contract No. ADM-281-88-0002). Rockville, MD: Editorial Experts.

National Institute on Drug Abuse. (1991). *Drug abuse and drug abuse research: The third triennial report to Congress from the secretary, Department of Health and Human Services.* Rockville, MD.

Nye, S. G., & Kaiser, L. B. (1991). *Employee assistance law answer book.* New York: Panel Publishers.

O'Connell, R., & Fried, P. A. (1991). Prenatal exposure to cannabis: A preliminary report of postnatal consequences in school age children. *Neurotoxicol Teratol, 13,* 631-639.

Ogden, J., Hedges, H., Milstead, R., Sanders, J., & Mohler, J. (Eds.). (1977). The role of labor in developing and using alcoholism treatment facilities. *Labor Management Alcoholism Journal, 4*(6), 3-32.

O'Gorman, P. (1991). Codependency and women: Unraveling the power behind learned helplessness. In N. Van Den Bergh (Ed.), *Feminist perspectives on addictions* (pp. 153-166). New York: Springer.

O'Hare, T. (1992). The substance abusing chronically mentally ill client: Prevalence, assessment treatment, and policy concerns. *Social Work, 37,* 185-187.

Orlinsky, D., & Howard, K. (1986). Process and outcome in psychotherapy. In S. L. Garfield & A. E. Bergin (Eds.), *Handbook of psychotherapy and behavior change* (pp. 311-381). New York: John Wiley.

Ozawa, M. (1980). Development of social work services in industry: Why and how? *Social Work, 25,* 464-470.

Paolino, R. (1991a). Common drugs of abuse: Pharmacology and phenomenology. In R. H. Coombs & L. J. West (Eds.), *Drug testing: Issues and options* (pp. 50-66). New York: Oxford University Press.

Paolino, R. (1991b). Identifying, treating and counseling drug abusers. In R. H. Coombs & L. J. West (Eds.), *Drug testing: Issues and options* (pp. 215-234). New York: Oxford University Press.

Paolino, T. J., & McCrady, B. S. (1977). *The alcoholic marriage: Alternative perspectives.* New York: Grune & Stratton.

Pape, P. (1992). Adult children of alcoholics: Uncovering family scripts and other barriers to recovery. In E. M. Freeman (Ed.), *The addiction process: Effective social work approaches* (pp. 43-53). New York: Longman.

Parad, H. (1984). Time limited crisis therapy in the workplace: An eclectic perspective. *Social Work Papers: Industrial Social Work, 18,* 20-30.

Parad, H., & Parad, L. (1990). *Crisis intervention, book 2: The practitioner's source book for brief therapy.* Milwaukee, WI: Family Service America.

Patterson, C. H. (1985). *The therapeutic relationship: Foundations for an eclectic psychotherapy.* Monterey, CA: Brooks/Cole.

Peck, M. S. (1978). *The road less traveled.* New York: Simon & Schuster.

Perlman, H. H. (1964). The work role. In H. H. Perlman, *Persona: Social role and personality* (pp. 59-86). New York: Columbia University Press.

Perlman, H. H. (1975). In quest of coping. *Social Casework, 56,* 213-225.

Perlman, H. H. (1982). The client as worker: A look at an overlooked role. In S. H. Akabas & P. A. Kurzman (Eds.), *Work, workers and work organizations: A view from social work* (pp. 90-116). Englewood Cliffs, NJ: Prentice Hall.

Pilat, J., & Boomhower-Kresser, S. (1992). Dynamics of alcoholism and child sexual abuse: Implications for interdisciplinary practice. In E. M. Freeman (Ed.), *The addiction process: Effective social work approaches* (pp. 65-78). New York: Longman.

Pilat, J., & Jones, J. (1985). A comprehensive treatment program for children of alcoholics. In E. M. Freeman (Ed.), *Social work practice with clients who have alcohol problems* (pp. 141-159). Springfield, IL: Charles C. Thomas.

Piotrowski, C. (1978). *Work and the family system.* New York: Free Press.

Pokorny, A. D., Miller, B. A., & Kaplan, H. B. (1972). The brief MAST: A shortened version of the Michigan Alcoholism Screening Test. *American Journal of Psychiatry, 129,* 342-345.

Prather, J. E., & Minkow, N. V. (1991). Prescription for despair: Women and psychotropic drugs. In N. Van Den Bergh (Ed.), *Feminist perspectives on addictions* (pp. 87-99). New York: Springer.

Presnall, L. (1981). *Occupational counseling and referral systems.* Salt Lake City, UT: Utah Alcoholism Foundation.

Quadland, M. C. (1988). Compulsive sexual behavior: Definition of a problem and an approach to treatment. *Journal of Sex and Marital Therapy, 11,* 121-132.

Rapaport, L. (1970). Crisis intervention. In R. Roberts & R. Nee (Eds.), *Theories of social casework* (pp. 267-311). Chicago: University of Chicago Press.

Reamer, F. G. (1992). The impaired social worker. *Social Work, 37,* 165-170.

Reynolds, B. C. (1951). *Social work and social living.* Washington, DC: National Association of Social Workers.

Rodgers, F. S., & Rodgers, C. (1989, November-December). Business and the facts of family life. *Harvard Business Review,* 121-129.

Roman, P. M., & Blum, T. C. (1987). Ethics in worksite health programming: Who is served. *Health Education Quarterly, 14,* 57-70.

Rounsaville, B. B., Dolinsky, Z. S., Babor, T. F., & Meyer, R. E. (1987). Psychopathology as a predictor of treatment outcome in alcoholics. *Archives of General Psychiatry, 44,* 505-513.

Rush, B. as cited in National Institute on Alcohol Abuse and Alcoholism (1990).

Saltzberg, M., & Bryant, C. (1988). Family systems theory and practice at the workplace. *Social Work Papers: Industrial Social Work, 21,* 16-28.

Satir, V. (1967). *Conjoint family therapy.* Palo Alto, CA: Science & Behavior Books.

Schuckit, M. A. (1987). Biological vulnerability to alcoholism. *Journal of Consulting and Clinical Psychology, 55,* 301-309.

Schuckit, M. A., Irwin, M., Howard, T., & Smith, T. (1988). A structured diagnostic interview for identification of primary alcoholism: A preliminary evaluation. *Journal of Studies on Alcohol, 49,* 93-99.

Searles, J. S. (1990). Behavior genetic research and risk for alcoholism among children of alcoholics. In M. W. Windle & J. S. Searles (Eds.), *Children of alcoholics: Critical perspectives* (pp. 99-128). New York: Guilford.

Seilhamer, R. A. (1991). Effects of addiction on the family. In D. C. Daley & M. S. Raskin (Eds.), *Treating the chemically dependent and their families* (pp. 172-194). Newbury Park, CA: Sage.

Selzer, M. L. (1971). The Michigan Alcoholism Screening Test: The quest for a new diagnostic instrument. *American Journal of Psychiatry, 127,* 1653-1658.

Selzer, M. L., Vinokur, A., & van Rooijen, L. (1975). A self-administered Short Michigan Alcoholism Screening Test (SMAST). *Journal of Studies of Alcohol, 36,* 117-176.

Siporin, M. (1975). *Introduction to social work practice.* New York: Macmillan.

Siporin, M. (1985). Current social work perspectives on clinical practice. *Clinical Social Work Journal, 13*(3), 198-216.

Skinner, H. A. (1982). The Drug Abuse Screening Test. *Addictive Behaviors, 7,* 363-371.

Sloane, R. B., Staples, F. R., Cristo, A. H., Yorkston, N. D., & Whipple, K. (1975). *Psychotherapy versus behavior therapy.* Cambridge, MA: Harvard University Press.

Smelser, N. J., & Erikson, E. (Eds.). (1980). *Themes of work and love in adulthood.* Cambridge, MA: Harvard University Press.

Smith, C. (1991). Healing the feminine: A feminist residential model for treating chemical dependency. In N. Van Den Bergh (Ed.), *Feminist perspectives on addiction* (pp. 115-123). New York: Springer.

Smith, M. L., Glass, G. V., & Miller, T. I. (1980). *The benefits of psychotherapy.* Baltimore, MD: Johns Hopkins University Press.

Steidinger, J. (1986). The current state of evaluation practices in Employee Assistance Programs, San Francisco. *Employee Assistance Quarterly, 1*(4), 51-65.

Steinglass, P. (1987). *The alcoholic family.* New York: Basic Books.

Stellman, J. M., & Daum, S. M. (1973). *Work is dangerous to your health: A handbook of health hazards in the workplace and what you can do about them.* New York: Vintage.

Stern, D. (1985). *Interpersonal world of the infant: A view from psychoanalysis and development.* New York: Basic Books.

Straussner, S. L. A. (1988). Comparison of in-house and contracted out employee assistance programs. *Social Work, 33,* 53-55.

Tabakoff, B., Hoffman, P. L., Lee, J. M., Saito, T., Willard, B., & De Leon-Jones, F. (1988). Differences in platelet enzyme activity between alcoholics and controls. *New England Journal of Medicine, 318,* 134-139.

Tarter, R. E., Alterman, A. I., & Edwards, K. L. (1985). A vulnerability to alcoholism in men: A behavior-genetic perspective. *Journal of Studies in Alcoholism, 46*(4), 329-356.

Teare, R. J. (1987). *National survey of occupational social workers.* Silver Spring, MD: National Association of Social Workers, Commission on Employment and Economic Support.

Titmus, R. M. (1966). *Essays on the welfare state.* London: Allen & Unwin.

Tolson, E. (1988). *The metamodel of clinical social work.* New York: Columbia University Press.

Trice, H. M., Beyer, J. M., & Hunt, R. E. (1978). Evaluating implementation of a job-based alcoholism policy. *Journal of Studies on Alcohol, 39,* 448-465.

Turnbull, J. E. (1988). Primary and secondary alcoholic women. *Social Casework, 69,* 290-297.

U.S. Department of Health and Human Services. (1987). *Alcohol and health: Sixth special report to the U.S. Congress* (DHHS Publication No. ASDM 87-1519). Washington, DC: Government Printing Office.

Van Den Bergh, N. (1991). *Feminist perspectives on addictions.* New York: Springer.

Videka-Sherman, L. (1985). *Harriett M. Bartlett practice effectiveness project.* Silver Spring, MD: National Association of Social Workers.

Walsh, J. A., & Ruez, J. F. (1987). Murder in the workplace: Responding to human trauma. *EAP Digest, 7*(5), 34-37, 66-69.

Walsh, J. M., & Trumble, J. G. (1991). The politics of drug testing. In R. H. Coombs & L. J. West (Eds.), *Drug testing* (pp. 22-49). New York: Oxford University Press.

Washton, A. M., Stone, N. S., & Hendrickson, E. C. (1988). Cocaine abuse. In D. Donovan & C. A. Marlatt (Eds.), *Assessment of addictive behaviors* (pp. 364-389). New York: Guilford.

Watts, T. (1981). The uneasy triumph of a concept: The "disease" conception of alcoholism. *Journal of Drug Issues, 11,* 451-460.

Weaver, C. A. (1979, July). EAPs—How they improve the bottom line. *Risk Management,* pp. 22-26.

Webb, N. B. (1990). Consultation in crisis situations: Behind-the-scenes help for the helpers. In H. J. Parad & L. G. Parad (Eds.), *Crisis intervention book 2: A practitioner's sourcebook for brief therapy* (pp. 293-312). Milwaukee, WI: Family Service America.

Wegscheider, S. (1981). *Another chance.* Palo Alto, CA: Science and Behavior Books.

Weiner, H. J., Akabas, S. H., & Sommer, J. (1973). *Mental health care in the world of work.* New York: Association Press.

Whitfield, C. L. (1989). Codependence: Our most common addiction—some physical, mental, emotional and spiritual perspectives. In B. Carruth & W. Mendenhall (Eds.), *Codependency: Issues in treatment and recovery* (pp. 19-36). Binghamton, NY: Haworth.

Willette, R. E. (1991). Techniques of reliable drug testing. In R. H. Coombs & L. J. West (Eds.), *Drug testing: Issues and options* (pp. 67-91). New York: Oxford University Press.

Williams, R. L., & Tramontana, J. (1977). The evaluation of occupational alcoholism programs. In C. J. Schramm (Ed.), *Alcoholism and its treatment in industry* (pp. 109-135). Baltimore, MD: Johns Hopkins University Press.

Windle, M., & Searles, J. S. (1990). *Children of alcoholics: Critical perspectives.* New York: Guilford.

Winfield, F. E. (1988). Workplace solutions for women under eldercare pressures. *EAP Digest, 8,* 33-38.

Woititz, J. (1983). *Adult children of alcoholics.* Hollywood, FL: Health Communications.

Work in America: Report of a special task force to the secretary of Health, Education and Welfare. (1973). Cambridge: Massachusetts Institute of Technology Press.

World Health Organization. (1978). *Mental disorders: Glossary and guide to their classification in accordance with the ninth revision of the International Classification of Disease.* Geneva: Author.

Wyers, N. L. (1988). Economic insecurity: Notes for social workers. *Social Work, 33,* 18-22.

Yasser, R., & Sommer, D. (1974). One union's social service program. In *Social Welfare Forum* (conference proceedings) (pp. 112-120). New York: Columbia University Press.

Young-Eisendrath, P. (1988). Mental structures and personal relations: Psychodynamic theory in clinical social work. In R. A. Dorfman (Ed.), *Paradigms of clinical social work* (pp. 43-73). New York: Brunner/Mazel.

Ziter, M. L. P. (1987). Culturally sensitive treatment of black alcoholic families. *Social Work, 32,* 130-137.

Zucker, R. A., & Gomberg, E. S. L. (1986). Etiology of alcoholism reconsidered: The case for a biopsychosocial process. *American Psychologist, 41,* 783-793.

INDEX

AA. *See* Alcoholics Anonymous
Ackerman, R., 162
ACOA. *See* Adult Children of Alcoholics
Addiction Severity Index, 96-97
Addiction theory, 37, 45-50, 71-72, 73
Administration, 23-32
 advisory board, 31-32
 and in-house marketing, 27-29
 and organizational assessment, 23-26
 and program evaluation, 29-31
 and program policy, 26-27
 union, 18
Adult Children of Alcoholics (ACOA), 38, 43, 160-163, 165-168, 198
Advisory board, 31-32
African Americans, 80
Aftercare, 111-112, 144-147
Ageism, 192-193
AIDS, 92, 185-187
Akabas, S., 1, 4
Al-Anon, 70, 113-115, 165, 198
Alcoholics Anonymous (AA), 3, 6, 47, 70, 104, 113-115, 198
Alcoholism, 28, 30, 44
 and addiction theory, 37, 45-50, 71-72, 73
 and EAP development, 1-2, 3, 6-8, 10-11, 12-13
 and fetal alcohol syndrome, 82, 86, 93, 162-163

in occupational practice, 197-198
 programs, 15, 17, 69
 See also Chemical dependence; Family issues; Substance abuse; 12-Step programs
ALMACA. *See* Association of Labor and Management Consultants on Alcoholism
American Psychiatric Association, 68, 81
American Society of Addiction Medicine (ASAM), 79-80
Amphetamines, 90-91
Anastas, J., 149, 152
Anthony, E., 162
Antoniades, R., 17, 19
ASAM. *See* American Society of Addiction Medicine
Assessment, 34-35, 51, 58-76
 and client input, 63-65
 and diagnostic classification, 68-69
 and family system, 71-73
 and substance abuse, 79-80, 81-85, 98-99, 146-147
 and workplace system, 73-76
 health, 65-68, 69-71, 83-85
 interviews, 94-96
 organizational, 23-26
 process, 60-63
 tests, 96-98

See also Referral; Theoretical concepts;
    Treatment
Association of Labor and Management
    Consultants on Alcoholism
    (ALMACA), 192
Ausubel, D., 47
Axel, H., 97

Backer, T., 7, 103
Bakalinsky, R., 17, 199, 200
Bateson, G., 44
Beattie, M., 43, 159, 165, 166
Beck, D., 127
Bell, P., 80
Bergin, A., 31
Beschner, G., 107
Beutler, L., 128
Billings, A., 81
Bissell, L., 198
Black, C., 38, 43, 159, 166
Blackmon, P., 80
Blankfield, A., 84-85
Blum, E., 46
Blum, T., 1
Brennan, K., 177
Brice, G., 149
Brisbane, F., 80
Brown, S., 34, 47, 84-85, 95, 114, 148, 163
Brown, V., 83
Buckstein, O., 83
Budman, S., 59, 132, 134
Burden, D., 151
Burrows, B., 50

Cacciola, J., 96-97
Carter, I., 4
Cermak, T., 158
Chan, A., 166
Chemical dependence:
    and addiction theory, 37, 45-50, 71-72, 73
    and assessment, 69, 81-82, 146-147
    and EAP development, 1-2, 6-8, 10-11,
        12-13
    and external providers, 19, 102, 104

in occupational practice, 197-198
    See also Alcoholism; Family issues;
        Substance abuse; 12-Step programs
Children of Alcoholics (COA), 160-163,
    165-168
    See also Adult Children of Alcoholics
Christner, A., 79-80, 102
Clark, L., 26
Cloninger, C., 49
COA. See Children of Alcoholics
Cocaine, 7, 88-90
Cocaine Abuse Assessment Profile: Addic-
    tion/Dependency Self-Test (Washton),
    96
Codependency, 157-162, 163-165
Collins, B., 158
Confidentiality, 20, 192, 194, 199-200
    and evaluation, 29-30
    and referral, 54-56, 77n
    and treatment groups, 143, 144
    See also Ethics
Contract programs, 19-21, 22
    See also External providers
Coombs, R., 98
Cork, R., 162
Corrigan, E., 107
Counselor-client relationship, 56-58
    and children of alcoholics, 165-168
    and codependency, 163-165
    and external providers, 19-21, 102-105
    and family issues, 153-155
    and in-house programs, 15-17
    and member assistance program, 17-19
    and occupational practice, 193-195
    and organizational assistance, 169-172
    and referral, 106-112
    and substance abuse, 79, 84, 94-97
    and treatment, 98-99, 125-128
Cox, W., 47
Crisis intervention, 132-136, 170, 176-184
Critical incident debriefing. See Crisis
    intervention
Cunningham, G., 16, 37, 64, 102, 104-105,
    107, 109, 110, 111, 118, 123, 125-
    127, 145, 169, 190, 191

"Current Labor Statistics" (*Monthly Labor Review*), 151

Dallas Morning News, 105
DAST. *See* Drug Abuse Screening Test
Denial, 95-96
Depression, 83-84, 86
De Rosa, J., 6, 200
DeSoto, C., 85
Detoxification, 84-85
Developmental theory, 38-40
DFWA. *See* Drug-Free Workplace Act
Diagnostic and Statistical Manual of Mental Disorders (DSM-II-R) (American Psychiatric Association), 68-69, 77n
Diagnostic classification, 28, 53, 59, 68-69
  and dual diagnosis, 83-85
  and substance abuse, 79-80, 81-83
Donovan, D., 81, 146
Dorus, W., 84-85
Drake, R., 83
Drug Abuse Curriculum for EAP Professionals (U.S. Department of Health and Human Services), 85
Drug Abuse Screening Test (DAST) (Skinner), 96
Drug Abuse (U.S. Department of Health and Human Services), 93
Drug-Free Workplace Act (DFWA), 12, 82, 97, 185
Drug testing, 17, 78, 79, 96, 97-98
DSM-III-R. *See Revised Diagnostic and Statistical Manual of Mental Disorders*
DSM-II-R. *See Diagnostic and Statistical Manual of Mental Disorders*
Dual diagnosis, 83-85

EAP. *See* Employee Assistance Program
EAPA. *See* Employee Assistance Programmers Association
EASNA. *See* Employee Assistance Society of North America
Ecological system, 43, 71-72
Eldred, C., 107

Employee Assistance Program (EAP)
  client change in, 6-8
  development of, 1-5
  future of, 12-13
  organizational change in, 8-10
  professional change in, 10-11
  term definitions in, 5-6
  See also Occupational practice
Employee Assistance Programmers Association (EAPA), 104, 192
Employee Assistance Society of North America (EASNA), 104
Engel, F., 176, 177
Epperson-SeBour, M., 184
Erickson, P., 90
Ethics, 63, 70, 116, 169
  and drug testing, 97
  and EAP development, 4, 11, 13
  and external providers, 105-106, 145
  and member assistance program, 18
  in occupational practice, 198-202
  See also Confidentiality
Evaluation, 29-31
External providers, 19-21, 22, 101-115, 170
  and aftercare, 111-112, 144-146
  and client education, 110-111
  and EAP development, 8-10
  and individualized referral, 106-109
  and mutual referral, 109-110
  as resource base, 102-105
  as self-help groups, 113-115
  ethics of, 105-106, 145
  monitoring, 112-113
  See also Referral; 12-Step programs

Family issues, 148-168
  and workplace, 150-155
  assistance for, 148-150
  chemical dependence, 155-157
  children of alcoholics, 160-163, 165-168
  codependency, 157-162, 163-165
  See also Alcoholism; Chemical dependence; Substance abuse; Theoretical concepts
FAS. *See* Fetal alcoholism syndrome
Fausel, D., 198

Feldman, S., 1, 8
Fetal alcoholism syndrome (FAS), 82, 86,
    93, 162-163
Fewell, C., 107
Fienstein, B., 5
Figley, C., 176
Fine, M., 146, 184
Fizek, L., 107
Ford, D., 35
Frank, F., 5
Frank, J., 37
Frank, P., 158
Freeman, E., 47, 68, 80, 84, 94, 106, 162-
    163
Freud, S., 38-39
Fried, P., 93
Friedman, E., 45, 149

Gadon, B., 149
Galinsky, E., 148, 152
Gallo, C., 176, 177
Garfield, S., 37, 194
Garmezy, N., 162
Germain, C., 43
Gilman, A., 85
Gilman, R., 187
Golan, N., 66, 134, 135, 181
Gold, M., 89
Goldstein, E., 39
Googins, B., 4, 150-151
Greene, S., 131
Grissom, G., 26
Gunther, J., 80
Gupta, S., 83

Haley, J., 43
Hartman, A., 73
Helzer, J., 83
Hepworth, D., 44, 68, 72
Hewitt, P., 186
Hispanics, 80, 107
Holmes, T., 132
Hughes Act, 3
Human behavior theories. See Theoretical
    concepts

ICD-9. See International Classification of
    Disease
Inciardi, J., 80, 90, 91, 107
In-house:
    marketing, 27-29, 136, 192
    programs, 15-17, 22
Insurance, 12-13, 68, 102, 186-187
International Classification of Disease
    (ICD-9) (World Health Organiza-
    tion), 68-69, 77n, 81-83
Intervention, 35, 65
    crisis, 132-136
    organizational, 6, 55-56, 170, 176-184
Isaacson, E., 156

Jaffe, J., 88-89
Jayaratne, S., 37
Jerrell, J., 29
Johns, A., 82

Kaminer, W., 113, 158
Kammerman, S., 152
Kanter, R., 17, 41, 72, 148, 151, 152
Kantor, D., 43
Katz, S., 113, 114, 158
Klerman, G., 131
Kohn, M., 41
Koss, M., 59
Kurtz, L., 80, 106-107, 114
Kurzman, P., 18, 169, 194

Laing, R., 44
Lambert, M., 31, 36, 59, 125
Lambert, S., 150-151
Lazarus, A., 37
Leavitt, R., 2, 7
Lesieur, H., 50
Leukefeld, C., 162-163
Levinson, D., 40
Levy, S., 107
Lewis, J., 44
Litigation, 28, 70, 97, 103, 199
Lowenstein, S., 39
Lundberg, M., 41

MAC. *See* McAndrew Alcoholism Scale
Madanes, C., 43
Madden, S., 91
Maiden, P., 22
Maluccio, A., 127-128
MAP. *See* Member Assistance Program
Marijuana, 92-93
"Marketers Complain of Sex Offers" *(Dallas Morning News)*, 105
Marketing:
    and external providers, 21, 170
    in-house, 27-29, 136, 192
Marlatt, G., 47, 145-146
Masi, D., 1, 3
MAST. *See* Michigan Alcoholism Screening Test
McAndrew Alcoholism Scale (MAC), 97
McClellan, A., 96-97
McClellan, K., 7, 21, 29
McFarlane, A., 176, 182
McGilly, F., 4
Meltzoff, J., 31
Member Assistance Program (MAP), 5, 17-19, 22
Meyer, C., 43
Michigan Alcoholism Screening Test (MAST) (Selzer), 96
Miller, M., 47
Miller, T., 55
Minnesota Multiphasic Personality Inventory (MMPI), 97
Minorities, 25
    and developmental theory, 39
    and discrimination, 107, 192
    and substance abuse, 80, 92, 96
    See also Women
Minuchin, S., 43
Mitchell, J., 181
MMPI. *See* Minnesota Multiphasic Personality Inventory
Moncher, M., 92
Monthly Labor Review, 151
Moos, R., 164
Mortimer, J., 40
Moss, H., 48

NA. *See* Narcotics Anonymous

Narcotics Anonymous (NA), 70, 104, 113
Nathan, P., 46, 47
National Association of Social Workers, 70, 104
National Council on Addiction and Drug Dependence (NCADD), 79-80
National Institute on Alcohol Abuse and Alcoholism, 47, 48, 49, 82, 86, 95, 102, 162, 166
National Institute on Drug Abuse, 83-84, 89, 90, 92
Native Americans, 80
NCADD. *See* National Council on Addiction and Drug Dependence
Nicotine, 92-94

OAP. *See* Occupational alcoholism program
Occupational alcoholism program (OAP), 5
Occupational practice, 189-202
    and burnout, 193, 196
    and clientele, 193-195
    and professional identity, 10-11, 198-202
    and workplace, 191-192, 195-196
    careers in, 190-191
    chemical dependence in, 197-198
    discrimination in, 192-193
    skills for, 196-197
    relationship; Organizational assistance
    See also Employee Assistance Program; Counselor-client
Occupational social worker, 2-3, 4-6, 10-11, 32n
    See also Occupational practice
O'Connell, R., 93
Ogden, J., 17
O'Gorman, P., 158
O'Hare, T., 84
Opiates, 91
Organizational assistance, 169-188
    and client service, 172-174
    and counselor-client relationship, 169-172
    and crisis intervention, 176-184
    and EAP influence, 184-185
    and external providers, 21
    and in-house programs, 16

and policy, 185-188
to work groups, 174-175
Osterea, 92
Ozawa, M., 171

Paolino, R., 88, 89
Paolino, T., 164
Pape, P., 159
Parad, H., 132, 133, 181
Peck, M., 71
Perlman, H., 40, 41, 72, 122
*Pharmacological Basis of Therapeutics,
   The* (Gilman), 85
Pilat, J., 162-163
Piotrowski, C., 151, 152
Pokorny, A., 96
Post-traumatic stress disorder (PTSD),
   176, 181-182
Prather, J., 91
Presnall, L., 1, 3
Privacy rights. *See* Confidentiality
Professional issues. *See* Occupational prac-
   tice
Program models, 14-22
   blended, 22
   contract models, 19-21, 22
   in-house, 15-17, 22
   member assistance program (MAP), 5,
      17-19, 22
   See also External providers
Psychotherapy, 70, 111, 117
PTSD. *See* Post-traumatic stress disorder

Quadland, M., 50

Rapaport, L., 133
Raskin, 49
Reamer, F., 198
Referral, 51-52
   and confidentiality, 54-56, 77n
   and counselor-client relationship, 106-
      112
   and substance abuse, 78-81, 98-99
   management, 7, 28-29, 52-55
   self, 7, 29, 30, 55-56

See also External providers
Religion, 70-71
*Revised Diagnostic and Statistical Manual
   of Mental Disorders* (DSM-III-R)
   (American Psychiatric Association),
   81-83
Reynolds, B., 18
Rodgers, F., 150-151, 152
Roman, P., 12
Rounsaville, B., 84
Ruez, J., 183-184
Rush, B., 47

Saltzberg, M., 149, 150, 153-154
Satir, V., 44
Schuckit, M., 48, 80, 84
Searles, J., 166
Sedatives, 85-88
Seilhamer, R., 155, 162
Selzer, M., 96
*Seventh Special Report to the Congress on
   Alcohol and Health* (National In-
   stitute on Alcohol Abuse and Al-
   coholism), 49
Siporin, M., 35-36, 37
Skinner, H., 96
Smelser, N., 40
Smith, C., 107
Social Work Code of Ethics (National As-
   sociation of Social Workers), 70
Steidinger, J, 29
Steinglass, P., 44, 148, 156, 157, 162
Stellman, J., 42, 69
Stern, D., 39
Stimulants, 88-91
Straussner, S., 16, 19
Substance abuse, 28, 78-99
   alcohol, 85-87
   and addiction theory, 37, 45-50, 71-72,
      73
   and assessment, 69, 79-80, 94-98, 146-
      147
   and diagnostic classification, 79-80, 81-
      83
   and EAP development, 1-2, 6-8, 10-11,
      12-13
   and mental disorder, 83-85

and referral, 78-81
and treatment, 98-99
and women, 80, 84, 90, 91, 92
in occupational practice, 197-198
nicotine, 92-94
racial differences in, 80
sedatives, 87-88
stimulants, 88-91
See also Alcoholism; Chemical dependence; Family issues; 12-Step programs
Suicide, 86-87, 90
Systems theory. See Theoretical concepts

Tabakoff, B., 48
Tarter, R., 49
Teare, R., 192
Theoretical concepts, 33-50
and addictions, 37, 45-50, 71-72, 73
base for, 35-38
developmental, 38-40
ecological system, 43, 71-72
family system, 71-73, 43-45
necessity of, 33-34
workplace system, 40-43, 73-76
Titmus, R., 195
Tolson, E., 36
Treatment, 34-35, 58-59, 116-147
and aftercare, 111-112, 144-147
and counselor-client relationship, 98-99, 125-128
and education, 124-125
crisis intervention, 132-136
empowerment, 123-124
for substance abuse, 81, 98-99
group services, 136-144
problem-solving strategies in, 118-122
short-term, 116-118, 128-132
validation, 122-123
See also External providers; 12-Step programs
Turnbull, J., 80, 84
12-Step programs:
Adult Children of Alcoholics (ACOA), 38, 43, 160-163, 165-168, 198
Al-Anon, 70, 113-115, 165, 198
Alcoholics Anonymous (AA), 3, 6, 47, 70, 104, 113-115, 198

Children of Alcoholics (COA), 160-163, 165-168
Narcotics Anonymous (NA), 70, 104, 113

Unions:
administration in, 18
and drug testing, 97-98
and EAP development, 4, 9
and programs, 2, 5, 17-19, 22, 32n
U.S. Department of Health and Human Services, 85, 93, 102

Van Den Bergh, N., 80
Videka-Sherman, L., 31

Walsh, J., 98, 176-177, 182, 183-184
Washton, A., 88, 89, 96
Watts, T., 47
Weaver, C., 73
Webb, N., 183, 184
Wegscheider, S., 38, 166
Weiner, H., 6, 18
Whitfield, C., 158
Willette, R., 97-98
Williams, R., 29-30
Windle, M., 48, 162, 165-166
Winfield, F., 149
Woititz, J., 38, 43, 159, 166
Women:
and codependency, 158
and developmental theory, 39
and discrimination, 151, 192
and fetal alcohol syndrome, 82, 86, 93, 162-163
and substance abuse, 80, 84, 90, 91, 92
stereotyping, 90, 96, 107
Workaholic, 40, 42
Work in America: Report of a special task force to the Secretary of Health, Education and Welfare, 42, 69
Workplace:
and family, 150-155
environment, 69-70, 177
systems, 40-43, 73-76

World Health Organization, 68, 81
Wyers, N., 152

Young-Eisendrath, P., 39

Ziter, M., 80
Yasser, R., 18

Zucker, R., 49

ABOUT THE AUTHOR

GLORIA CUNNINGHAM, Ph.D., is an Associate Professor at Loyola University (Chicago) School of Social Work, where she designed and directed the Occupational Social Work Program. She was active in the development of employee assistance practice through the National Association of Social Workers/Council of Social Work Education (NASW/CSWE) National Task Force for Industrial Social Work and the Occupational Social Work Committee of the Chicago Area Chapter of NASW, where she served as its first permanent Chair. She earned her M.S.W. at the Loyola University School of Social Work and her Ph.D. at the School of Social Service Administration, University of Chicago. She was among the first women to be appointed to the U.S. District Court Federal Probation and Parole Service, where she provided direct services to offenders and their families and participated in education, training, and writing in the field of criminal justice. In addition to her continuing interests in occupational social work and employee assistance, she also teaches courses at the master's and doctoral levels in general clinical social work. Her current research interests include the occupational experiences of women professionals with special emphasis on issues of discrimination and harassment.